4042

THE OTHER SIDE
OF LENNON

THE OTHER SIDE OF LENNON

by

SANDRA SHEVEY

SIDGWICK & JACKSON
LONDON

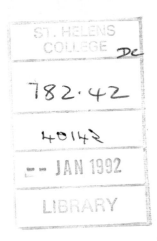
First published in 1990 by
Sidgwick & Jackson Limited
1 Tavistock Chambers, Bloomsbury Way
London WC1A 2SG

ISBN 0 283 06003 4

Typeset in Great Britain by
Hewer Text Composition Services, Edinburgh
Printed by Mackays of Chatham plc, Chatham, Kent

To Reg, who makes me feel like Marilyn Monroe

CONTENTS

ACKNOWLEDGEMENTS

In writing this book I should like to express my gratitude to the following:

Dr John Gallwey for taking time out from AIDS research to be interviewed; Robert Whitaker for sharing insights about the tours; David Nutter for his contributions; Vic Lewis for his candour; Raymond Feather for observations about Lennon's childhood; William Pobjoy for making the trip into Liverpool and escorting me around Quarry Bank; Eleanor Bron for giving interviews, which she hates; John Junkin for his largesse and affection for John; Horst Fascher for information on John's German period; Alan Livingstone for background on Capitol's signing of the Beatles; Walter Shenson for his anecdotes; Sir David Napley for information on Lennon's obscenity bust; Nic Knowland for recounting his cinematographic experiences; Nicky Hopkins for his own account.

The fabulous Beatles Convention for the job they do in enriching the Beatles cult with an excellent programme of guest speakers and events; BBC radio for access to *Lost Beatles Tapes*, also *McCartney on McCartney*; Channel 4 for allowing me to view the Larry Parnes documentary; BBC-TV for allowing me to view Brian Epstein footage; the *Beatles Monthly* magazine for information; Jonathan Cape's publicity department for all Lennon reviews; *Daily Mirror* files for access to microfiche dating back donkeys' years; Ansbacher and Co. for the release of the prospectus for the Beatles' bid to buy Northern Songs; the British Library Manuscript Collection and Hunter Davies for allowing access to Lennon's original manuscripts and first drafts, which provide illuminating insights into revisions.

Don Short for lacking discretion; Kenny Lynch for catching light in a bottle; Jonathan Hague for his confidences; Jack Douglas for his revelations; 'Apple' girls Alison Boone and Alex Crockett for their candid accounts of life as Kenwood housegirls; James Rushton (Brian's valet/PA) for his disclosures; Ken Partridge for his contacts; Carey Wallace for her sources.

John Lennon and Yoko Ono for their honesty and forthrightness in an interview which at the time (1972) mystified me.

1

Would You Believe,
Willy Russell?????

When John Lennon was asked to write a brief autobiographical sketch to accompany the catalogue for his series of erotic lithographs, *The Honeymoon Suite*, he failed to mention his famous association with the Beatles. The truth is that John was ashamed of his contributions to the greatest rock group in the world. He hated it, and all the false, meretricious nonsense that it involved. To John, the Beatles was a hollow victory, an opinion which he sought to justify during the twelve-hour marathon interview I had with him and Yoko Ono at their brownstone apartment in Greenwich Village in 1972.

Like most Beatles fans, I had expected to meet in John the apotheosis of my maiden crush – the personification of those English rock ballads enshrining wonderfully bucolic values, the greatest lyric poet of the age. In short, a Beatle.

Instead, to my surprise – even shock – I met a kind of Willy Russell hero: bitter, sarcastic, downbeat; putting down popular music (of which he was king) as a sort of placebo for the real stuff; cruelly mocking those who found charming the offbeat, casual ways he had of ingratiating himself into the heart of an audience. During the time we spent together, which was considerable, I was subjected to searing attacks on my own tastes in music and personalities (which valued highly both Lennon and the Beatles) and bullied into committing myself to a tentative affection for the new John and his message music.

It was only following John's death and my decision to make an attempt at writing a biography of him that I came to find, in researching his life, the discrepancies between his version of events and the observations of friends, colleagues and lovers. It is with consequent satisfaction, eighteen years after interviewing John, that I can now begin to understand what he was talking about then.

Fundamental to any understanding of John's bitterness after the dissolution of the Beatles and the McCartney lawsuit is an appreciation that the Beatles never evolved into the group which John had originally envisaged when he first formed the band. During the period of guidance by their manager, Brian Epstein, John's eruptions at various intervals threatened to sabotage that patina of respectability painstakingly created by Brian.

The John Lennon who led the Beatles to success back in the early sixties at the Hamburg clubs was completely different from the boy who took America by storm. The original Lennon, calling his group the Savage Beatles, was comparable more to Sid Vicious than to what he had become under Brian's management. Greasy, tough, attired in black leather with a kind of Hell's Angel magnificence, Lennon used to swagger around the stages of those Hamburg clubs stoned on pills, booze or both. It wasn't inconceivable for him to eat, spit, fart, piss or masturbate on the stage, where he was compelled to play gigs for six or seven hours at a stretch. His ad libs had none of the playfulness he was to project as a Beatle. At this time in his career he was raw, raucous, angry and insolent, screaming out foul language, racist insults and obscenities against the Germans (and Nazis).

Of course, when Brian got them in hand, this all changed and Lennon was compelled (for the sake of the group) to adopt middle-class standards of speech, dress and behaviour. Of all four Beatles, it was John who most resisted Brian's attempts to make them over. It was only (and even then reluctantly) when he saw that Brian was right and that they could gain greater audiences, acceptability and more money by playing it straight, that he allowed himself to be changed.

John's anger at having compromised with himself was plainly visible when I interviewed him. Five years after Brian's death, and throughout his association with Epstein, it was Lennon alone who threatened to blow the act by allowing those privately racist, aggressive and violent aspects of himself to receive public attention.

I have always said that John Lennon was the greatest advert the Church of England ever had, and whilst he was rigorously anti-Church (he baulked when Cynthia had their son Julian christened without his permission) he was pro-God – which had little or no mitigating effect upon the American public, which sought to crucify him for his remark about being 'bigger than Jesus'. Whilst the same thing was said by Marshall McLuhan (who became in consequence a media guru), and whilst it was a comment made in Britain and about Britain for the *Evening Standard*, and was taken out of context when reprinted in an American publication, John's provocative remark elicited death threats serious enough for Brian Epstein to rush from his sick bed and over to the United States where the Beatles were about to start on a tour. Cancellation was barely avoided by John's reluctant and resentful offer to apologise publicly for the remarks.

This, then, the other side of Lennon, surfaced on any number of occasions, but firmly took root when John started doing avant-garde stuff with Yoko (whilst still with the Beatles) and then began writing experimental rock after the group broke up. Previous to the Yoko–John collaboration, Lennon showed himself up on two principal occasions, both overlooked by the press and over both of which he was ostracized by Epstein. The first was publication by Jonathan Cape of John's book of humorous Liverpudlian sketches, many of which had first appeared in Bill Harry's 1960s' magazine *Mersey Beat*. The book was widely reviewed, often well, but still failed to have the impact of the songs and never became part of the Lennon cult. To my mind these sketches are crude, lewd, adolescent, racist drivel, which whine on about pro-fascist ass-tight Christ figures and make generalized offensive remarks about 'niggers', 'Jews' and so on. Doubtless they have an audience and could become an acquired taste, but the fact that they were written by the same wide-eyed, honey-tongued, bucolic balladeer of Strawberry Fields, Penny Lane, Norwegian Wood and Savoy truffles makes one speculate about the extent to which his Beatles songs were revised.

It is worth noting that this book, *In His Own Write*, came to Jonathan Cape via the back door, without any acknowledgement of Lennon's contributions. Only later was it disclosed that he was its author. At the celebrated Foyle's literary lunch where John was feted and rudely chose not to speak, Brian Epstein publicly repudiated the book by saying that he had not encouraged John to write it nor had he involved himself with its publication.

The second attempt was the play at the National Theatre (then at the Old Vic) which was based on this book and John's second, *A Spaniard in the Works*. The reviews were appalling. The three-play bill did not run, and this at a time when the Beatles could do no wrong and everything that Lennon touched turned to gold.

There is an interesting bit of Lennoniana hidden away in the British Museum archives, contributed by Lennon biographer Hunter Davies, which threatens to give the game away. It is a rough draft of 'Strawberry Fields', originally called 'Calderstones Park' (one of Liverpool's many areas of parkland), and bears so little resemblance to what eventually came out that one has trouble believing that John actually wrote a lot of the work attributed to him. The Calderstones ditty is full of self-conscious references about being seen (necking) and being forgiven (he had a rough time as a schoolboy).

One merely has to compare John's independent work with what he wrote as a Beatle. Leaving aside for the moment the popular convention (such as the images), there is little doubt that his Beatles work is stronger. He has denied it, but the lyrics alone show us that he simply had more to say as a Beatle. The transparency of using politicism as a substitute for ideas is pathetic, but in Lennon's case, and considering the euphoric hype attending the group's success, it is disgraceful.

Whether, as a neighbour of John's suggested, the lyrics to his songs were cribbed from church hymns and old English ballads, or effectively rewritten by one of Brian Epstein's team, a definite transformation appears to have taken place between his first and last drafts, making the former almost unrecognizable. Having listened to some of the tapes of the recording sessions he did at the Record Plant in New York City, during the time he was recording solo or in tandem with Yoko Ono, I observed that in his later life the transition was greatly reduced and the first and second takes of songs were not unlike what was eventually released. But the Beatles stuff was revised beyond recognition.

If one gets past the soft sell, it will be seen that at root John was not a particularly creative person. His dependency upon the talents of the EMI producer, musician George Martin, has been documented elsewhere. When the Beatles left Martin, or vice versa, Lennon, by then a mature talent, borrowed heavily from the Zen ideas formulated into life exercises in Yoko Ono's book *Grapefruit*. He also relied upon the musical judgement of producer Phil Spector. It was Spector who fought John every step of the way on 'Imagine' (bringing in the violins) and on 'Happy Xmas (War is Over)' (using the sounds of bells and the choir).

So how is Lennon great? Like the Irish revolutionary Charles

4

Stewart Parnell – or worse, like Hitler, representative of a type of small-minded fascist bigot thriving in situations of deprivation and stress, bullying those with more than he, unremitting even when his means greatly exceed theirs?

When, after Brian's death, the Dream tumbled down around his ears, what did Lennon do? He took off his clothes, parading naked on album covers and cavorting around in bed nude in hotel rooms, in the hope that the shock of seeing him naked would divert people's attentions from his musical paucity. He produced erotic lithographs (some said shocking), which were confiscated under the Obscenity Act, of him and his wife in intimate conjugal poses. He made dirty movies – or a send-up of dirty movies, which to me still seem dirty.

And when those old stand-bys of shock failed to grab public attention, Lennon went even further. He became a political renegade. The last quarter of his short life was devoted to a peace campaign which, whilst it may have contributed to creating an atmosphere of embarrassment toward America's involvement in Vietnam and to speeding up its withdrawal, fundamentally served John's selfish purpose to become a cult figure: youth's spokesman – a working-class hero. His music at this time was barely musical. It was cant, doggerel, diatribe. His rationale that things had become so bad that there was no time for lyricism seems a cheap attempt at self-justification. John's solo albums championed causes and people about which he knew little: Angela Davis, John Sinclair, feminism, Attica State. Musically inept, politically valid, he had become a focal point. The next step would be to run for political office. In short, Lennon had abandoned his role as youth poet and balladeer for that of candidate.

Why was he shot? There are many theories, including the cybernetic idea that the CIA brainwashed Mark Chapman (co-incidentally also the surname of an early Beatles drummer, Norman Chapman) into killing John because he posed a political threat to the status quo.

Whilst the FBI does not admit to having any involvement in John's murder, it continues to deny access to information about John which would categorize him as a security risk. This protectiveness, though understandable, does however give verac-ity to those prejudices which serve to justify the defence – oh, that was *not* the reason.

Reading those parts of his FBI file which are in public domain, I came to realize the extent to which Lennon was committed to ending the Vietnam War and the means he used (including paid protestors and petitions) to embarrass the US government into winding down the hostilities. I also became aware of the compulsive and almost exclusive dedication to political change he evinced in a country which had not wanted his residency in the first instance and only accepted him after great perseverance on his part. When he died he was in the process of organizing a protest for the factory workers and was drafting a film script about James Hanratty, a man whom John believed was falsely executed for a crime he did not commit.

But even if it is true that John's murder was CIA-determined, it has about it a sense of poetic justice. The ultimate cock-rocker past his prime, crapping on the system that made him a god, allowing him to live in a style which Lennon himself admitted was wildly excessive by comparing it to *Satyricon*; back-stabbing the producers and managers who made it happen by denigrating their contributions and by saying that the Beatles did not evolve the way he had wanted and therefore the group was nothing and of no importance; assailing the Church whilst promoting drugs, nudity and other exhibitionist folly.

'Lennon – he was a swine, a yobbo,' said one British rock singer. If not a swine, he was clearly a fraud – one of the most scandalous farces perpetrated on the public by the rock music industry. But let us not forget that it is we – the media, the fans, the public – who go along for the ride. How did it happen? This book attempts to tell the tale.

2

Will the Real John Lennon Please Stand Up?

I was asked to meet John and Yoko at their brownstone apartment on Bank Street in Greenwich Village in September 1972, shortly after their arrival in the States and whilst John was waging battle with the US Immigration Department to get permanent residency. He had been busted for drugs in Great Britain and had resolved never to return to a country which, because of this, seemed to him to be ungrateful for the contributions he had made both to the economy and to the arts.

At first glance Bank Street seemed a rather unprepossessing residence – one big sitting room with a kitchen alcove en suite, and a back room or series of back rooms leading off it. May Pang, the Lennons' secretary and John's subsequent lover, was with them at this time and has confirmed that the apartment was indeed small and that there was only a bedroom and a bathroom leading off the main room.

This, for the Lennons, must have been similar to what John's sixties' bachelor pad in London's Emperor's Gate was like. I didn't know it, but the Lennons were also ensconced at the St Regis Hotel where they let both offices and a home suite during the intervals they were completing filming of *Imagine*. Bank Street was now their bohemian pied-à-terre.

Projecting a working-class persona, John rambled on about monogamy, role reversal, short hair and limited audience appeal. It was common knowledge during his first marriage that he fooled around, said John's Liverpool art college chum Jonathan Hague, imparting to me a story about his making a play for one of Jon's friends when John was both married to Cynthia and also seeing Yoko. It was only a year after our interview and his protestations

7

of fidelity that Mr Contentment took off with May Pang on that legendary 'Lost Weekend' in Los Angeles.

Lest anyone suppose that his romance with May was intended to replace Yoko, they have only to consider that the famous reconciliation with Ono at Elton John's Madison Square Garden concert saw John with not Pang in tow but yet another girl.

Monogamous? No way. Lennon was naturally promiscuous. He had married sex, casual sex and sex with assorted (although limited) mistresses. May Pang was one. And whilst the public may wish to believe that she was but a brief interlude in John's life, the fact is that he never stopped loving her, slept with her until the end of his life (long after his famous reconciliation with Ono) and gave her as a keepsake his prayer book (which she still cherishes).

The release of the album *Some Time in New York City* was the reason for our interview. Sales were low, and John was hoping to stimulate interest by chatting it up. The album was formula Lennon with its low lyrical content and obligatory indecencies, such as the use of the pejorative term 'nigger' in the title of the track 'Woman Is the Nigger of the World', focusing attention not upon quality but upon controversy.

Realising now that it was as if to see a parson de-frocked, at the time I could only puzzle about Lennon's rancour over his audience (and critics) awaiting the return (or resurrection) of the old Lennon. About this he was furious. 'One criticism levelled at me,' he complained, 'was: "Please give us some more images, John." I wrote "images" for my own sake. It is like asking some film-maker to make films like you did ten years ago. Don't make 'em the way you do now, 'cause I like the ones you made ten years ago. Well, if you don't like the films I'm making now – don't buy it and do not bother me with it 'cause I know what I'm doing and I'm not looking for maximum audience at the expense of my own mind any more.' He pauses: 'Discussing something which happened on forty minutes' worth of plastic six months ago which was just one evening in my artistic life is just one piece of shit. It is just another meal. It is like discussing one fuck forever.'

Was the Beatles' swansong to the studio where they became superstars, and the greatest-selling Beatles album of all time, *Abbey Road*, a one-night stand?

'To me *Abbey Road* is just a slick job of work done by four professionals who knew what they were doing. As an artist it was a complete and utter bore for me to produce *Abbey Road*. And I don't care if I never make anything that people like as much as *Abbey Road*. I think *Abbey Road* was nothing.'

Of his most successful solo LP to date, *Imagine*, John was no less generous.

'*Imagine* was a child's lyric – very simple. It was couched with violins and a nice melody which was more acceptable than quote one with just as simplistic a lyric but without the violins.'

If Lennon impaled the image of his former self, Yoko annihilated it without demur.

'The success of the Beatles reflects the naiveté of the period. It reflects the naiveté of that age when male chauvinism and things like that were not in question. The fact that everybody in the world admired four young boys with a Peter Pan image without any question as to whether the wives were in the background struggling – they preferred that no women were around them.'

Lennon's social availability was a great deal more than myth, for as I discovered after the interview, he kept a London pad in Emperor's Gate (while the wife was hid away in the country with their son) for freewheeling encounters. (Singer Kenny Lynch has great stories to recount about John's swinging London days, which will be discussed later.) But here and now let me say that during that famous Helen Shapiro tour, when the boys began as a back-up group and ended up as headliners ('Please Please Me' had zoomed to Number One), there was that thing about John never admitting he was married. In the course of our interview Lennon himself came clean about his 'secret marriage' to Cynthia.

'I was married before I left Liverpool and I was probably doing it as well but I was definitely influenced to keep quiet about it. And this is what would happen in a press conference or we would be sitting in the dressing room and they'd come in and ask: "Are any of you married?" And so I wouldn't have to lie, someone would always butt in when I answered. George or someone would butt in with: "Oh, go on!" Or he'd make a crack about it. Something like that.'

Whereas Yoko emphasized the edge that male superstars have over their female counterparts, John turned round the argument to his own advantage, proving to us that a man suffers the same sort of humiliation as any Playboy bunny.

'Let us not pick on Elvis but he was a big hero for people from my age group. Was Elvis a slave dressed in his tight leather pants and bangles any less or more than the females? I wouldn't know.

9

We are all whores. We're high-brow whores. A different class of whore.'

Whilst at the time I considered John's comparison to be a colourful bit of rhetoric, in the course of my research I have come to appreciate its greater significance. Many of the stories about John from friends and associates portray him as a savage bully. One chap had a hit song entitled 'Come Outside'. Consequently, every time his path crossed with John's, Lennon would chant: 'Come out. Come out.' Another man, Jewish, recalls that Lennon would talk to him in a mock-ethnic accent. Others bore the resentment of John's dislike of suit-and-tie men. Still others were the butt of his anti-intellectual jibes. There is every indication, unpleasant as it may be, to suggest that Lennon sought to intimidate others with his confidence, wit and physical appeal.

Apparently Lennon was converted from all this when he met Yoko – his saviour, with whom he could be classical and pure. Theirs was a relationship I do not pretend to understand completely, mostly because they said so much and told one so little. The truth is, I think, that John had run dry of ideas. Belting thirty (old for a rock star), he drew upon Yoko's fecund imagination, financial genius and merchandizing skills. Daughter of a Japanese banker, Yoko managed their money to advantage, sparing John the necessity of either writing or performing. Desperately in love with him, she lacked the competitive edge of a collaborator, and coped with his ego in a loving and nurturing way. Understandably, John was euphoric about the partnership.

'The only thing ever lacking in working with another artist and they were usually male – whether it was Stuart Sutcliffe (my art school friend) or Paul McCartney (my musical friend) – is that the relationship only goes as far as the front door and after that you are alone in bed. It is a plus and not a minus. The plus is that your best friend can also hold you.'

Of course the funny thing is that John was very much a locker room male. He often roomed with men. Even when the Beatles had become so big that they were offered the choice of private accommodation, John chose to share (not with Paul, his collaborator, but with Ringo). He went off with McCartney to Paris on the £100 his aunt had given him for his twenty-first birthday, although he and Cynthia were practically engaged. A few weeks after the birth of their son, Julian, John persuaded Brian Epstein to allow him to tag along on Brian's proposed Spanish holiday – an excursion which earned John the 'homosexual' label from Liverpool locals. Contrary to the opinion that Brian was on the make for John, I believe it was John who tried to involve himself with Brian, believing as he did that he was irresistible to both sexes and, more importantly, needing the confidence of Brian to maintain his supremacy as founder of the Beatles pop group. It is of no small significance that during Brian's management a publishing company was set up by him for Lennon and McCartney (although Harrison wrote too), and that the number of songs by Starr and Harrison per album were seriously limited.

It may sound crass, even incredible, but on scrutiny it appears that Lennon's liaison with Ono was anti-climactic, John playing the role of a male Alexandre del Lago, anguishing over his lost youth – a played-out hustler, the very embodiment of the type of tin pan Elvis god which he hated.

So what about the hip politics? The feminist transition, rather than being a natural evolutionary change, was pursued more out of desperation – a safety net. The mantle failed to hang right, and when I talked to John I was aware of his difficulty in coming to terms with his new image. He admitted it took him four years to adjust.

'Even though I could sing "Woman Is the Nigger of the World" and could accept the stuff intellectually, there is still an emotional reaction that happens without me even knowing. And that is the real hard thing. It's like starting to have to become ambidextrous. I was amazed that I ever got through it. I can't put it in words. I almost pulled the plug on it.'

More surprising, the Beatles' image as a band of hard-drinking, fun-loving, sex-crazed English schoolboys became transparent when John frankly revealed his true feelings about the opposite sex.

'Like most men I found women terrifying, which you don't know how to deal with.' About his first marriage he said, 'Whatever anybody else had, that was what it was. And what I have discovered is that I never had a relationship with a woman before. I had no idea of what it was to have a relationship with a woman.'

The effect of the then typical English single-sex education left its mark, and it was not until he met Yoko that John was able to relax with his naked body. Hence, perhaps, the obsession. (Ironically, nudity was something which Brian Epstein felt comfortable with from an early age, and may be one source of John's resentment.)

'I was with both sexes up to when I was aged seven, and then they split us. From ages seven to eleven and from ages eleven to sixteen (which is when I left school) I had no communication with women. Whether it was a wolf whistle or a bit of snuggling in the park and a run home, that is *not* a relationship. But you have a relationship with other men on the football field or whatever. You are only taught how to have a relationship with other men. So I had no idea. A woman was just something you met at a party. You either date them or you don't date them. You didn't discuss music or you didn't discuss rock 'n' roll with them.'

Biographers are keen to suggest that Lennon, during his marriage to Cynthia, was a wife-beater. Cynthia's friends deny this allegation and have told me categorically that it is absolutely untrue. However, Lennon himself admitted frankly to charges of physical cruelty to women.

'The He-Man was supposed to smack her across the face. In all the movies they propagate the smack in the face. She succumbs in tears and you make love. Most of the guys I knew in Liverpool thought that is what it was about. If she didn't lie down first, you smacked her in the face and then you got what you wanted. That was the Tough Guy. You not only dressed like James Dean and walked around like that but you acted out like those movies. It is a relief not to have to be *machismo* or whatever it is. It is not much fun.'

During the course of the interview there was a lot of chat from Yoko about how flexible and liberated John was but one thing said – suggesting chauvinism in the household – rankled, as it still does eighteen years later. Objecting, Yoko began: 'We go to a restaurant and usually they serve the woman first. A waiter was starting to serve me and the manager came up to him and said, "John first." I was very surprised but I guess the way they think is: "He is a superstar. Forget about the slave wife." That bit. It is similar to being married to Brigitte Bardot in a way. There is that side to it. The sex symbol bit.'

Whether the Lennons arranged to have me interview them in their spartan artists' pad, with its lack of status or wealth, may only be supposed. I did not know then that they had booked rooms at the smart St Regis Hotel and could not suppose that within a few years they would practically buy up the Dakota apartment building, along with farms in upstate New York and homes in Long Island and Palm Beach, Florida. Today Yoko Ono lives in a style and manner befitting the Rothschilds. At this stage, however, the couple were talking about lack of possessions and carping about being ripped off by staff using taxis rather than buses, since they were working for the inexhaustibly rich Lennons.

Their message during the interview, purely and simply, was politicism. We may not be great, but we are committed. They sought to portray themselves as the martyred American spies Julius and Ethel Rosenberg – sacrifices to the Cause. 'It is like Jesus,' said John, seeing no humour in the comparison. 'It is like if Jesus had a good PR man he might have been able to do what he did and not die on the Cross. Should he have done what he did and ended up on the Cross? Or should he have been voted in in Israel?'

He paused: 'What we are saying is: Be naked. It's nicer and it is easier if we weren't and we might prolong whatever is going on longer if we don't reveal ourselves. But whatever is going on, it is time to be completely naked and run the risk. The same argument was given to us about "Two Virgins" [the nude cover]. Be more subtle. Why didn't you make it a pop album? Why did you have to be naked? You shouldn't have done it. If we put it out now [after *Hair* and *Oh Calcutta*] it would be a joke. Back then it was direct and no holds barred. It is guerrilla warfare of the mind.'

John's disenchantment with material wealth may derive from the inequality which for many years prevented the Beatles from seeing much of the money which their records generated, due to a paltry royalty agreement. (It is estimated that the Beatles, responsible for 50 per cent of the revenue of Capitol/EMI, generated a billion billion in income.) Worse, John lost battles to secure ownership of both Northern Songs (the publishing company which Brian Epstein had started for them) and NEMS (which controlled much of their finances following their breach with Brian and after his death). Bidding for control over rights to their own songwriting, they failed in a bid against ATV for dominance of the company, unable to convince the outstanding shareholders that they were indeed serious about or capable of managing their own affairs. The fact that Epstein had built into the group's renewed EMI contract a clause giving his company, NEMS, a continuing 25 per cent following the termination of his role as their manager made purchase of NEMS after his death an absolute necessity. Here too Lennon found himself stonewalled by Brian's mother Queenie and brother Clive. Ignoring the Beatles' bid in favour of a stronger one from Triumph Investments, the Epsteins sold for twice what the Beatles offered. Both battles will be discussed later, but for now suffice it to say that the encounters served to underscore Lennon's contempt for big business.

'My auntie used to say, "I'd sooner be rich and miserable than poor and miserable." That's rubbish. They are always saying – "Well, you are allowed to protest." If you really start saying something that goes against the grain, you are put away. Who has said anything? – Kennedy, Martin Luther King – you can name them on five fingers. Where are they now? I don't care what – a madman or a conspiracy or whatever the game is. Five people said something and really tried to do something and they ain't here.

'People say Britain is free. Free – relative to what? Russia, maybe. Britain is a colony of America the way Japan and every- where else is. I am not screaming about it. It is a fact of life. This is not a revelation or a political statement. America is what Britain was. *This* is the Empire.'

He paused. ' "Working-Class Hero" is about us all. In the old days the working class or the Third World, or women, or whatever, were allowed to be boxers or jugglers. And in my generation they could be Albert Finney or John Lennon. But it is the same game. The blacks were supposed to dance and sing or run track or be great boxers and the same from the class that I came from. The working–class hero was allowed to sing, as long as he did it like Elvis. As soon as you rock the boat they try to put you back in your place. Refusing to be the myth is the bit. "Get back in your place, boy. You had your lucky break. You got your cash. We said that you are all right. Now, what else do you want?" Well, that ain't good enough for me. I woke up. I don't want to be Joe Louis and they say nice things when you are dead. You have to play the game on all levels.

'I am not being hit because of the work that I'm doing. I am being hit because I refuse to be a good boy, to accept my gratis health food given by the State and carry on the Old Tradition of becoming one of them. Whoever *they* are. The Establishment. Or grow up.'

He paused again. 'People put their arm around me at Immigra- tion and say, "Grow up boy." Grow up means: Shut up, clean up, dress up and die. Then you are allowed to live half-dead, which is what most people do. That is the difference between a real artist and people going through the motions. I refuse to be half-dead.

'English men,' he huffed, 'are wimps. They have a reputation for being effeminate and sadist. And they don't get that through loving Mommy. I'll tell you that.'

The myth defiled, the search for the real Lennon – the *other* side of the flamboyant public personality – has led to a fascinating voyage of discovery which I shall now share with you.

3

Life of Brian

That the Beatles succeeded to the extent they did is amazing, considering that much of what Brian Epstein had envisaged for the group was in direct conflict with John Lennon's personal vision. It is no hollow accolade which Epstein biographer Ray Coleman bestows upon Brian when he refers to him as 'the man who made the Beatles'.

But it was more than differing visions which separated John and Brian. It was the divergence in background and upbringing which comprise British class politics that set them forever apart. As the years progressed, rather than growing closer they grew farther apart as John's bullying and resentment of Brian were perversely fuelled by the gracious gestures by which Epstein sought to ingratiate himself with the boys.

When Brian met John, he was a successful twenty-seven-year-old director of a small family business which specialized in furniture and had just introduced a musical department popular with young record buyers.

Although in trade, Brian conducted himself in the manner of a gentleman. And why not? His upbringing was privileged in a way that was only possible before the war for people of middle-class means, imposing an unbreachable divide for members of the working class, difficult to comprehend today.

Brian, as they say, was 'posh'. As a child he was cared for by a nanny who used to push his pram in Calderstones Park. He was loving, wanting to please and to be pleased in return. He adored his family, revered family life and was the kind of boy you would expect to marry and raise a family. As it was, not finding the right girl was a lifelong disappointment, and it is with poignancy that one considers his congratulatory note to his younger brother when he married. The family did much together, often going off to Southport for the Jewish holidays, the High Holy days, where one Liverpool chum of Lennon's remembers seeing Brian acting 'very grown-up and posh'.

Raised as an orthodox Jew, Brian never ceased to be religious, and often on his return to Liverpool (after he had established his office in London) he would attend Greenbank Synagogue with his parents, prompting an Israeli visitor to exclaim in the middle of the service: 'Look! There is Brian Epstein, the Beatles manager.' Brian is buried nearby at Long Lane Cemetery in the Jewish burial ground, and it is not uncommon to see visitors who never knew Brian pay homage to the grave, where they lay ferns and other greenery.

His aunt Stella Canter recalls Brian as a child. 'The Epsteins lived in Liverpool when Brian was growing up, and every Sunday my father would go to visit the grandchildren and I would go with him. He worshipped them. So did the boys' parents. They were *lovely* children. Brian was the elder. The general feeling is that it was a happy house. My brother and sister-in-law were very much in love and I think the boys grew up in a very loving atmosphere.'

Loving and elegant, for the Epsteins had not only a nanny but a maid too. And lots of lovely china, silver and glassware. It was undoubtedly from his family that Brian developed a taste for 'gracious living'. The term became a standing family joke. 'We used to have a joke about "gracious living",' recalls Mrs Canter. 'Brian used to talk about gracious living. We were on holiday somewhere and staying in a house which was too ghastly for words. I wrote to Brian and said, "This is *not* what *you* would describe as 'gracious living'." '

Jewish holidays were times when the family got together, and Mrs Canter recounts that it was on one such occasion that she first heard a record by the Beatles. 'It must have been on Rosh Hashanah and Brian said to me, "I want you to listen to this." I think it was Radio Luxembourg. He said, "There is a new group out that I'd like you to hear." It must have been "Love Me Do". I remember listening to the group and Brian saying, "What do you think?" In those days I was very much a Sinatra fan. I said "Wow" when I heard it. "I'm sure the kids will love it." But "Love Me Do" was not my cup of tea. I was afraid of voicing my opinion at the time, because I was obviously not in the same generation. And Brian stuck to his guns and said, "I think they're great".'

She pauses. 'Later on I became quite a Beatles fan. Some of their music was terrific. Lyrical, melodic and nostalgic to this part of northern England because they used local things – Penny Lane and all around there, Strawberry Fields.'

Did Brian clean up the Beatles?

'They were pretty scruffy in those days and Brian was keen on altering their image. I think they were rebellious but I do not think Brian minded that. I remember once asking him when hearing a John Lennon song, "What does he mean? Does he mean what I think he means, Brian?" And Brian replied, "He means exactly what he says".' (Mrs Canter thinks the song was 'Norwegian Wood', but it was probably 'Day Tripper' with the muffled reference to 'prick tease'.)

She continues, 'Whatever they did that he didn't agree with he wasn't going to have the Beatles put down. And he stood up for them all the time – about smoking pot, the Vietnam War and the Maharishi.'

And gay sex?

'I was *shocked* when I read it all, because that part of his life was a mystery to me.'

Did he ever bring the boyfriend to the house?

'Never!'

In researching the prelude to Brian's death, I was surprised that neither his mother, Queenie, nor his aunt Stella knew that months before he died Brian had suffered a nervous breakdown and had been confined to the Priory Hospital in Putney, south London, for treatment. During the time that he was reported to be in fine form escorting his mother round London following his father Harry's sudden death, he was himself oscillating between sanity and neurosis, barely released from medical care. And yet in responding to my queries about access to Brian's psychiatric records, his mother states in writing that she did not know her son had received psychiatric care.

Confirms Stella, 'I didn't know that he had been to the Priory clinic. At the time of his father's death he was obviously very distressed – very anxious for his mother. He persuaded her to come and live in London where he could make her feel useful. And he used to take her out. He was so busy worrying about his mother.'

Did she subscribe to the 'suicide theory'?

'People say he did away with himself, which is absolute nonsense. He was taking these tablets. His Mum once said to me, "It's difficult. He would take a sleeping tablet and then somebody would phone up. And he'd come back and take another one." And in the end the verdict was that he died of an *accumulation*, certainly not a suicide. That was the last thing. It was more than he could cope with. Because at the time all that he was concerned with was looking after his mother and seeing that she was okay.'

She sobs, 'A young man in his prime, aged thirty-two, with everything to look forward to, coming to an end like that. And years later people are looking for something dirty. When he was alive, nobody wrote anything nasty about him.'

If our code for social conduct is formulated during our schooldays, there was every indication that Brian would become a model of goodwill and fair play. Both his lifelong commitment to socialism (and passive resistance) and precocious eroticism (love of nudity) were manifest at an early age. Whilst he did not always fall in with the others at Wrekin College, his public school, his oddities were tolerated by both the masters and the boys.

Although not a Harrow or an Eton, Wrekin is very much a public school in the traditional sense, a bit of heaven – a Shropshire idyll called 'the garden school' because of its prodigiously lovely gardens. Here boys are trained in every possible discipline. Study, dining, religious instruction, amateur dramatics and sports are pursued with a team spirit both supportive and reassuring.

Whilst Lennon was often chastized by masters and senior boys at Quarry Bank (and was either 'slippered' or caned), Brian was cherished by his teachers, says the wife of his housemaster, remembering him with affection.

Another Wrekin boy, son of a Liverpool fruit and vegetable supplier, Brian Johnson remembers Brian Epstein with mixed feelings. It was Johnson who was ignominiously quoted about having fought with Epstein over a bar of chocolate and, having only received a small bit, lashed into him about being 'a stingy Jew'. Chatting to me in 1989, Johnson clarifies the story: 'I could just as well have said, "You old Scotsman." There was no harm meant. I don't think there was any anti-Semitism at Wrekin. We were all boys who had been born in the middle thirties, so we had all been through the war. We knew about the Holocaust. We had all seen the pictures of Belsen.'

Actually Johnson's friendship with Epstein was sustained longer than Ray Coleman's book makes out. They were not merely

Wrekin rivals or fellows. They had a friendship outside school which endured until Epstein's involvement with the Beatles.

'I remember seeing Brian during the school holidays from time to time. He had a source and used to get trade show tickets for cinemas or previews. There were three or four Liverpool cinemas for local reviewers and I remember going to a couple with him. And we'd go to the Basnett bar afterwards for a drink. Lots of theatre people went there. It was outside the Playhouse and the Royal Court.'

At Wrekin Epstein tended to be posher than most boys: his hair nicely cut, his clothes neatly tailored. Often he would return to the boys' dorm with stories about some fancy place he had visited with his family at the weekend or on holiday.

'He liked "gracious living",' recalls Brian. 'I can remember his mentioning trips to London with his parents. He would ask if I had been to London with my parents, and I said yes. "Have you been to Bagatelle?" Bagatelle was a restaurant nightclub run by Edmundo Ros, the band leader. That was pretty elegant for post-war Britain. We still had rationing at that time. I said "Yes." He was surprised. We got into an animated discussion of London restaurants and nightclubs.'

Johnson's path crossed again with Epstein's when the latter was working at NEMS. It was, eerily, the last time. The memory is acute. 'I recall I was in a restaurant near the NEMS Whitechapel office one lunchtime. It is a Mecca restaurant (now operated by Grand Met) which used to serve English food, have linen tablecloths, waitress service and a bar. I used to go there with my brothers. I saw Brian in a far corner and went over to have a word. He was there with his brother Clive. He said, "Do you come here every day?" I said, "Actually we do." We had a family business with offices in different parts of the city. I sensed he was envious of that. And I said, "We must get in touch and have dinner or whatever." He said, "Right. Let's do that." And that was the last I saw of him.'

Problems upon leaving the pubic school cocoon are summed up by Johnson: 'I think the Beatles looked at Brian as an officer. I think he was a good one. There would be antagonism. What they were doing was helping to break the mould of the class system. What would be going on in the group between the officer and the ranks? Pick out the weakest point they could find.'

Whereas some public school boys tend to lose a little of that finesse in the real world, Epstein remained the very essence of a public school boy until the day he died. His speech, dress and grooming set him apart, and it was obvious from his diction alone that he was a cut above. His hand-made suits and the silk cravat he wore (almost as a mascot) around his neck, as much as that fabulous camel-hair coat, alienated any chance of getting in with Liverpool lads. His nails were manicured, his hair coiffed, and the lingering smell of aftershave suggested to one and all that Brian was a man of means.

Although he was very social, his affairs failed for any number of reasons, including suspected infidelities about which Brian was sensitive. He used to race around town in a Ford Zodiac (before trading it in for a van to trot the Beatles around Britain), squiring some lady to a fancy Liverpool nightspot. He had a bachelor pad in the unfashionable Liverpool 8 district (which to his regret failed to see much action), and a dinner jacket — something which struck both Lennon and McCartney as indicative of style.

Sadly, Epstein had little or no instinct for choosing the right girl, if one reads between the lines in Ray Coleman's account of his life. Singer Alma Cogan was crazy about Brian, but he apparently couldn't quell his unreciprocated affection for Cilla Black, whom Coleman mistakenly records as being married to Bobby during the time that Brian was in love with her (they married after Brian died).

Brian's PA at Kingsley Hill, Sussex — the house he bought seven months before he died — was James Rushton, who confirms Brian's unreciprocated passion for Cilla. 'There was a side to Brian that was sensual. Cilla Black wrote to Brian saying she wouldn't come down to Kingsley Hill to stay with him, 'cause he said that her work was a load of crap. What he said was that her talent was not that great and that she was bloody lucky to be in the situation she was. True to tell, Brian's comments were fanciful since he pursued Cilla's career until the end of his life.

Black has never suggested that there was the slightest hint of intimacy between her and Brian Epstein. However, Brian's devotion to her career until the end is documented in police testimony. 'During the past period also, so far as his business affairs were concerned he had been even more diligent than usual and had paid even more attention to them than in the past. Examples of this are of his persistent attempts to reach one of his prominent artistes who was abroad, as he was very excited about a number of plans he had evolved and wanted to get *her* views on them as soon as possible.' Cilla Black was the *only* prominent 'her' in Brian's stable. (Cilla, incidentally, *was* out of the country at the time of Brian's death.)

Perhaps it is envy at not snagging a man who went on to become a multimillionaire and who, after he has made it, barely remembers who you are. But some girlfriends quoted in other publications about their relationships with Brian have been less than loyal.

In contrast, girlfriend Joanna Dunham, changed since those youthful days at RADA, summons up a picture of Brian close to the truth. He was precociously amorous and he did drink. 'We had been going around together. It wasn't really a sexual relationship, except that we *did* kiss and hold hands. In those days, the sixties, the Pill hadn't happened and I lived in London in a flat with three other girls. We didn't sleep with anybody until we married, which was not unusual in those days. There were people who did, but they were the exceptions.'

Why did it end?

'I remember that he asked me to a party one night. He said he had something important to tell me, and that he would when he arrived. I could tell he had been drinking. The party was in Golders Green at the home of his uncle. It was a fabulous house with a long and winding road leading from the door. When we got there it was all Brian's family and I didn't know anybody. I got to feeling isolated. The atmosphere cloistered me. I ran out of the house. I couldn't stand it.' She pauses, 'I never learned what it was he had to tell me. Perhaps it was that he was gay. But we mustn't speculate.'

Dunham's path crossed with Brian's when she left RADA and went on tour to Liverpool. 'He was very sweet,' she recalls. 'He sent me masses of flowers in my dressing room. It was a classy thing. He was very sweet to me. He took me out to lunch.' Their last encounter was by mail when Dunham was by then married with two children. 'One day a gift arrived by special messenger. It was a book of the Beatles. He sent it around with a note, saying, "Thought you might like this." '

Epstein's panache must have been provocative for someone of John Lennon's working-class background – a boy with one good Sunday suit whose idea of a good time was to spend the night with a girl in Blackpool. All of John's defences came to the fore with Brian. He bullied, tormented, abused, scandalized and even

— Albert Goldman speculates — assaulted Brian, a blow which the biographer concludes resulted in his death.

Was class rivalry that intense? Raymond Feather, now with the BBC, was a neighbour of John's when they were kids and the families lived near to each other in Menlove Avenue. He is able to characterize for me the antipathy between people of different faiths and classes in what is essentially a racist environment. 'John never mixed with Jews,' he said. 'He didn't know anything about Jews. His image of Jews was based on ignorance. He never knew blacks although he liked their music. And there is a big black community in Liverpool. But the blacks never went to the Cavern, for example. It was a "white, working-class club". The blacks in Liverpool spoke with a Liverpool accent and were a two-hundred-year-old community of West Africans. The Jewish community dates back to 1700, although there was a big migration in 1900.'

Adding insult to injury, Epstein was not only a Jew — he was a rich Jew. 'Epstein was a business Jew from a family of business people. Very different in social class to Lennon. Epstein came from a big furniture family which owned record shops. Company directors. And living in a completely different part of Liverpool.'

John, on the other hand, militantly working-class, bridled against Brian on principle. 'John was proud. There is a very cultured working class in Liverpool — very Irish in many ways. John was born working-class Liverpool but never grew up working-class Liverpool. (His aunt was lower middle-class.) And yet his sympathies remained. I never found him that way, but I imagine that John could be hostile to "the rich" 'cause he was emotionally hurt as a boy. And sometimes he used to be a bit extreme.'

He pauses. 'People like John didn't like the rich. They resented the Jews. He didn't identify me as a Jew. He didn't know me as a Jew, just as a neighbour. He vaguely knew I was Jewish. He probably identified me more as middle-class. And himself as working-class. *That's* why he baited Brian. Not because Brian was a Jew, but a *bourgeois*.'

Coming from an environment where all faiths and classes freely intermingled made it difficult for Epstein to assimilate working-class Liverpool aggression. Perhaps he didn't take it seriously. Incidents suggest he believed he could become part of their circle. On at least one occasion he tried to emulate them

23

by dressing up (or down) in black leather. Virginia Harry, married to then-editor of *Mersey Beat*, recalls Brian strutting into the Cavern one afternoon suited out in leather togs, and looking absolutely ridiculous. 'We all turned our backs on him, and he sheepishly sneaked out,' she recalls.

Says Feather, 'John Lennon was everything Brian was not: bold, dynamic, free of his parents and family ties. Independent. Couldn't give a bugger about anything.' Brian yearned after that freedom, and in its pursuit he had left the family home and taken a flat in town without benefit of wife and marriage. Recounts Feather, 'To his family he was a bit of a black sheep. He tied his star to the Beatles and left the security of the family business to work on their behalf. He left everything. He was a "rootless person". But he *couldn't* break into their group.'

He pauses. 'The pop groups had their own culture and they weren't going to let him in. Firstly, he was five years older than Lennon. He was a different class, intellect and education. He would do everything to help John and he'd probably kick him in the guts. Whatever he gave him he'd say was crumbs and be resentful.'

Years after Epstein accomplished the miracles of making the Liverpool group not only Number One in Britain but the first British pop group ever to become Number One across the Atlantic, he is reviled in his home town as a greedy moneymaker. A local tour operator, identifying the family home, proffers information about the family originally being Polish immigrant Jews and Epstein being a queer.

An Epstein stalwart, Feather admits that Brian wasn't interested in pop music, although he ran a record department. 'Epstein was a businessman. Marketing John more effectively and making money out of them were his goals. Realizing the potential which the groups were beginning to have on the national scene, his aim was to make them respectable and try to market them in London and New York. He cleaned them up – changed their hairstyles and sent them to a private tailor. He *didn't* send them for elocution lessons, although he might have done. 'Cause in those days Scouse was dreadful, and was *non grata* at the BBC. *I* did go for elocution lessons, and when John's auntie found out she said that *he* should go too. She wanted him to be respectable and suburban.'

Bill Harry agrees that Brian knew nothing about pop music when he began managing the Beatles. 'He'd invite me up to his NEMS office and pick my brains about which groups I thought would succeed,' recalls Bill. His wife Virginia concurs: 'All Brian did was to make money off the Liverpool people. He gave nothing back to the community.'

Liverpool businessman Sam Leach is of the same opinion. Having wanted to promote the Beatles himself, he found that he lacked the capital to merchandise them on an independent record label. 'Brian financed the group. He put up money for what was needed. Being Jewish was a big help in the business. He had a lot of contacts. Most of the agents are Jewish. But I don't think that Brian ever played that up. They didn't really like him. They didn't look upon him as a Jew. He didn't sound Jewish.'

His motive for involvement with the group, whether artistic or financial, earned Epstein a reputation about which he was justifiably angry: that of money-grubber. Even the BBC in an interview implied that he took an exorbitant percentage of their gross. Unlike some managers, who *can* take up to 40 per cent, Brian never took more than 25 per cent off the top. And yet a side man whom I interviewed, having played on a number of Beatles sessions, repeated the misconception that Brian Epstein took excessive fees. Happily on BBC radio, years after Brian's death, Paul McCartney set the record straight in one of the best interviews with him I have ever heard.

Whereas Leach is critical about Brian's lack of business skills, citing as an example his cock-up of a merchandising deal which cost the Beatles 90 per cent, he fails to recognize successful manoeuvres which Brian made on their behalf.

The Beatles were perceived by Epstein as junior partners in the family firm, and his agreement with them was never more than a golden handshake – he failed to sign the management contract, so as to give the boys their freedom if and when they wanted it. Yet it wasn't pure altruism, for there doesn't seem to be a copy of the contract on which the boys' signatures are co-signed by parents or guardians.

Examples of where Brian's devotion succeeded include the 15 per cent royalty he got by asking for a percentage of the *wholesale* price. He also set up Northern Songs, a publishing company, for John and Paul, in which he took but a minor financial interest. Although he failed to secure for them controlling shares (a situation which ran amok when the company, then public, fell prey to a takeover bid) he did realize substantial capital for them (upon which there was no capital gains tax) by floating the company. Before his death, whilst losing the management of the Beatles, he helped them set up their own company, Apple – although he thought the boys would be wiser investing their money in blue chip department stores, and told them so.

Although they threatened many times to get a new manager, the Beatles waited until the legal expiry of their contract in 1967, two months after Brian's death, before making any such commitment. Although the stories are legion about managers and agents trying to obtain a copy of the management contract so as to lure them away, in the era when they succeeded in becoming 'bigger than Elvis Presley' they remained firmly with Eppy.

Early on, when there was some dispute about the parity of one of the clauses, Epstein put it out for a second reading without hesitation. David Harris, now a District Registrar of the High Court, was the solicitor at Silverman, Livermore who drafted the contract which has now become a standard artist-manager document. 'I remember Brian rang me one day out of the blue and said he was interested in a group called the Beatles. I laughed. What a name. He wanted the contract prepared before the end of the year. I knocked it out – charged less than £20. It was an effective contract and used thereafter for other artists – Cilla Black, Jerry Marsden.'

So what about the query?

'We sent it for a reading to Henry Lachs (then a barrister and now a judge). Brian wanted to be satisfied that it was fair. I instructed Lachs to peruse the contract and advise. He said it was more than fair.'

In the last year of his life, Brian, knowing that the Beatles intended to get a new manager, nevertheless negotiated their renewed EMI contract with diligence. Legal adviser Alan Leighton Davis, then of Goodman Derrick and Company, recalls: 'The whole thing took many months. It was a well thought out business manoeuvre. We had specialists' advice and so on – plotting the stratagem over the EMI contract. It was not just a case of it being routinely signed. Firstly there was the decision of whether to go with EMI again, get a new label or produce through NEMS or Apple. But they had this splendid man at EMI called George Martin. They thought highly of him. They started to go ahead with him.'

Was it out of spite that Brian inserted in the contract a clause overlooked by the boys, giving NEMS 25 per cent of their gross for the duration of the document whether or not Brian continued as their manager?

I asked NEMS director Vic Lewis about it, since it ultimately produced a storm in a teacup when discovered and cost the group about £1.5 million to get them out of the contract when NEMS was sold to Triumph Investments following Brian's death. Lewis is indignant. 'Why weren't we entitled to 25 per cent? After all, we negotiated the contract, didn't we?'

The story goes that it was this issue which sent John bolting back to London on the weekend of Brian's death from Bangor, North Wales, where he was in retreat with the Maharishi – the 'something' which Albert Goldman says 'had aroused his passion'. Could he have demanded to see a copy of the contract and beaten Brian to death when he saw that he was obliged to pay 25 per cent? During their entire association Brian vetted each and every thing the Beatles signed, once castigating his personal assistant, Wendy Hanson, for allowing the boys to sign something on their own. They trusted him implicitly, and it wouldn't have occurred to them to vet a contract which he had drawn up.

Entitlement as much as money was the motive, with Epstein feeling bereft when the boys began negotiating with Allen Klein.

'Allen Klein was always around the corner,' says Vic Lewis. 'He made offers. I think Yoko was part of Allen Klein's set-up to get in with John.' He pauses. 'I knew Allen Klein. I had worked with him over Donovan. I thought it would have been a bad thing if he had got the Beatles.'

Another subject of controversy and a keen source of irritation for the Beatles was the consolidation of NEMS with the Robert Stigwood Organization in January 1967, boosting the NEMS banner with such important stars as The Who, Cream and the Bee Gees.

'The Beatles were furious,' Lewis recalls. 'I told Brian he shouldn't have done it – brought in Stigwood. That could have upset him. Stigwood is a very ambitious man. I told Brian: "You might find out that you haven't got the Beatles and that Stigwood has got the Beatles and the Bee Gees." They would never have gone with him. Stigwood came in over my head from the start, which I thought was wrong, and he took over Brian's Argyll Street offices. Probably in the discussions the Beatles had with Brian they said, "We don't like that guy Stigwood, so stop mentioning him to us." So in a while Brian said, "God, what have I done?" The Beatles for a start didn't want Brian to mess around with the Bee Gees.'

Or Cream either for that matter, for it was touch and go as to whether Alistair Taylor, Brian's PA, would get to accompany them on their important debut USA tour; Epstein resisted until the very end. Recalling events at the Beatles 1989 Convention in Liverpool, Taylor says, 'Stigwood went white. He said, "Okay, Alistair, you go with Cream to America." I said, "No way, Robert. I work for Brian." I got a telegram from Brian saying, "Under No Circumstances Will You Leave for America. Brian Epstein." On Sunday morning I got a call from Brian, "Alistair, you would love going to San Francisco. It is a marvellous city. You must go." So we get to the airport and the Pan American lounge and someone came to me with a message that Brian Epstein was downstairs. I said, "You must be joking. Are you sure?" So I went out and looked over the railing and there he was, immaculately turned out and standing there. I said, "Do you want a drink?" He said, "No, no, no. I just came to apologise." This is unheard of, unheard of, for Brian. "Terribly sorry that you were angry and that I upset you." I said, "Come on up." He said, "No, no, no. I just want to make sure that you are all right." '

But the rigours of Brian's coming to terms with his loss of the Beatles had already set in. He was emotionally involved, feeling led down the garden path and dumped. Can't buy love? He tried to keep them by making them expensive gifts, giving dinner parties and so on. Vic Lewis confirms, 'Brian was a great father figure. Anything that any of the boys' girls wanted – cars or furniture – Brian would make sure that everything was done. He liked the idea of the dependency of the boys upon him.' He pauses. 'At first Brian made the Beatles, but then they made him. And they could have felt "After all we've done, he's going to muck around with something else".' But the Beatles had stopped touring, so what did it matter about Cream or the Bee Gees?

Epstein's obituary in the *Jewish Chronicle* suggests that he was led astray by sex and drugs. Before his death, about the time of the release of the *Sergeant Pepper* album, he signed a London *Times* petition for the legalization of marijuana. Ironically, drugs would be his epitaph. Was there sex between John Lennon and Epstein? My source says yes – it was rumoured that, when they got high, John had oral sex with Brian.

Observations by a Stigwood client departing the stable at the time of the merger are revealing. 'I know that Stigwood wanted to take over the Beatles when he first heard John sing some rock 'n' roll song. He called it rock 'n' roll shouting. He was bedazzled. This was way before the takeover. But at that time Brian Epstein was in good shape and it took Stigwood a long time to get round to it.'

Under psychiatric care and in and out of mental hospitals during the last year of his life, Brian often unburdened himself to his PA at his house at Rushlake Green in Sussex, James Rushton. Something was eating Brian – was it Lennon going on about managers living off their clients' immoral earnings?

Says Rushton, 'Brian liked to walk, and we'd take five-mile walks when Brian would confide in me about his troubles. He was sensitive. He felt insecure. He felt cheated that he hadn't got a talent. I would tell him that he was mad, that he had got an immense amount of talent, that he was mad.'

Progressively more incapable of coping with the Beatles, Epstein sought the counsel of Stigwood who advised him to deal with the boys legally. This evolved into him saying *he* was going to take over the Beatles, which is what he always wanted. 'Stigwood told me,' says my source, 'that his idea was to get Brian to take off and he would take over the Beatles. Brian could take a back seat and be a figurehead. That was his aim. A contributing reason for his not succeeding was that Lennon did not want him.'

So why did Brian get on well with Lennon? According to this inside source, a number of rock agents, managers and record company executives comprise a gay Mafia. 'Brian was more of a gentleman and less of a fag than the others.'

This, then, is precisely *why* he suffered worse at the mercy of his pop groups. 'I think that John enjoyed making him suffer – putting him through hoops. That is the position of a manager – the man you love to hate. John tried to blow his mind. Brian was a vulnerable person. He was getting more and more fucked up. He was emotionally and psychologically getting screwed up. John had a killer instinct. He enjoyed making Brian suffer. If you take a sensitive soul like Brian, put him in an environment of tough, working-class Liverpool lads – rough trade – you're going to make him suffer. He was out of his depth.'

The homosexual myth which plagued Epstein unremittingly throughout his life is actually based on little factual evidence. The two legal encounters involving compromising homosexual situations, from which he was vindicated, stigmatized him unfairly. Businessman Sam Leach recalls that, when it was suggested that the Beatles might sign up with Brian, there was a lot of foot-kicking under the table and sly winks at John. When an in-house photographer went on holiday to Paris with Brian, there was that same sort of tittering by members of Epstein's office staff at what was clearly a non-sexual situation.

Beatle drummer Pete Best, outspoken about Epstein being on the make, talked to me about Brian's unsolicited advances to him. 'Brian asked me to spend the night with him.'

At his flat?

'No, at an hotel.'

Why, when he let a flat in town for precisely that purpose?

'We were all going to Blackpool.'

All?

'John, Cyndy, Brian and I all drove to Blackpool for the evening and we debated staying over.'

Oh, so there were others?

'Yes, but Brian addressed his remark to me.'

Other stories are open to interpretation, too. A self-confessed reformed homosexual, George Melly told me a story as an example of Brian's homosexuality. 'I was asked by Brian to lunch after I had written a particularly nice review of Lennon's book for the *Observer*.' Melly was having a dinner party and asked Brian to come to his house instead. At the party Jonathan Miller began describing his visit to the Scotland Yard 'black museum' of criminology and, in Cockney dialect, began imitating the constable describing the exhibits. 'Now you see here, sir, where the semen has seeped in on one side of the panties and the semen . . .' Recounts Melly, 'Poor Brian grew more and more embarrassed. Finally, just before we were having our pudding, he abruptly jumped up, left the table and went home.'

The obsession that Brian was homosexual, a closet fag, grew rapaciously throughout his short life. Lennon was compulsive about fuelling the rumour and began looking for ghosts. Epstein's PA-cum-valet recalls being interrogated by Lennon about his relationship with Brian. 'I remember meeting John one time at Chapel Street. Brian was having a bath when he arrived. So we chatted. He had an aura. You could be looking over there but when he entered the room you knew. It was uncanny. Because he wasn't beautiful. Brian was better looking than any of the Beatles.'

He pauses. 'Lennon asked me if I was paid. He was intrigued as to what my relationship was with Brian. He asked if I was gay, and if I was screwing Brian? I wouldn't give him any information. He asked what my function was. I said I am developing it. He asked again if I was gay. I said, I am, but is that relevant? He asked about Brian. I said, "I share a house with him." '

When Peter Brown went over to become the Beatles' PA, James Rushton went to work for Brian both at his Georgian house in Chapel Street, Belgravia and his country estate, Kingsley Hill in Sussex. At present a psychiatric nurse, Rushton came to work for Brian after jobs with several notable eccentrics. At Kingsley Hill during the last months of Brian's life, Rushton was witness to the many changes in mood and personality which resulted from Epstein's problems.

The property was a Georgian farmhouse of elegant appearance on five or six acres with lovely gardens, a pond and a paddock flanked by a wall and two gates on each side. The drive wound in and around the back part of the rose garden and barn. Adjoining was a charming old oasthouse which Brian used as a staff cottage, and a garage which he turned into a theatre to view films.

Furnished with the help of his PA, the house featured lovely, expensive antiques such as four-poster type beds from Mallett's of Bond Street, fine silver and Persian carpets. The music room, in the attic, was psychedelic, and housed a mahogany Mellotron machine with hundreds of tapes. But the main attraction of the room was the Star of David in reeds which Brian had placed on the wall. When John Lennon first saw it he went blue. Recalls Rushton, ' "The room is great, Brian," he said, "but what did you have to crap it up for with that Jewish star?" Brian was hurt. Lennon couldn't resist putting him down. He didn't say anything. It was something else which he had done which was wrong. He was so unsure.'

Like most of Brian's team, Rushton was kept at arm's length from the boys. 'They were Brian's exclusive domain,' he says, 'and everyone was kept well away when they came around. Once on Ringo's birthday he had sent me to buy a £1500 lead statue for Ringo's garden. I transported it to Kingsley Hill where the party was held and then to Ringo's. When I returned, the party was underway. Brian told me to go and then called me to return (he felt badly), so I sat there having tea with Ringo.'

More frequent encounters occurred at Chapel Street, where Rushton recalls events during that final year. 'Lennon started hanging out with Brian. They'd go to the Saville Theatre (which Brian owned) and Crockford's gambling club.'

When Lennon wasn't probing Rushton's relationship with Brian, he was sounding off about politics: was Brian paying him enough?

'He called me "James",' recounts Rushton. 'He talked to me as if I was an equal, which I thought I was. In those days I wasn't a Communist. I was left-wing, anti-wealth, although I lived amongst it. All of my acquaintances were incredibly wealthy. But I hated wealth that was wasted. We discussed politics. He was not dogmatic. He listened to what I had to say.' He pauses. 'The Beatles, I do not think, considered Brian one of their chums. He was a businessman in the class mould. And yet he supported them in their crusades against the Vietam War, organized religion, legalization of drugs, gay rights, to the anger of others in his stable of artists. When he came out for marijuana, Cilla got angry 'cause her parents objected. And Lulu objected too. I hated her. She was completely anti-drugs.' Occasionally there were quarrels, Rushton recalls: 'One time Brian told John, "You can't say these things." John said, "Don't give me that crap." Brian said, "People might misconstrue." He had an *image ideal*. He idolized them, but he wanted them in a certain way.'

Was the opulence of Kingsley Hill as incredible as it sounds?

'There were people there most weekends. If you are in that profession, people come around. As well as great food and wine there were legendary pot cigars – specially rolled marijuana joints in the cigar boxes which Brian reserved for the Beatles. I remember one time starting to light one and was cautioned, "Remember, they're narcotic." '

Were there ever any drug busts?

'Rich people have always had immunity from the law,' says Rushton.

What was Epstein like when he let his hair down? Rushton's account casts a new light.

'He had a trick of disappearing when we had company. He went to bed. He liked things to be nice. I'd try to make them special – food and flowers. We'd have plain English food. He liked sweets – puddings. He loved port. He would drink a bottle after dinner, roll a joint, put on a record and go to sleep. Other times he'd lock the bedroom door and get stoned on acid.'

Was he paranoid?

'We never rowed. But we did once. He accused me of thinking he was gay. "But Brian, you are," I thought. But I did not say it.'

Curiously, Brian was not the prig which many suppose. His nights at Chapel Street were spent drinking and gambling. He had three cars – a big Rolls, a Bentley Continental and an Austin

Princess with a walnut interior. He had a butler, a housekeeper and a gardener in the country, and two more staff in town. 'The country couple left when I arrived,' volunteers Rushton. 'They couldn't cope with pop stars running around naked and jumping into the pond at 1 or 2 a.m.' He pauses. 'But most of it was for show. Brian would take out a girl. They'd go to the theatre, return to his house for drinks and then his chauffeur would take her home. We'd go to Crockford's to do a bit of gambling.'

Whilst it is Lennon whose behaviour toward staff was regimental and imperious, demanding that his chauffeur wear a uniform and so on, Brian's was democratic and without pretensions. Rushton recalls: 'When the previous butler and housekeeper left, I interviewed for their replacements. The first couple to apply were too professional. The man called me "Sir". I took him around the house and grounds, and to show him the oasthouse which was close to this pond, and there were ducks. He said [mock upper-class affectation]: "Sir, may I suggest ducks-crested!" Brian would not have stood that pomposity. No way. So I asked Brian to meet the villagey couple I had interviewed. He was delighted with them.'

Actually, many of Brian's friends considered him to be lacking in taste – or what taste he had to be 'naff'. Rushton agrees: 'He did have a fondness for a kind of gauche simplicity. I remember one time I told the gardener I'd like some flowers around. He asked what I'd like. "Daffodils," I said. The man stuffed the vase full of daffodils. Brian recognized its own beauty. To me it was insensitive to put all the daffodils in this vase – plonk. But to Brian it had a special charm. He liked the fact that it wasn't pretentious.'

If Brian's house parties were naff, the weekend which Robert Stigwood spent at the house would be described as 'supernaff'. Rushton remembers, 'They were all outrageously dressed in this simple little sleepy Sussex village. Stigwood was wearing a pair of trousers which were too short and he had all these cowbells around his neck. Brian wore a flowered shirt and tight jeans. I wore beads. We went to this Warbill-in-Tun pub before lunch for drinks, Stigwood leading off in his open-top Bentley followed by a Rolls, a big American job, a Rolls, and so on.

'We had this thing at the pub and then we had lunch. Very naff. Pudding was individual trifles with things on them. Then we had supper. And then everybody left. Brian went to bed at 10 p.m. A few pop stars remained. And Stigwood stayed. I didn't know

33

what the scene was. It was quite funny. We all sat there staring at one another.'

Prior to his death and during the year that he was under psychiatric care Epstein discussed his turmoil candidly with Rushton. 'He asked me about psychiatry and if I believed in its curative powers. But mostly he talked about quitting the business. He had already decided to get out. Allen Klein had been making overtures – trying to muscle in. Brian brought in Stigwood as a way of coping.

'Weeks before he did so he told me he was getting out. I said, "Why? Has something happened?" He said, "I'm just getting out." That is how he talked. He was planning to retire. I think he regretted buying the Saville Theatre and hoped to sell it.'

The events of the weekend of 27 August 1967, Brian's death, are mystifying as there are so many versions of the truth. The most common is that Brian intended to spend a comfortable weekend in the country with NEMS directors Peter Brown and Geoffrey Ellis, and that when the boys he expected to show up didn't he went back to London in search of fun.

Rushton refutes that account. 'That weekend was going to be a big business sort-out. The Beatles were away, but that didn't matter since they were the product.'

The events leading up to Brian's departure for London and subsequent death are recounted by Peter Brown in police testimony:

I last saw him on Friday the 25 August 1967 between 10 a.m. and 10.30 p.m. I had been invited with Mr Geoffrey Ellis who was also a director of NEMS Enterprises to stay for the weekend at Kingsley Hill, Rushlake Green, Sussex and we arrived at 8 p.m. in time for dinner. Brian was already there, having arrived earlier in the afternoon. He was extremely interested in having related to him business matters which had occurred during the day and asked for a full report on the activities of the artistes. He showed no sense of being disturbed in any way and the meeting was a friendly and happy one.

After dinner we had coffee in the drawing room and while we were having coffee he made a telephone call and after his call he said he had telephoned a friend in London and that some people might be coming down later, giving me the impression that it was doubtful if, in fact, they would come due to the lateness of the hour and the distance that we were from London.

About half an hour after this he then said to us that he was going out for a little while and that he might even go to London. He then left the room and returned with a jacket on. We both urged him not to go out at that late hour and I walked with him to the garage trying to persuade him not to go and he assured me not to worry and that if Geoffrey and I went to bed he would be back already in the morning when we got up.

An item in the *Sunday Mirror* alleges that Epstein received a late-night business call which brought him back to London with haste.

Biographer Albert Goldman writes in *The Lives of John Lennon* that just before Brian's death Lennon had come round to Chapel Street. 'Something had aroused his passion and he had behaved in his accustomed manner, seizing Brian's arm and twisting it up behind his back as he bent him forward. John was preparing to bugger Brian. . . .' He goes on: 'John demanded that arrangements be made immediately to get him out of the country. . . .'

Goldman sets the incident in the context of Brian's mother Queenie's visit to Chapel Street, which ended on the Thursday before the weekend when he died. However, when I asked Mrs Epstein about any violence between John and Brian she said there had been none. Since the police files which would report such incidents are kept for no more than five years, I cannot validate Goldman's allegation.

When I wrote and asked Yoko Ono to confirm the allegation as recounted by a third party, Marnie Hair, I received no reply.

Whilst I did manage to contact the doctor who first examined Brian, I could not establish any evidence of violence to the body (but for minor bruises noted by Goldman and chronicled in the coroner's report). I did pick up one piece of information from an in-house photographer who recounts that he was told by Brian's valet, Marney* there was a suggestion of violence, since the curtains were in shreds. And yet the consensus is that there was

---

* The man's name is actually Lonnie Trimble. An American, he was not Brian's valet at the time of his death, but was present at the scene and refutes any suggestion about the curtains being shredded.

Interior designer Ken Partridge, who did up Brian's Chapel Street house and also John's Kenwood mansion in Surrey, says that he was called to Epstein's place on several occasions previous to his death to repair something which had been damaged during an assault.

no violence nor foul play, and that any bruising was minor and therefore irrelevant.

One of the first to arrive at the scene was composer Don Black (*Aspects of Love*), who shared an office with Brian. The two men had a brotherly affection, Brian being proud as punch of the 'Jewish' songwriter who had won an Oscar (*Born Free*) whilst merely a neophyte in showbusiness. Black categorically denies that there was anything on Brian's body to suggest violence.

And yet the rumour persists. Could Lennon, troubled about the 25 per cent accruing to NEMS long after their separation from Epstein, have demanded of Brian that he revise the contract, insisting on his return from the country at 10.30 on Friday night? Could the disagreement have led to obstinacy, precipitating violence and resulting in accidental killing? Perhaps. Ironically Lennon's roadie, Malcolm Evans (who could have furnished some answers), died in Los Angeles in a shoot-out some years ago.

Curiously, one newspaper account actually mentions the papers and objects on the bed adjoining Epstein's in the room where he died. Contracts?

Dr John Gallwey, the first doctor on the scene, says not. 'I remember papers found on the adjoining bed. There were letters – one letter in particular, gushing with affection. It must have been from a fan but could have been otherwise.'

From a man?

'No, a woman!'

The profile compiled by psychiatrist Dr John Flood, whom Brian had consulted occasionally in the four months preceding his death, makes allegations which serve not only to compromise Brian but to suggest suicide. Writes Flood: 'The patient had always shown some signs of emotional instability and over the last five years he has had a meteoric rise to success as the manager of the Beatles and various other artists. The patient was homosexual but had been unable to come to terms with his problem.'

In short, Epstein was a closet queen. But if he was in the closet, how could he have been out? What about bruising to the nose and wetness to the back? Whilst the coroner's report makes no mention of sodomy, the police report does disclose that there was wetness beneath Epstein's body.

If a murder occurred, it is dubious as to how and when. Firstly, Epstein's bedroom door was locked from the inside, which means that the murderer had to have got out through the bedroom window. Secondly, when? Saturday was the staff's day off. However, his butler claims that he saw Brian alive on Saturday night. Quoted in the police report as having gone to Brian's room on Saturday, 26 August 1967 at 5 p.m. to give him a meal, Antonio Garcia concludes that Epstein seemed 'perfectly normal. He was in bed and using the telephone.'

Peter Brown says he contacted staff on Saturday afternoon (when Brian was asleep) and again at 5 or 5.30 p.m., when he succeeded in speaking to Brian. 'He was very apologetic. He said that he had gone to bed late and had taken quite a number of sleeping tablets to enable him to sleep. He still felt drowsy. I suggested that as he felt drowsy he should come back to Sussex on the train and we would meet him at the station. He said he probably would do that, but he did not feel at that time even able to do that. I then went on to remind him that a friend of ours, whom he did not think was in London that evening, was in fact there, and suggested that, if he did not want to make the effort to come to Sussex, he had dinner with him. We did not hear anything from him and assumed that he had decided to stay in London. This was, in fact, the last we heard from him.'

Brown then discloses that on the Sunday after returning from the pub for a drink he received a frantic call from Brian's butler. Apparently Epstein had not been out of his room at all on the Saturday. His door was closed and the intercom was off. Brown asked the man to bang on the door, which he had already done, and, while had had been unable to reach him, he had spoken to Mr Epstein's secretary, Joanne, who was coming to the house. 'I told Antonio to telephone me the moment Joanne arrived, which he did. I then told Joanne to telephone my doctor and ask him to call me the moment he arrived at the house. When my doctor, Dr John Gallwey, arrived at the house, I told him and advised him to break the door down, and hung on while he did this. Dr Gallwey then came back and reported to me what the position was.'

Gallwey, currently pursuing AIDS research at the Radcliffe Infirmary in Oxford, recalls the events of the weekend when Epstein died. 'I remember getting a telephone call either from Peter or Joanne on a Sunday lunchtime when I was having lunch with some friends. Either Peter or Joanne rang me up and said that they were at Chapel Street. The couple there, who were either Spanish or Portuguese, had been unable to rouse Brian. They had knocked on the door but they had been unable to contact him. What should they do, and would I go around? I went around. It was no distance at all. They were old friends of mine. And Joanne was there and Peter Brown was at the other end of the telephone in Sussex. I knocked on the door. Brian had a double door which closed off a sort of suite. That was locked. I said, "We shall have to break down the door." It looked pretty solid, but it was paper-thin. We just went in.'

Could he recall the death scene?

'I remember seeing Brian lying on his left side curled up surrounded by papers, letters and a number of other things.'

Could Dr Gallwey tell how long he had been dead? Had lividity set in?

'He was lying on his side and he was dead. There was no vomit. There was nothing around at all. He was discoloured. He had been dead for a while.'

Dr Gallwey says that the curtains were not shredded and does not recount blood oozing from his nose (alleged in the police report). He confirms that the sheet *was* wet beneath Epstein's back, but states this to be 'normal body excretions'.

He confirms there was post lying on the adjoining bed, but argues that the police tried to read something into some letter Brian had received from a lady (probably a fan). 'The policeman said, "Couldn't this be a love letter? And might not this be relevant?" The writer had been expressing a fondness for Brian and the policeman was trying to read something into it.' This crucial bit of evidence was distorted by the press who reported a 'Dear Pat [Boyd?]' letter found at the bedside, reaffirming the myth that Brian was odious to women and was vainly pursuing those who spurned his advances for those of George Harrison.

He pauses, 'The police inspector looked around and said, "I have to release this information to our press room as soon as possible." Brian's lawyer, David Jacobs, had by then arrived. He said they could release the information and the policeman seemed exceedingly interested in getting this through to their press office. That seemed to be the main thing he was interested in.'

Concludes Dr Gallwey, 'I stayed for one and a half or two hours, until a firm of undertakers arrived. When I left there was a barrage of reporters who took absolutely no notice of me. I wondered how they found out what had happened so quickly.'

A smart sixties' West End London doctor whose clients included people in showbusiness, Gallwey knew Brian (through Peter Brown) socially too. Giving me his opinion about why Brian was a loner, he says, 'Firstly he was not a physically attractive person. Not physically sexually attractive. Secondly, I think his interests were with people who would not have found him sexually attractive. He liked "straight" boys on a sexual level.'

And Lennon?

'He offended his success ethic. If he was ashamed of anything he was ashamed of his success (earning so much money). You could blame it on your entrepreneur. I always felt that he unfairly categorized Brian as being to blame for his fall from grace.'

He pauses. 'It is difficult to look back all those years ago. But I know that Brian was very hurt by his rejection of him. I think it was from discussions with Peter and Brian. He was hurt at the end.'

About John, whom he remembers as 'aggressive', he summons up an incident at a party given by Lionel Bart in a house which looked like a mausoleum. 'Lionel had extraordinary parties, and to this one he had invited the entire English football team, to whom the Beatles were hippies. Somebody in the Beatles and somebody in the English football team fell out with each other. I don't think it came to fisticuffs, but they were angry with each other.'

The cause of the death: an accidental and accumulated overdose of drugs.

On the weekend of Brian's death James Rushton had left for his cottage in Lewes so as to be out of the way during the business meeting. On Sunday night someone from the office had rung to say that Brian had died. Recounts Rushton: 'I went back to Kingsley Hill but nobody was there. I had some friends of mine who had in a way kind of adopted me – one was a social worker. They came over to Kingsley Hill to comfort me.'

Dr Gallwey recalls that he went from the house to see Lionel Bart, who was one of Brian's closest friends, to tell him before he found out otherwise. 'I went in and he said, "John, I've just seen on television that Brian's dead." The speed with which his death was announced says nothing for our media, and it caused great distress to his family.'

Recounting his own version of those dreadful events, Alistair Taylor remembers that he had just returned home on Sunday from a successful US tour with Cream when he got a telephone call.

'It was Joanne, Brian's secretary. "I have just had Maria and Antonio on the phone and they can't raise Brian. Can you please meet me at Chapel Street?" My wife blew her stack. I had been away a week already. She objected, "You have just got back from a fourteen-hour flight. You have been working like a dog for this man all these years. Do not go." I said, "I've got to go, luv." Admittedly I was delayed. Finally I arrived. Joanne opened the door. I heard noises. I got hold of the doctor and Brian was lying there asleep. The doctor just said: "He's dead." On the side of the table were six bottles of pills, all half full, all with the lids back on. Now if you are going to commit suicide you are not going to screw the lids back on. There was a glass of bitter lemon and a plate with some chocolate digestive biscuits on it. There was correspondence on the bed. But Brian Epstein did not commit suicide. I concur with the autopsy report that he took one pill too many.'

Not only did Brian's death write the closing chapter in the Beatles saga, it revealed with transparency the darker side of the sex, drugs, love and peace trip embraced by Lennon as part of his cult.

4

The Emperor without Clothes –
the Myth Laid Bare

Brian's death was liberating for Lennon, since he was, as Epstein's New York lawyer, Nat Weiss, remarked, 'the only person he knew who could dominate John'. His loss, and consequent lack of control over the Beatles, was a tremendous burst of freedom for John. Tentatively adapting to McCartney's ideas for the group, such as *Magical Mystery Tour* and *Let It Be*, which he later disparaged as 'granny stuff', Lennon was merely waiting his time to let his real self emerge.

If fame depended upon unity of purpose, the Beatles needed something to conceal the rift which was growing between them. What evolved, in reality, was a pursuit of different directions which left them fragmented as a group, and whilst they made a tacit effort to stay together, the unlikelihood of that working was apparent.

While Paul's conservatism gave John a chance to shout 'Foul', Lennon's smouldering radicalism manifested itself in ways which shook not only the group's partnership but their friendship too. It was Lennon taken to abstraction, and whilst in the past there had been Brian to sort it out, once they were bereft of him John's ego brought down the greatest pop group of all time. 'He doesn't want us any more,' McCartney was quoted as having said to Jane Asher following the arrival of Yoko Ono. On other occasions, such as John's 'We are bigger than Jesus' whopper, Paul had been kind: following Brian's despatch to the States to save the upcoming tour and to remove John from the danger posed by the Hard Right, he quipped: 'Had he done it right, he [Brian] would have been photographed with Billy Graham.'

The Beatles legend does not stand up well to scrutiny when you consider the hundreds of Lennon-McCartney songs unreleased in EMI archives. One only has to listen to a couple of Lennon's personal favourites which got by, such as 'Dr Robert' and 'What's the New Mary Jane', to see that in many instances he was a very poor lyricist. Out-takes from the *Let It Be* sessions illuminate the difference between the idea and the reality of the song 'Get Back'. The original, entitled 'Don't Want No Pakistanis', is a nasty, trite piece of racism against both coloured minorities and Common Market countries. Its ethos is National Front, with Lennon tossing in a tagline about 'the Common Market being too common for me. Ha, ha'. When the song was released, its baser elements eliminated, it became a witty, women's lib put-down about Sweet Loretta Fart, a lady who didn't know her place. But when and how this new song emerged is closeted in secrecy, for we do not share in its evolution. More important and to the point, its sentiment and style are in complete opposition to its origins. This, perhaps, is why Lennon was sardonic about the whirlwind of Beatlemania, dismissing it blithely as 'a one-night stand'.

If, as has been suggested, Harold Wilson's Labour government was concerned with re-establishing class as an impetus to mobility, the Beatles were the very essence of the campaign. Lennon talked about his contempt for both America and 'fascist Britain', but at heart he was contemptuous of race, sex, nationality and class. If alive today, he would have rationalized a way to accept £7 million to do an American Express commercial.

What he was, at heart, was an embittered, divisive individual whose capacity for lyricism was on a par with his nihilist cartoons and polemics. That this side of Lennon failed to emerge during his Beatles years is to the credit of his manager, his musical producer, his music publisher and others dedicated to his welfare. Later on it was Yoko Ono and Phil Spector, plus various musicians, who covered up for John's lyrical and musical paucity.

Did anyone ever consider why Lennon, at the height of Beatlemania, felt compelled to publish songs under a pseudonym to see if they would sell? Can you imagine Tim Rice doing it? And yet this is precisely the case with 'Woman', published under the pen-name of Bernard Webb. The song, recorded by Peter and Gordon, reached Number 23 in the charts.

Without the hype, purveying the kind of repressed sex to which Lennon said he owes his fame, Lennon was at best a hack writer with an audience of two hundred thousand, earning £30,000 a year. His solo singles failed to reach Number

One in the charts, only achieving universal recognition *after* his death.

It is obvious from everything I now know about John that he must have despised the Beatles hype, perceiving it as an idealized version of Britain marketed for tourists. Many of the people and places Lennon sang about nostalgically were actually very painful experiences which he did not *want* to gift-wrap. The song 'Penny Lane', for instance, a nostalgic bit of English whimsy about bus shelters, barber's shops, a nurse selling poppies and an eccentric banker, is nothing but an advert for British tourism. It had no reality for Lennon, who hated the war (and declined to make an appearance at the Arnhem graves on the group's first Hamburg visit), and for whom the Liverpool Penny Lane district was a grim reminder of his own mother's desertion. It was here that Julia lived with her lover and John's two half-sisters, after John had been turned away from their home. Similarly a song like 'Julia' (*White Album*), which idealizes the woman who rejected her son by not insisting that the boy should live with them, is given truer voice in John's solo 'Mother', in which he rails against the lady for having turned him away. ('You had me but I never had you.')

So who is the real John Lennon? And where do his origins begin?

John says it all when quoted after the break-up, 'I've spoiled my image. People want me to stay in my bag. They want me to be lovable. But I was never that. Even at school I was just Lennon. Nobody ever thought of me as cuddly.'

Harrison confirms, 'People are only allowed to read the hype and see pictures, like a chauffeur carrying parcels for you out of Harrods and putting them in the back of a Rolls Royce. It's like a party political broadcast on behalf of the extremely rich people.'

The truth was shrouded in secrecy, and although the Beatles were doing it at the time, everyone kept mum. No one wanted to sabotage the myth that the Beatles, like the Stones, were respectable. 'Throughout the age of Beatlemania,' wrote one critic, 'the press never let slip a word about the Beatles' promiscuous sex lives or their predilections for pills, marijuana and later LSD, despite that these predilections were common knowledge among the journalists who followed them around.'

The marijuana claim, and Lennon's drug bust for possession, came to a head in July 1967 a month before Brian Epstein's death when the Beatles (and their manager) signed a *Times* petition to legalize the weed. It elicited the indignation of the British people, among them Home Secretary James Callaghan who, when police conduct in Lennon's drug bust was later protested about in the House of Commons, turned a deaf ear believing that they had behaved appropriately.

Rolling Stone called it artistic suicide, but at the time Lennon was committed to disassociating himself from the Beatles mop-top image and to revealing to the public the darker side of his character. Nudity, obscenity, drugs and radicalism, once private preoccupations known to family and friends, became public obsessions.

The record makes Ono the cause of John's dissipation, but research reveals Lennon's anti-social side on any number of occasions before meeting her.

The infamous 'Butcher's Sleeve' of Capitol Records' compilation of singles left off earlier albums, *The Beatles Yesterday and Today*, released in June 1966 – a prelude to John's own anarchistic *Two Virgins* – created such a stir that five hundred thousand had to be withdrawn and the cover re-shot using a steamer trunk. The inside story was recounted to me by Don Short, then a *Mirror* writer who became the Beatles' Father Confessor.

'Brian Epstein showed me the cover and asked what I thought. I said it was awful and would damage the Beatles' image. He said he was going to have the copies destroyed. And he did.'

The picture shows the group in white surgeons' gowns, or perhaps butchers' overalls. They are draped with pieces of raw, red meat and mutilated baby dolls – bits of dolls' arms and legs. Paul is unshaven and George is pulling a demonic face. Record company executives and industry people called the cover 'sick and depraved'.

While the same idea was to be a huge success for punk singer Alice Cooper with his album *Billion Dollar Babies*, it was an absolute travesty when the Beatles did it.

Twenty-five years on I discussed the furore with Robert Whitaker, the in-house Beatles photograher who shot what today is a valuable collector's item at the auction galleries.

Whilst photographers Robert Freeman and Iain Macmillan got a lion's share of the Beatles covers, Whitaker's work is relegated to several of their American sleeves, none of which feature with distinction the collage art for which Whitaker is renowned. Having come to Brian Epstein's attention on account of the work he did superimposing contrasting images over one central image, Whitaker perversely took his chance on what is essentially *not* his style of cover. Perhaps the 'butcher' images should be super-imposed over a more commonplace image for contrast.

In the course of our interview Whitaker showed me the evolution of the photo – the many lead-ups to the final shot – and explained some of the thinking behind it and why the reaction was so volatile.

An attempt to deromanticize the boys, the photo session tried various poses before deciding on the one used. Others include a girl with sausages coming out of her pelvis, supposedly an umbilical cord. 'The point was,' says Whitaker, 'to show that the Beatles are as human as we all.' The chosen photo of hacked-out bits of meat, bones, teeth and eyes came about because, he says, 'of the enormous popularity of the Beatles and the way children would scream over them'.

The session was totally ad libbed. 'I just put the dolls in front of them, let them play. Harrison is doing his thing. John Lennon is unpacking Ringo. I wrote two million on the box but it could have been six or ten million. John could see what I was doing and was amusing. Paul hated it. George and Ringo thought it was weird. But they went along with it. Brian [Epstein] was there. He let it go on.'

Whitaker continues, 'Capitol released it and it got banned. And when it was banned we hurriedly had to shoot another cover to paste over the top of this one. We switched to a shot of the group in a hotel room with a huge steamer trunk – one of them sat inside it, one sat on top of it. I had to do it in Brian's office in Argyll Street. The transparencies were then sent out to the States and they were pasted over the old covers.' He laughs. 'It is represented in galleries as "a peeled butcher's cover", because people would steam off the new cover for a peek at the original.'

While at the time the cover was criticized as being 'in bad taste', it is now renowned as the only 'pop art record cover'. 'My cover is not obscene,' protests Whitaker. 'It is not about cutting people up. It is trying to show that we are limbs and so on – quite a lot of deep thinking in that. It was never meant to be offensive or anything like that.'

That Lennon was the Beatle most receptive to his ideas is reassuring, and although Whitaker does not recall any excessive politicism on Lennon's part, he does say that he spoke privately against America's involvement in Vietnam, demanding why a capitalist society could say it had the right to judge other people and wanting to know what was the difference between that and the USSR. ' "Two forms of oppression do not make a right," he said,' says Whitaker.

A very 'inside' Beatles person, Whitaker can say with authority that McCartney is surprisingly vain. He also boasts a cartoon of Brian, John and George captioned (over Brian): 'I've written a very lovely song I'd like you guys to sing', and claims distinction for having photographed Yoko Ono, before John knew her, knitting at a UFO rally in London's Tottenham Court Road.

Present at Yoko's debut show in Britain at John Dunbar's Indica Gallery, Whitaker recalls how impressed John was by ' "the very bright woman doing things, forms of cybernetic art, that were terrific". As their friendship progressed he became more and more interested in her because Yoko talked about the kind of art John was interested in. John was a fairly prolific painter, writer and drawer, and I do not know if he got the full form of stimulation that he required or could have got off Cynthia at that point in her life. Yoko being an original artist, which John was, he could feed off her. They were hugely fond of each other's conversation. Hugely stimulating.'

But depressive too, says Whitaker, contrasting times with John and Yoko with visits to Lennon's Weybridge home when he was married to Cynthia. 'I recall there was a knocker on the door – a woman's ass or bosom – that the house was being rebuilt, and they lived in the attic. This is where John and I painted together. It was very quiet in the house, I must say. There was a swimming pool outside and it was very much somebody else's house which they bought. They were advised by their accountant to buy a nice house somewhere – to start spending their money wisely.

'John was funny and great fun. He thought about other people immensely. Friends of the Earth. I remember how unhappy Brian was that he had been ousted by the Maharishi. But the Beatles were more interested in getting their minds right. John grew up having met the Maharishi – he became aware of Transcendental Meditation, Bed-ins, Peace-ins, and so on. John was always a profound underground artist.'

A bit of a kook too. 'He had an imaginary friend,' says Whitaker, 'and when he performed and bowed he would always talk to this little man on the floor. I never heard quite what he said because the kids were always screaming.'

Having seen the 'butcher's sleeve' prints, I asked if it might not have been simpler to use candids which made John look ridiculous? There is a favourite photo of Brian's where John is lying on his back drinking wine out of a bottle. In his own book of photos of the Beatles' first US tour, photographer Dezo Hoffman tells how steamed up John got by a photo Dezo had taken of him leaping out of a swimming pool with hair as flat as a duck's posterior. Whether, as has been suggested, the Beatles wore wigs and John did not like being caught undressed, or whether he simply didn't fancy being the victim of Dezo's candids, is not known. We know from Hoffman's account only that he objected.

The need not to reveal but to humiliate describes Lennon in later years. His own erotic lithographs of Yoko Ono called *The Honeymoon Suite*, commissioned by an American art illustrator and done by John whilst under the influence of mescaline, were confiscated under Britain's Obscenity Act.

On view at the London Arts Gallery in New Bond Street from 15 January 1970, the set of fourteen prints was displayed in its entirety for the first night only, making that event something of an historical one. Following the removal of the offending eight the collection was not seen together until years later when other exhibitions were mounted, the law case having long since been settled in Lennon's favour. Subsequently they have been on view in cities around the world, in tandem with Lennon's sketches and drawings. There was a good exhibition in London in 1989, diminished only by the fact that the drawings had been coloured in by Yoko.

The John Lennon prints case was heard at Marlborough Street Magistrates' Court on 1 April 1970. Writing about the case in *Not Without Prejudice*, defence solicitor Sir David Napley says his case was based on two points: that the prints were not indecent by standards of propriety recognized today, and that they did not tend to annoy 'passengers'. Writes Sir David, 'The magistrate dismissed the summons saying he was not satisfied that the art gallery was a public place or that those visiting it were "passengers" under the terms of the Act.'

Before my own interview with John, I obtained a set of the prints and asked him to sign it. My own reaction at a vision of carnality expressing sentiments more worthy of Henry Miller was one of indignation.

And the public reaction? A married woman declared she was stunned by 'a drawing of Lennon and his wife having sexual intercourse. I left the gallery with my head down.' Another witness, a man, said the lithographs of 'Yoko Lennon in the nude with an exaggerated bosom and another which showed her performing an oral act on Lennon' startled him.

Was it honesty Lennon wanted, or perversity? The latter seems truer, judging from Lennon's support of *Oz*, a sixties' underground magazine originated by Whitaker, Martin Sharpe and Richard Neville, which got busted for its 'School Kids' issue (1970) featuring on the cover a photo of two black women experiencing orgasm, intercut with a photo of a public schoolboy in blazer, tie and glasses. The photo, discouraging for its racist and sexist overtones, was the cause of a prosecution that resulted in victory. The legal costs were covered by a campaign mounted by Lennon and friends; John donated the lyrics to a song written for the cause: 'God Save Us', recorded by Bill Elliot and the Elastic Oz Band in 1971.

The underground magazine revelled in exhibitionism, fetishism, nudity and, marginally, iconoclasm, forming a link to Lennon's own counter-culture mentality. 'That's why I talk about school on my LPs. I'd like to incite people to break the framework, to be disobedient in school, to stick their tongues out, to insult authority.'

But there is a thin line between freedom and anarchy, and Lennon was eager to confront people with things they found morally or socially unpleasant as if to punish them for his own childhood frustrations.

The charges against *Oz* include: publishing an obscene article, sending indecent publications through the post, and the archaic and rarely used count of 'conspiring . . . to produce a magazine containing divers lewd indecent and sexually perverted articles, cartoons, drawings and illustrations with intent therefore to debauch and corrupt the morals of young children and young persons within the realm and to erode and implant in their minds lustful and perverted desires.'

One critic objected, 'I found objectionable many of the illustrations and portions of the text. Ignoring the four-letter words there are portions of the text which I find obscene, the advertisement "Suck" page 27. I found there were several mentions of drugs and of freedom of sexual behaviour which were objectionable.'

Another wrote:

Largely destructive of accepted beliefs and fails to put forward alternative constructive proposals for society. The bulk of the illustrations, i.e. those which portray sexual behaviour, appear to me to be the work of sick minds in that they are intentionally pornographic and emphasize the sordid and deviant forms of

48

sexual behaviour . . . the acts would be outside the experience of most children and could only result in some children being corrupted. In other words they appear designed to encourage the picture of perverted sexual behaviour. The use of the illustrations of young coloured girls on the front cover involved in homosexual practices is a particular nauseating example, so too is the use of the childhood character, Rupert, in the cartoon on page 14–15. The frequent references to drug taking, smokes, weed, acid trips and spinach craze would seem to accept the principle that drug taking is normal practice and fail to draw to attention the dangers involved in the use of drugs . . . The illustration on the 'inside' back cover and 'incest with my mother' is obviously a degrading and perverted example of the intention to corrupt.

Earlier evidence of Lennon's pathology is found in his play *In His Own Write*, an adaptation of his books *In His Own Write* and *A Spaniard in the Works* and co-authored with Victor Spinetti and Adrienne Kennedy. First published by Jonathan Cape in March 1964 at the height of Beatlemania, the books, translated into a play, were much improved by omitting racist and sexist references to wandering Jews and mammies.

Mounted in 1968, the play not surprisingly failed to attract either critics or audiences. But when John's first book, *In His Own Right*, was published in 1964 it received a much more active reception which could have damaged the group's image. The *Times* review was superlative, but other reviews called it 'illiterate, rude and lewd'.

The question is: could Lennon have kept his soul in its accustomed style on £30,000 a year? Arriving late on opening night at the National Theatre in the flashiest chauffeur-driven Rolls Royce imaginable, Lennon interrupted the triple bill of three period farces by his entrance with Yoko Ono.

Submitted to the National by literary director Ken Tynan, a Lennon fan, who had already asked him to write up for *Oh Calcutta* (to be staged in 1970) an account of his masturbation experiences in the countryside around Woolton as a boy with Peter Shotton, the play was perceived to have screen potential, eliciting that famous caution by Sir Laurence Olivier, then artistic director, about protecting his sale of rights.

Ronald Pickup, portraying the central character 'Me', talked to me about his experience in the role and of meeting John Lennon.

'I can remember Victor Spinetti [co-writer and director] saying, "Now, look, John is going to come today and he is going to be as shy and frightened as you are. All of you help him." And he was. He came with Yoko and they stood at the back. He did look terribly shy. We did a run-through, and he said, "That was great. Nice to see you." He *was* nervous. A bunch of girls in the cast turned to jelly, but he was still shy. Although the way we used to rehearse was far from awesome. We used to rehearse in an old warehouse in a back street near the Old Vic. A bunch of actors wearing jeans and tee-shirts. It was his people and Victor was there. But he was shy.'

Was he pleased? 'Like a lot of writers he was pleased that something was being done with his work and that there were things he perhaps did not realize. Victor brought so much to it. I very much let myself be putty in Victor's hands, because it was a new thing to me.'

Hailing from Chester, with Liverpool as his stomping ground, Pickup endeavoured to use a bit of Scouse dialect in his interpretation of the role. 'It was the first time I had done an absolutely contemporary part, although it was not in a naturalistic setting. Victor said, "Come on. Be yourself." The way it was written is so much directed to the audience. Straightforward Lennon stand-up comedy. Telling the audience the events in this strange Lewis Carrollese way of his. And then galloping off into his fantasies.'

In the course of preparing, Pickup was escorted to the EMI recording studios where Lennon was working on the sound effects for the show – Dickensian effects and a Sherlock Holmes spoof with slides and rear-screen projections. 'Victor took me to see them where they were having a session in the Abbey Road days. They were wonderful to watch, because they were in this huge studio behind glass. I popped into the control room and said hello. They would stand and chat in corners and strum away a bit. I could have sat and watched for hours. Yoko was there. She said, "Hello, nice to meet you" and that was all.'

Was he a fan? 'Absolutely! We are the same age, so I was well aware of who Lennon was. He was a king. He was a symbol of liberation, rawness, vulnerability and this strong, satirical sense which the sixties represented for all of us. He was the king.'

Steadfast despite bad reviews, Pickup believes the critics failed to understand the play. 'There is this wonderful cheeky attitude of giving the finger to the Establishment – the send-ups of everything. I remember John saying, "I want that sound effect that you get when you are listening to a play on the radio about Sherlock Holmes and it is as if there is a carriage going by every window all the time." He is absolutely right. They are crackers about sound effects (the foghorn from the ship – the sound of the coach and horses).

'There is a lovely scene toward the end where they are sitting around the table with this dreadful non-conversation going on. You get an idea of that dreary side of life. "Dad" was a shadowy figure played by a bluff actor – didn't have a lot to do. Mr Guy-next-door down for a pint at the local, back to the HP sauce. Listen to the wireless and the sound of the coach and horses.

'When the audience catch on they love it. They absolutely love it. They are making the connection with the real word. Very exhilarating. Cheeky. Childish. Unpretentious.'

Was Lennon pleased with the production?

'He didn't come backstage after the play. But that could have been because of the audience and the press. There were problems. It was as if royalty was there. They were all looking at Lennon. He fled.'

Describing his own idea of the play, Victor Spinetti declares: 'This play is about the growing up of any of us: the things that helped us to be more aware – reading of comic books, going to school, a first visit to the theatre, visits to the cinema, going to church, and the effect of all the things that pour into a home via the TV and the radio.

'We invented a family who were confirmed TV addicts, rarely speaking to Me, the central character, so he created his own fantasy world and spoke to his own families.'

And John's feelings?

'He said it took him back to his childhood and he remembered the things he thought about when he originally wrote the books . . .'

Despite the play's elimination of vulgar references to minorities, the general incomprehensibility of its send-up of parents, school, media, Church, war, State, business and other institutions put critics at odds, resulting in negative reviews and a short run.

Drama critic Irving Wardle wrote:

The second half of the programme consists of *In His Own Write* adapted from John Lennon's two books of subcultural word games and cartoons. Victor Spinetti has assembled Lennon's unconnected pieces into a montage of working-class provincial upbringing. We go into fantasies of boys' comics and Sherlock Holmes, a burlesque *Hamlet*, nonsense sermons and launching ceremonies, nightmares and quarrels with the inert family grouped inert round the television set and giving voice to feeble sounds of good cheer at Xmas and blinkered parental advice . . . what it leaves you with is a soporific flow of mindless punning that is closer to Prof. Stanley Unwin than to Joyce.

The *Queen* reviewer agreed: '*In His Own Write* is adapted from John Lennon's nonsense verse and shows that he is best employed as a Beatle.'
Another reviewer:

. . . the Lennon piece, after the interval, is rather tiresome. Its amiable phantasmagoria of a boy's world just before the war, during it and afterwards might be moderately amusing if condensed for a revue; but it seems wildly out of place on the stage of the National Theatre. It is hampered, moreover, by its persistent jabberwocky-jargon – a joke that palls . . .

Tom Maschler, managing director of Jonathan Cape which published the book in 1964, went to the 1968 opening of the play, having remained friends with John over the years. 'I often went to his house, firstly in Emperor's Gate, Kensington, and then at Kenwood until he and Cynthia got divorced.' Maschler remembers Lennon in the finest sense without any of the racist put-downs for which he was notorious, such as his references to Brian as 'a rich Jew fag' ('Baby You're a Rich Man').
'I think John's mind was by far the most interesting. He charmed me. He entertained me. He had an original way of seeing things.'
At the first night Maschler talked to John about the adaptation. 'I think he was disappointed. He liked this girl (Adrienne Kennedy)*

* Maschler's comments about Lennon endorsing the project on account of a 'platonic' affection for Kennedy are unconfirmed by the playwright. Kennedy told me when I spoke to her in New York that she had given the play to Maschler, who passed it on to Spinetti, who showed it to Ken Tynan at the National. The original writer credits went to Kennedy and Spinetti, but when Lennon came into the project after a holiday with Victor in Morocco on 29 December 1967, Adrienne's name was excised, on account of her not being a member of the Writers' Guild of Great Britain. Only after lengthy meetings at Apple was the matter resolved, with writer credits going to all three. It was Tynan, in tandem with Olivier, who conspired to pull the play after its brief critically unfavourable run.

very much. I do not mean that he had a relationship but he liked her and she liked his books and wanted to adapt them for the stage. He was charmed by her. She loved the books so much and wanted to do it. He let her have it. I do not think she succeeded in making it into something else.'

The book, as noted, came to Maschler's attention in 1964 via the back door. 'I commissioned a man named Michael Braun to do a book about the pop scene in Britain,' he recalls. 'He came into my office one day and showed me these writings. He didn't tell me who they were by. They were on hotel notepaper, and this that and the other. I just roared with laughter. I thought they were absolutely wonderful, but potentially totally unsaleable. How do you sell these kinds of ditties, good as they were. I said, "Who wrote it?" He said, "John Lennon."'

'Of course I knew who he was, because I grew up in the southern suburban area of Wimbledon, and when they performed it was the most incredible scene you can imagine. There were twenty ambulances outside. One in four keeled over with excitement.'

The book sold barely a quarter of a million copies at a time when Beatles albums were going gold. The reviews, save the one comparing Lennon with Edward Lear and Lewis Carroll, unmasked Beatlemania as hype and Lennon as the emperor without clothes.

'Lennon first makes his million,' wrote one critic, 'then writes. There must be a moral in that somewhere, but at the moment it eludes me . . .'

Another said: 'Would this book have been published if it had been written by a Beatles fan? Possibly not, so it is a happy accident that it was written by a Beatle.'

Still another: 'Unfortunately there is no indication given of John's age at the time of writing (and drawing) and readers cannot be sure if the material has been dredged from the pages of Quarry Bank high school or his kindergarten magazine.'

Barry Broadfoot wrote in the *Sun*: 'This book won't be read by the Beatles fans, for largely, it is unreadable. And if it ever was recorded by the Beatles, it would kill Beatlemania dead.'

Another item: 'Much of the writing is sick humour . . . some of it is vicious, a lot of it drivel, but there is an underlying sense of frustration of intellectuals to thrive on and find hidden truths.'

Tom Hungerford wrote: 'If any but John Lennon had unleashed that on a publisher he would have been committed to the booby-hatch in short order . . . the moral of *In His Own Write* is that you can fool a lot of the people a lot of the time if you try hard enough and you've got the gall . . .'

Carped another: 'He takes delight in physical deformity, in violence and in putting people to death (you can make what reflections on his Merseyside background you like out of that).'

But the cruellest cut must be an account of his presence at the Foyle's literary lunch held at the Dorchester Hotel, where he refused to speak. One critic protested:

> Mr Osbert Lancaster, always clever and amusing and a brilliant speaker, was the chairman and made a scintillating speech. The author, who is of course one of the famous Beatles, sat next to him and refused to make a speech or even say a few words. The only other speakers were Mr Brian Epstein, to whom the Beatles owe so much of their tremendous success as he is their brilliant young manager, and another Liverpudlian Mr Arthur Askey, who quickly had the whole room laughing.

(Ironically, when Yoko's book *Grapefruit* came out there was no Foyle's luncheon; an excuse was made about necessary lead time.)

But it was in the music of his later period that Lennon's darker side obliterates any remnant of respectability, with its indulgence in nudity, pornography, obscenity and drugs.

He had flirted with censorship in the past – crusading for sex, drugs, gay lib (Britain's Consenting Adults Bill passed in 1967, the year Epstein died) and Jesus – and his songs had at one time or another been banned in the USA, Australia, South Africa and Britain. It was with Yoko that he annihilated any remaining traces of the early Lennon with his release of the anarchistic *Two Virgins* in November 1968, recorded in May that year between midnight and dawn at his house in Weybridge when Cynthia was on holiday in Greece. It took five months to get the Beatles' permission for its release; the fact that they approved is immaterial, since seeds were sown which would mature in 1970 when McCartney sued for dissolution of the Beatles.

The whole thing became ridiculous: each composing in different places songs which the other renounced. The partnership continued *de facto* until the 1975 final decree, raising in the meanwhile questions of copyright relating to songs written alone or with Yoko Ono. Whilst 'Cold Turkey', credited solely to John, formally ended a thirteen-year collaborative tradition, it was with

'Give Peace a Chance' that the collaboration really ended, since the song, credited to Lennon–McCartney, was written during John and Yoko's famous Montreal Bed-in when Paul was miles away.

It may be that John's inspiration to produce experimental albums derives from having met and heard Ono. However, an oblique insight into John's character comes from Peter Shotton in his chronicle of their friendship, and has nothing to do with purity or Yoko Ono.

Apparently before Epstein's death, during those months when he was having a nervous breakdown, Brian sent John a tape recording made in his house. 'I don't know why he sent it,' Lennon told Shotton, 'but he's trying to tell me something – fuck knows what! He just can't seem to communicate with us in his usual way any more.'

According to Shotton, the recording was 'barely recognizable as that of an human voice, alternately groaning, grunting and shrieking – and occasionally mumbling words which, even when decipherable, made no apparent sense whatsoever. The man on the tape was obviously suffering from great emotional distress, and very likely under the influence of some extremely potent drugs.'

Shocking? Yes, but no more so than the *Two Virgins* cover or the *Life with the Lions* account of Yoko's miscarriage, together with screams and tears, causing two women who as teenage girls had worked for the Lennons during the summer of their Golspie car crash to shudder when discussing it twenty years later. Alexandra Palmer, now Crockett, and Alison Tilley, now Boone, are now married with children. Having seen the original *Two Virgins* sleeve,* where John is erect, Alex says, 'When I asked about it I was told that "men aren't allowed to have erections on record covers" and so consequently the sleeve was discarded.' Adds Alison, 'Alex and I were given copies of *Two Virgins* and we were told it had been revised. We saw the originals – where John was having an erection. We had quite a few laughs, I must say.'

When *Life with the Lions* was released they were given a copy of the LP which features an actual audio account of Yoko's miscarriage, the couple having taken a tape recorder into their

---

* Apparently the Lennons deferred to the other Beatles and EMI by changing the sleeve, using a photo where John is inert. The original, decidedly, shows him erect.

room at Queen Charlotte's Hospital, Hammersmith in November 1968 to record the event. 'They gave us all a living recording of Yoko's miscarriage,' recalls Alison. 'It was the most horrible record of Yoko just screaming and squalling for John right through with the pains and when she loses the baby and them crying.'

Day help at the house Ringo leased from Peter Sellers and occupied by John whilst his own mock Tudor mansion was put on the market, Alex and Alison were each other's moral support. Alex recalls how different Lennon was from the press image. 'He was a moody person. I never felt relaxed in his presence. I never knew what to expect. You never knew if he would shout at you or make you laugh.'

Alison agrees, observing that Lennon wasn't Mr Nice Guy. 'He had a blue streak,' she says. 'Certain things he said. He wasn't nice at all. Yoko was more honest with you. John would say something and a minute later he would change his mind.'

In discussing the battle over the *Two Virgins* release with Andy Peebles in the BBC interview recorded in December 1980, just two days before John's death in the USA, he protested:

Two Virgins was a big fight. That was like nine months later it came out. It was held up for nine months. So [Sir] Joseph Lockwood [EMI chairman], he was a nice, nice guy. But he sat down at a big table at the top of EMI with John and Yoko and told me he will do everything he can to help us . . . Then when we tried to put it out he sent a personal note to everybody saying, 'Don't print it, don't put it out.' So we couldn't get the cover printed anywhere. It was really due out about nine months before it came out.

The album, released on Track in the UK and Tetragrammaton in the USA, was boycotted by many shops, and music papers refused to accept advertisements. In the United States, 25,000 copies were sold, with 30,000 copies confiscated by police from a warehouse in Newark, New Jersey.

Since it was released in the same month and year (November 1968) as the *White Album*, *Two Virgins* could adversely have affected Beatles' sales. Sidestepping the problem, critics referred to the former as mainstream Beatles, ascribing John's other stuff to an infatuation with the occult. The reverse, of course, was true, Lennon ascribing his only 'true' work to his collaboration with Ono. She was his source – the fountainhead of his genius.

'She can't be accepted. She is too far-out. It is hard for her to take. When I started telling her about what our life was like she couldn't believe it. She was like this silly eastern nun wanderin' around thinkin' it was all spiritual.' Yoko's spiritual exercises, compiled in *Grapefruit*, given to John during the early stages of their friendship when she sought his patronage as her sponsor, provided the source for innumerable Lennon compositions.

Give Peace a Chance, recorded between May and June 1969 and released one month later, rose to Number Two in the UK charts and Number Fourteen in the USA, selling two million records worldwide, causing at least one writer to wonder why, in view of its phenomenal success, Lennon could be persuaded by Allen Klein to compose separately from Yoko with Phil Spector producing.

Peace was recorded on an eight-track machine in Room 1742 of the Queen Elizabeth Hotel, Montreal. John and Tommy Smothers played guitars, Yoko banged a wardrobe while singing out the lyrics with John to the choral accompaniments of friends, visitors and passers-by including Allen Ginsberg, Rosemary and Timothy Leary, Murray the K, Dick Gregory, Petula Clark, Derek Taylor, and a rabbi, a priest, various members of the hotel staff, reporters, cameramen, a film crew and the Canadian Chapter of the Radha Krishna Temple.

The concept, tame by comparison with *Two Virgins* and *Life with the Lions*, was still inflammatory by Beatles standards, and whilst Lennon got away with *singing* 'flagellation' and 'masturbation', it is 'mastication' which appears on the sleeve notes.

None the less it is a significant achievement, proving that hand-made is as good as machine-made, and that personal statements can sell. Tragically, it was on the wings of its release that John and Yoko were involved in the Golspie car crash in Scotland during summer 1969, precluding their presence at the record's press launch at Chelsea Town Hall on 3 July, at which Ringo and Maureen Starr deputized for them. Had the course of *Plastic Ono* not been hampered by the untimely crash, who knows what direction John and Yoko's music might have taken?

The classic *Peace* was followed by 'Cold Turkey', ostensibly about heroin withdrawal but also about the breach following Brian's death. McCartney refused to claim any collaboration, so John took a solo credit for the first time since their partnership began thirteen years earlier. The single surprised with its movement into the UK Top Thirty where it stayed for six weeks, falling to Number Seventeen thereafter and prompting

Lennon's famous note accompanying the return of his MBE to Buckingham Palace.

Signing the note 'John Lennon of Bag Productions', he cited as reasons for its return 'Britain's involvement in the Nigerian–Biafran war, Britain's support of America in Vietnam and "Cold Turkey" slipping down the charts'.

Lennon despatched his chauffeur to his Aunt Mimi's house on the south coast to retrieve the medal when she was out – a somewhat ironic reciprocation of *her* secret visit to Kenwood when John and Yoko were away, giving rise to her remark, upon seeing a picture of the nude couple on the wall that she was 'worried about John'. Whilst the action is ascribed to John's anger at not getting a royal pardon for his 1968 drug offence, it was communicated to me by Buckingham Palace that 'we have no trace in this office of any such approach by Mr Lennon.'

A few months later, in March 1970, Lennon would further dishonour the distinction by giving an interview to the French magazine *L'Express* in which he talked about having accepted it in 1965 because 'our manager wanted it, and for the others'. He also said that he had been late in getting ready, that the Palace conceded to let them dress informally (no morning suits), that he was too nervous to bring his wife, that he smoked a joint in the loo, and that the Queen was prettier in person.

His new persona prompted one critic to write: 'To compare the hard assertive smilingly arrogant Lennon of 1964 with the howling, mortally wounded, pain-wracked animal who looms riddled with self-doubt and self-hatred out of your speaker . . . is quite a downer.' In discussing the prospect of being without mentor and manager Lennon was candid about his fears, recalling how press liaison Derek Taylor reassured him by pointing out in various Lennon–McCartney songs the bits which John had written.

The man who emerged on stage for the first time as a solo performer in September 1969 at the Live Peace in Toronto concert showed himself bereft of musical ability, singing talent and stage presence. The video which followed the event was documentation of his dependency upon Ono as guru, minder and nursemaid. Rather than being dominated by her, John was dependent upon Yoko, and while she was fond of saying she was probably 'a bad influence', the opposite seems nearer to the truth. She was, in no uncertain terms, the rising star to Lennon's has been of *A Star Is Born*.

Willing to welch on their commitment to perform, John and Yoko were got out of bed and put together by their PA, who rang the airport and delayed the plane for a few hours. Lennon complained of the primitive rehearsal conditions while sweeping into Varisty Stadium, Toronto in a limousine, entourage in tow. That the pregnant Yoko vomited before the show might be excused. But what about John? Singing mostly rock 'n' roll favourites, in the presence of Little Richard, Gene Vincent, Chuck Berry and Bo Diddley, Lennon demonstrated that he was unable to remember the words without a crib sheet held up by Ono. Unable to sing on key, his guitar playing falters, he caused us to wonder how much of Lennon was manufactured in the recording studio. He used offensive hand gestures not dissimilar to those he mimed in the *Let It Be* out-takes, when Linda McCartney and daughter Heather appear in the studio, and which have something to do with Jews.

Was help at hand? It is not insignificant that after Allen Klein's arrival at Apple as the Beatles' financial adviser Phil Spector emerged to produce John's next single, 'Instant Karma'. Klein has been quoted by McCartney in the famous Beatles court case as saying that: 'Yoko is the one with ambition', implying a resistance to the experimental music she made with John. It was Klein who suggested that John produce records of greater commercial appeal, using Phil Spector's famous 'wall of sound'. The advice produced friction, and PA Anthony Fawcett refers in his account of working for the Lennons to the quarrels which ensued at their Ascot home, some of which might have derived from disagreements over commercialism.

Whilst Lennon deferred to Klein and allowed Phil to produce a number of singles and albums, he later became so outraged over Spector's unilateral mix of 'Instant Karma' for release in the States (where it went gold) that he determined to produce his own songs. The duo worked together again in Los Angeles in 1973 on John's *Rock 'n' Roll* album, where Spector, as producer, declared his intention to remix the tapes, to which Lennon objected. From California where he resided during his Lost Weekend (about fourteen months) with May Pang, Lennon removed himself to New York where he began recording *Walls and Bridges*, finding that Spector had decided to return the tapes.

Initially keen on Spector when others opposed him, Lennon considered his mix of *Let It Be* to be superlative. Calling the tracks 'a pile of shit', Lennon was especially pleased with Phil's mix of 'Across the Universe', juicing up the original version heard on the World Wildlife Fund record. McCartney disagrees, blaming Phil for botching up 'The Long and Winding Road' by the introduction of violins and a woman's chorus. 'I would never have women's voices on a Beatles record,' McCartney said at the time.

Having seen *Let It Be* footage, I can only hazard to what extent Spector edited out the non-songs and intercut bits of Beatles whimsy, particularly John's, about 'passing the audition' and so on.

'Instant Karma', 'Happy Xmas/War is Over' and 'Imagine', all Spector collaborations, reflect well on Lennon. 'Imagine' rose to Number One, where it remained for three weeks.

Recorded in July 1971 in the eight-track recording studio Lennon had built at his Tittenhurst Park, Ascot home, 'Imagine' is credited to the Plastic Ono Band, referred to here as the Flux Fiddlers – a reference to his wife's New York City Fluxus experimental art group origins. The idea of a mythical band allows John to diminish the reputation of having been created by George Martin, Paul McCartney, Derek Taylor or anyone else, since the whole idea is based on the premise of changing players.

Compared with Ascot, Kenwood was the pits, jokingly referred to as a disaster of a house since many of the ideas didn't work. None the less the mock Tudor conversion featured an ample kitchen, a sun or music room and an upstairs loft used by John for painting and composing. The bedroom was created from two rooms, and featured a revolving bed which switched on at the wrong moments. John preferred to kip down anywhere and could usually be found asleep on the divan or a blanket on the sun room floor. Although the St George's Hill estate featured a swimming pool and a golf course, Lennon built himself a private pool and went to elaborate lengths to landscape the gardens. Housekeeper, gardener and chauffeur were in residence.

A robust house on a couple of acres in a security-tight celebrity enclave of Surrey, Kenwood was no match for Lennon's eighteenth-century mansion on 85 acres in Ascot, Berkshire. An architectural masterpiece, the listed building was not a house but a stately home with obligatory long drive, statuary, tennis courts, ornamental lake, gardens, parklands and, as a bonus, a cricket pitch. The mansion, with its Doric-pillared terraces and circular turrets, had the appeal of something in a windswept romantic novel.

Purchased from tycoon Peter Cadbury, it was first occupied by the Lennons around autumn 1969, following a lengthy period of refurbishment during which they based themselves at London's Inn on the Park Hotel, where Yoko celebrated a birthday. Sending flowers every hour, John also ordered a cake which was as high as the door to their suite.

In addition to a recording studio built to professional standards, the revamped house boasted wardrobes the size of department store stock rooms and a kitchen of hotel proportions. White was the prevalent colour throughout, and there was a carpet made of soft white fur specially woven in China and costing £100,000. Playing piano on several *Imagine* tracks – 'Crippled Inside', 'Give Me Some Truth', 'Oh My Love', 'How Do You Sleep' and 'Oh Yoko' – was Nicky Hopkins, a graduate of the Royal College of Music who had already played on 'Revolution' (*White Album*). Nicky recalls: 'The whole house was white. Too much white for me. Light of course. The studio was very comfortable. First proper studio I had ever seen in anybody's house. I had seen various half-hearted attempts, but this was a real pro job.'

The sessions, recorded during July 1971 at the eight-track studio which John jokingly referred to as Ascot Sound Studios because of his difficulties in getting planning permission for the conversion, were minimally hampered by a film crew photographing for a promotional video to be used by Capitol Records for the album's USA release.

The footage was eventually re-shot after the original director was dismissed, Lennon having decided following conversations with Capitol that a bit more glamour was needed. The Lennons' *Imagine* video, as separate from Andrew Solt's film of the same name, documents the transition from cinema vérité; the original director confirmed the change of image.

Much of the combat between Yoko, John and Spector was deleted. Hopkins talked about working with three dynamic egos. 'Yoko wanted *me* to play piano on *Imagine*,' he says. 'But John stuck to doing it because they were doing it for a video which I do not know if it ever came out. John was sitting at the big white grand piano. I would have played it in a more florid and complex manner, which is my style. I would not have played it that simplistically. And yet it is the simplicity of it that is so wonderful. It is a naive painting. A Gauguin.'

Hopkins played on 'Jealous Guy', the song which derives from the list of men Yoko had slept with before she met John, revealing

Lennon as a male chauvinist pig in his support of a double standard. Fond of sending up Yoko, he admits telling her: 'Do you know why I like you? You're like a bloke in drag. You're a mate.'

It is on 'Jealous Guy' that Hopkins had to fight for his music credit. 'When the album first came out the credits all swirled around on the inner dust sleeve. In the process my name got left off "Jealous Guy". That is the track I was most proud of on that album. I pointed it out to John, because it was one of the first copies that came out. He said, "I'll have them fix that." I thought: "I've heard that before."

'Several years later I was going through my letters when I found two copies of *Imagine*. I thought: "Why do I have two copies? I only keep one copy of anything." I thought: "Let's just check." Sure enough, one was without and one was with. So he had had it done.'

Recorded in July, released in October 1971, *Imagine* was done quickly and efficiently. 'The thing I liked about John,' says Nicky, 'is that whilst remaining a nice guy he was still able to get things done quickly without sacrificing any quality. He was direct with his communications and able to say what he wanted. He was a tremendous presence which you felt, and you wanted to work with the guy.'

Admitting that John had a bad memory, Hopkins recalls that Yoko handed out a lyric sheet to every song instead of the traditional chord sheet. While he doesn't come out and say so, Nicky implies that Yoko was overprotective. 'Even John referred to her as a mother type. He said Yoko was his mother. I never found anything to like about her voice. Or her work. I don't like that kind of singing.'

Preferring the Lennons as solos rather than as a team, Hopkins compares *Imagine* with *Double Fantasy*. 'Musically I didn't like the way the songs were mixed together on *Double Fantasy*. I think they were better when they were separate.'

Disagreeing with Hopkins, I cite Yoko's fecundity as an artist and note Lennon's dependency upon ideas original to her work in his creation of *Imagine*. The album's title song derives from *Grapefruit* instructions which tell the reader to 'imagine . . . this . . . or that . . .' Other Lennon songs, such as 'Mind Games', use Yoko's images – the cosmic 'yes' ('Yes is the answer').

I also argue that she faced greater censorship problems, for while John's 'Working-Class Hero' and 'Give Me Some Truth' replace four-letter words with asterisks on album sleeves, Yoko's 'Open

Your Box' was re-recorded (omitting any reference to 'legs') before EMI would release it. The song was also banned in the States because of the word 'box'. John told Andy Peebles: '"Box" in America means something to do with the female anatomy below the waist.' By the same token, Yoko's song 'Woman Is the Nigger of the World' was banned because of the pejorative reference to 'nigger'. And yet snickering references to Jews and niggers in John's own books and play, whilst meeting with criticism, were never censored.

A few weeks after John complained to *Disc and Music Echo* (18 January 1969) that Apple was losing £18–20,000 a week Allen Klein was brought in for the company clean-up. Bag Productions was formed on 21 April 1969. Ostensibly John wished to finance his own artsy events, many of which (clearly the films) were encouraged by Klein, who believed there was a market for them on the US college circuit. Whether or not the advances of monies had to do with fronting for film projects there was acrimony at the end, with Klein and ABCKO Industries suing John for a total of $508,000 over allegedly unrepaid loans.

Ace cinematographer Nic Knowland worked with John and Yoko on several of their films, including *Rape* (financed by Austrian television), *Apotheosis*, *Bed Peace Montreal* and *Imagine*. He rates Ono highly.

A respected underground film-maker before she met John, Yoko gained notoriety on the London scene for her low-budget experimental films such as *Bottoms*, featuring 365 bare backsides. The film was the first underground film to get a West End screening, though the then censor, John Trevelyan, objected on the basis that 'other bits of the anatomy had crept into the footage.'

Rebuked Ono, 'Many bottoms are unbecoming – boring . . . My film is no more boring than *The Countess from Hong Kong*. Besides, I would rather be bored than provoked into war.'

The films financed by Bags are expensive; Yoko herself admitted that she used to take pride in doing something small which she could not do as Mrs Lennon. *Imagine*, for instance, was shot in colour using as many as seven cameramen on what is only an hour-long film.

The popularity of her songs is not shared by the films, for, essentially minimalist, they prove too arcane for the average viewer. When she goes for big, such as with *Imagine*, it is minimalism on a large scale without characterization or continuity but with moot symbolism.

Knowland, who shot three-quarters of *Imagine* at Tittenhurst, recalls: 'It was complicated because there was a director who fell out with John and Yoko and his footage was put to one side.' It appears that John and Yoko, hero and heroine of their cult, took control, working up ideas in a cinema vérité way with the cameramen and crew. The documentary effect enhances Yoko (dressed to the nines) whilst diminishing John, who is photographed without make-up or 'key' light. And yet the observation palls, since it is reality which is thrust upon us – controlled by the film-makers – rather than us being allowed to glimpse an indiscretion or vanity in the midst of role playing. Still, the dramatic change is awesome for anyone who remembers John in *A Hard Day's Night* as a full-faced, plump, jovial Beatle. If his intention is to divest himself of Beatlemania, he more than accomplishes it here. Whether the Golspie car crash, in which John suffered multiple facial injuries which required seventeen stitches, changed him perceptibly, or if the physical change is the result of drugs, diet or photography, Lennon looks lacking in animation and virility. Firstly, he appears short. His clothes fit badly: the shirts and trousers are too small on his frame. His face lacks character, and the expression is ruthless and hard. Where has the cheeky smile gone? His movement is minimal but for sex encounters with Ono, which are devoid of affection and verge on the psychology of humiliation.

Recounting his experience, Knowland says, 'Yoko had strong ideas of what she wanted. She wanted to do things in an unusual-looking way. There was no shooting script, and the chess sequence was shot in an odd way. All white chess players. They were making odd moves – a suggestive manoeuvre by Yoko pulling her skirt up.'

Having first met Yoko when she approached him to shoot *Rape* while she was awaiting the birth of their first child, Nic recounts: 'I met her while she was in hospital. They were using it as an office. We had an editing machine so they viewed the film there. She was very satisfied. After the miscarriage she assembled the rushes at home.'

The closest she comes to making a feature by classical standards is *Rape*. And whilst the film is credited for its surpassing portrait of harassment, Ono fails to generate her deserved momentum as a cult figure. Misrepresented as tedious and dour, her sexual energy ignored, she becomes a dupe for the Madonnas of the world whose representation by the media errs in their favour.

Fecund and sexual, Yoko is portrayed as feminist and marginal.

Said to reflect the persecution which the couple experienced, *Rape* evolved out of the marriage between an international pop star and an underground film-maker. The Austrians who financed the film failed to understand it – the scenario would have been better if it had stuck more closely to the Lennons themselves. When, for instance, Yoko and John lunched in Paris with Salvador Dali, Yoko beat away fans with the warning: 'Those days are over. My husband no longer is a Beatle. Leave him alone.'

The storyline is improvisational, the camera following around London a Hungarian girl on holiday, without having told her (for purposes of authenticity) that she was being filmed. Being related to the television company executive provided Knowland with access to the flat where the girl was staying, making all the more terrifying the sense of impotence and fear.

Knowland recalls: 'We descended upon her in Chelsea at the flat where she was staying with her sister. We followed her along the street. After a while we let her go. Then we knew she was going to Highgate Cemetery. We picked her up at the cemetery. She was a bit surprised at the time. She got quite distressed at that point and wanted us to go away. We let her go. We had the keys to her sister's flat and waited inside for her to come back. When she came back, we just followed her and wouldn't let her go until she really broke down. We were inside the flat when she came in and found us. She was a bit distressed by this. She wanted to call the police and we wouldn't let her. She more or less broke down and this is where the film ends with her in a turmoil. We raped her – that was essence of the film. We intruded into her life with our camera!'

Is the film an allegory for Ono's own image subverted by a prejudiced camera eye perverting the truth of character and personality? McCartney has recently said about Ono: 'When I first met her I thought she was hard and pushy. Now I think the opposite.'

Honest or pretentious, the couple's efforts at film-making fail to enhance Ono's reputation, and important critics unfairly dismiss her work as 'silly' or 'chi-chi'. One critic attended a showing of her *Bottoms* film in Belgium; Yoko was snuggled inside one of her plastic bags with a teacup by the side containing a note scrawled with the caution: 'Yoko is not here.' 'I wonder,' said the man, 'if you kicked it whether she would still be not there?' A less hostile but equally disparaging reaction is recounted by a gallery owner to an idea of theirs for a show using receptacles of the rich and famous. To me the idea sounds wickedly original. But the director, finding the concept chi-chi, plumped for something by David Hockney instead.

Apothewatsis or *Apotheosis*, named by a gallery owner after seeing a rough cut, is John's first solo directorial attempt. It was shot twice – the first time at a deserted airfield in Basingstoke, and then at Lavenham in Suffolk, because John was dissatisfied with the first attempt.

The intention is to capture the couple's spiritual transcendency, the metaphor being a balloon basket.

The initial problem was that it proved impossible to construct a wooden platform on the balloon basket that would hold the heavy 35mm camera securely in place. A helicopter was eventually used instead, carrying cinematographer Nic Knowland as a passenger.

Since John wanted a slow-motion shot of himself and Yoko, starting at their feet, then panning up their bodies over their heads and on into the sky, they had to be photographed directly from the balloon as it started its ascent. Several times the wind almost blew the balloon out of control and everyone had to fling themselves on to the side of the basket to prevent it dragging across the ground.

Recounts Knowland, 'John knew a bit because he had been in films. He resented cosmetics and artificiality in cinema. We shot naturalistically and realistically. He liked that. He hated the phoniness of "big" films.'

There was no soundtrack, only natural sounds, John's apotheosis being the ascent of the spirit into the clouds.

Photographed on a cold winter's day, with three cameras set up in different parts of Lavenham village square, the film commences with a shot past John and Yoko wearing monks' habits. Recounts Knowland, 'You drift out and see the whole village, over the village, over the fields and into the clouds. This was a more trippy film than the heroin film [I assume he means *Imagine*]. We were in the clouds for some minutes and turned it into a wonderful skyscape. Absolutely no sound. Just the creaking of the basket, the sounds drifting up from the land – cocks crowing and cars driving around.'

Eighteen and a half minutes long, conceived in wide screen colour, the film was shown in the West End at Nash House on 3

November 1969 but was only briefly noted in the *Sunday Telegraph* on the 9th as 'a spiritual portrait'. Yoko and John rambled on for hours, culminating by saying that it is 'the best thing we have done'. 'John and I,' said Yoko, 'are thinking more and more in spiritual terms.'

5

His White Goddess

Had Cynthia Lennon not changed herself, she might have remained married to John. Yoko would have become his mistress. This was John's original intention. But as he writes in *Skywriting by Word of Mouth*, he divorced his wife 'to avoid having to live with [her] new nose. . . . They [We] got the new nose. And I got my dream woman. Yoko.'

Mirror newspaper archives put the change somewhere around 24 July 1967, which seems right since it means that from November 1966 (when John met Yoko) until May 1968 (when they made *Two Virgins*) Cynthia was trying to stimulate John's waning interest in her femininity.

The *Mirror* news item captioned 'Mystery of the Beatle Girl' talks about them going to Greece on holiday with the intention of purchasing an island. Observing that all appear to be accounted for but Cynthia, the report ruminates: 'Now it ought to be Cynthia Lennon, a girl who does not push herself into the forefront of any occasion. It looks like Cynthia Lennon. In fact, it *must* be Cynthia Lennon.'

Cynthia herself, in the book which Lennon tried to suppress, *A Twist of Lennon*, attributes their growing apart to the following: '[He] accused [me] of not loving enough, [of being] unfaithful, of looking or talking to a member of the opposite sex for too long.'

But in the 1972 interview I conducted with John, he told me plainly that his first marriage was like all first marriages and that the child – their son Julian – came out of a liquor bottle on a Saturday night. Elsewhere he has been quoted as saying how unhappy he had been: the only reason the marriage survived for six years was that he wasn't home a lot; and when he was, he and his wife had little in common. 'I cannot', he said, 'understand how my wife could say she thought we were happy.'

And yet there is ample evidence that Lennon was nuts about Cynthia, that the myth of their 'secret' marriage is vastly overblown, that he made no effort to disguise the fact that he was married, and that he was seen (according to numerous gossip column items) at nightclubs, on holiday, at social gatherings and at home with his wife. Closer to the truth is that John, an emotionally insecure boy, did not like change, and when his wife began to assert her individuality, emerging from behind his shadow, he bridled and bolted.

Jon Hague, a Liverpool art college painter friend of John's, was present in that famous photo of the four of them in Lettering Class (John, Jon, Cynthia and Phyllis McKenzie, now Fearon). He remained close to Lennon over the years, and was the recipient of a free meal in the days when Apple was losing 'up to £20,000 a week'. Both John and Paul financed Hague's one-man show at London's Royal Institute Gallery, 195 Piccadilly (4–23 December 1967), the same month as *Magical Mystery Tour* aired. John, incidentally, also bought him a house in Leamington Spa, near to where he was teaching at Coventry art college. Ironically, following his show, Hague gave up painting and became an antique dealer. He still lives in the Leamington house, which has been exquisitely refurbished.

In the months prior to the exhibition, Jon got to observe Lennon's relationships to both Cynthia and Yoko. 'Funny that when I was having my exhibition he said to me there was somebody else he was going to help with painting – this lady. He had just obviously met Yoko. I didn't know at what stage their affair was at.' (Yoko's Lisson Gallery show was actually two months earlier than Hague's, from 11 October to 14 November.)

The alterations in Lennon since art college days were apparent to Hague not only in the sense of physical change but in personality development too. 'I felt he was sort of a king. Suddenly he moved into a different league from me. He was like a different person. Where had this person come from? He wasn't the Lennon I knew. In his public manner he was completely confident. I was absolutely amazed to watch the person perform, and to conduct himself around the table. But he was still the same Lennon. I felt very humble in his presence. I admired everything he did, not just because I knew him.'

In view of the careful planning and preparation undertaken, Jon spent many Sundays with John and Cynthia at Kenwood. 'I'd roll up all my paintings, put them in my car and drive down to his house. I unfurled my paintings sitting on the floor.'

Was he impressed by the way they lived?

'It was a fabulous house, but John spent most of his time in the sun room living like a hippy with the mattress on the floor. He lived in this very domesticated suburban house, but like a student in one room.'

Was John remiss as a husband and a father?

'He was home on Sundays and played with his kid. But he was away so much. When I was there he took me up to the attic where he had his home equipment audio machines. I was totally unmusical and he kept trying to introduce me to new things. He played me records of Yoko Ono's Plastic Ono Band. I didn't like it. He said, "No one likes it." He was trying to do something new. I couldn't understand why he did this thing on Beatles records.'

Always preferring the company of equals, Lennon sought Ringo's company to Paul's, perceiving Paul as 'the younger boy'. 'I got the impression that John and Paul were not terribly great chums. He came around mostly with Ringo. I bumped into John a few times and he was always with Ringo. He picked me up once in the streets in London. He was with Ringo then. I remember when we were at college, in the canteen, Lennon said, "Do you mind if two of my friends from next door [the Liverpool Institute] sit at our table?" They happened to be Paul and George.'

Whilst Yoko Ono was named as co-respondent in the divorce proceedings which Cynthia brought against her husband, it is fair to say that John was sexually active with other women too. Hague recalls when John came to his exhibition and afterwards went on to a nightclub. 'There was a girl who had come down from Leamington with my lot. I knew her quite well. She fancied John. John wasn't exactly an angel as regards women. I wouldn't have expected him to be different. He was always interested in women. There were always girls hanging round the Beatles and he wasn't exactly disinterested. With this girl from Leamington he was keen to give it a go, although he was married. After that one night with John this girl was involved. There is no indication that John ever saw her again.'

But the earliest accounts place Yoko safely in the role of protégé without being any threat to John's marriage, even on those occasions when she came to the Kenwood house to discuss her work or to solicit John for money. To Lennon she was then just a fascinating oddball.

Having arrived in Britain in 1966 with her second husband, Anthony Cox, Yoko was a formidable figure in the art underground who had established herself in New York for her avant-garde Happenings as Queen of the Lofts. One only has to glimpse the *Grapefruit* exercises, such as Cut Piece, Disappearing Piece, Fly Piece or Clock Piece, to get a sense of the complexity of the woman's mind. Although from a wealthy family and related on her mother's side to the Japanese royal family, she led the life of an indigent artist film-maker having come to Britain because 'My growth in New York was being repressed.' Living just above the poverty line, the Coxes managed to finance films and shows which were, despite the reviews, some of the most original in London at the time. *Bottoms* was widely touted by the art underground and, though disparaged by the critics, influenced a whole battery of Establishment plays and films.

The Bags, the Bed-ins, the concepts – ahead of their time – continue to furnish the Establishment with ideas. I note that an upcoming American chat show features the interviewer in bed with her guests, an idea derivative of John and Yoko's famous Bed-ins.

Peter Owen, publisher of Ono's *Grapefruit* book in the United Kingdom, remembers Cox and Ono as part of the sixties' art underground, having seen them at parties and social gatherings. 'There was this party where she gave the host, the art critic of *Art and Artists*, a hammer and a board. It was a birthday present of her art work. She said it was her conception of art. She was into this gimmicky thing. The show where she met Lennon was at one of her Happenings.

'Cox, I didn't talk to him. He didn't make any real impact on me. I didn't talk to either of them. She stood out more than he did. Perhaps because she was Japanese. But she dressed oddly. I believe she always had on this hat. I was not particularly impressed with them.'

Lack of acceptance placed pressure on the Cox marriage; newspaper accounts told of quarrels and tears on any number of occasions, such as during the *Bottoms* screening when the soundtrack wasn't right.

John's primary interest, aside from being Ono's patron, was to teach Ono how to meditate as a way to save her marriage.

Having first met Ono on the night before the opening of the

Indica show, Lennon admits he was intrigued by the lady's reputation for bags and uninhibited sex, and when she began to
assault his sensibility with her 'psychic games' he found himself
irresistibly attracted to her femininity. As well as giving him a
copy of *Grapefruit*, which he kept by his bedside, she used to
send along sexy gifts, such as a red plastic tampon, to stimulate
his libido. On other occasions she would scribble notes, or write
love letters on exquisitely perfumed notepaper.

The truth came out in May 1972 when Leslie Anthony, John's
chauffeur since 1965, sold his story to the *News of the World*.
Impaling the myth of love at first sight, Anthony presented a
picture of an artist who wanted financing for the art and film
shows which she and her husband were mounting.

Actually Lennon came to Ono's show in November 1966,
entitled *Unfinished Paintings and Objects*, at the invitation of
John Dunbar, the gallery owner, whose introduction of John
to Yoko, whilst of historical significance, has never been widely
acknowledged. When I asked Dunbar (who seems to have departed
from the art scene in the role of gallery owner) whether he intended
to undermine John's marriage to Cynthia. He replied simply that
he enjoyed bringing together people of similar minds.

From Anthony's account it appears that John's presence was
out of deference to Dunbar, whose gallery he wished to patronize.
'John wanted to buy some "daft exhibit" consisting of a couple of
wires taken from an Army tank that lit up at each end. He paid
£600. He also paid £200 for a magnet swinging in the middle of
a bit of plastic.'

First impressions? Posterity records that Yoko says John was
unshaven. He concurs.

But one observer hints that there was some distress caused by
the way this chauffeur-driven pop star proceeded to handle the
exhibits prior to opening night. For instance, he wanted to hammer
a nail into the virgin painting and take a bite of the apple. When
this was refused he agreed to mount a ladder and peer through
a spy-glass at the ceiling for the answer to his cosmic question.
The reply was 'Yes', although the artist's name was O-no.

According to Anthony, at one point she clung to him, talking
in her funny, high-pitched voice until he fled. 'She came tripping
out after him into St James's and begged to come along to the
studios where we were going to record. A few days later she
turned up at Abbey Road studio and was let in. John groaned
about what a pest she was.'

Pest indeed? If Yoko were perceived as anything less than Transcendent Perfection, would John have risked breaching a cardinal rule: No women in the studio? Jon Hague recalls: 'I was there when Yoko was in the studio and in fact had to take her out for a Japanese meal. I don't know why, I didn't have anything to do with Yoko, really. Whether she was bored and wanted to go, or whether it was something else, I was sent out to have a meal with her. I was told by John that they didn't want her in the studio – that they didn't want anyone around. John was breaking the rules. He was arrogant and just decided he was going to go and do what he liked. Yoko obviously wanted to come. She insisted upon coming and he had obviously given way. It caused a lot of friction by her being there.'

The presence of Ono precipitated McCartney's famous walk-out. One EMI observer, with a first-hand view of the crisis, recalls: 'I can't remember the first time when John came into the studio with Yoko. Suddenly, instead of just John and Paul working in the studio as they used to, where they literally wrote the material in the studio – they played each other chords and bits of things and lyrics, and then they got George and Ringo to work out the arrangements and riffs – from this point in time Yoko appeared in the studio right at John's side. In the early days she didn't say anything. But not long after they had her in the studio, she started to interfere with some of the songs and have input into what she thought they should do.

'I remember when she turned to Paul and said, "Why don't we try it this way?" He exploded and asked John: "What the hell is going on? We haven't had anyone in the studio before. Why have we suddenly got somebody interfering in the way we work? Either she goes or I go." John said, "She's not going", and Paul stormed out. It was about a week before they could get Paul back in the studio. That was the beginning of serious friction.'

According to my source, John said he needed Yoko there. He thought she had some good ideas. 'She was obviously at the time supplying him with something he needed – stability, sex, drugs. I know that it caused tremendous friction with Paul and it was the beginning of the end of the relationship. It became a bit of a thorn in their side.'

What did Brian Epstein say about it?

'He wasn't happy about it. But by then Brian wasn't having the control over the Beatles that maybe he might have done earlier.

He might have taken John to one side privately without anybody around and said, "This really isn't going to work out." And John probably told Brian that he insisted upon her involvement and that it was a take it or leave it situation.'

Whether Ono influenced John or merely confirmed his leanings toward the occult in terms of sex, drugs and mysticism, her participation grew to the point where John insisted she be included in the *Let It Be* sessions, asking for a microphone to be placed near her chair. Their drug bond was strong, too, with the couple making on-camera jokes about needing heroin 'to relax' and comparing drugs to sex ('shooting is exercise').

While McCartney didn't sue for dissolution until 1970, the seeds of discord were planted as early as November 1966, and it appears as testimony to McCartney's equanimity that he didn't allow himself to be manipulated into hasty action, but waited until the time was right for him to quit. In due course he survived not only the indignities of the recording sessions for John's *Two Virgins, Cold Turkey* and *Instant Karma*, but the suggested delay in releasing his own debut solo album because of its conflict with a Beatles release. John, however, had for the past few years continually upstaged Beatles releases with his own product.

Another witness to the Beatles recording sessions was Savile Row tailor Tommy Nutter, who designed the wedding costumes for John and Yoko: those unisex pants suits in white gabardine which were not worn on the wedding day since John could not find the trousers and Yoko decided to wear a skirt.

Nutter was a room-mate of Peter Brown, John's Apple PA via NEMS following Brian's death and prior to assuming presidency of the Robert Stigwood Organization's New York office. Backed by Brown, Nutter opened his first shop in Savile Row opposite the site of his current one, and called it simply Nutters. Lennon was his first client, and Tommy still has the invoice for the clothing purchased. 'They had about half a dozen suits each, of three pieces – waistcoat, trousers and jacket: single-breasted with a waistcoat and wide lapel and lightly flared trousers. That was the look then. Not the big shoulders that I have become known to do. Hers were identical.' (Tommy's suits are also visible on the sleeve of EMI's *Abbey Road*.)

Acquainted with Lennon during the period of his obsession with nudity, he recalls: 'I think it was Yoko who got John to come to a tailor. It was her idea, but he didn't need any pushing. He was happy to go into that look. Unisex. He was going along with anything she did anyway. The two of them used to walk around the shop with nothing on. I didn't find it particularly attractive, I must say. So that was quite embarrassing, really – in front of other people in the middle of the shop. They were looking for patterns and fabrics. It was hard not to look. It was not something which would particularly excite me. I was just trying to get them covered up as soon as possible.'

Body shapes?

'John was thin, but with puppy fat. A little bit round-shouldered and sunken-chested. Fitting Lennon I had to build up one shoulder, since one is lower than the other. Yoko has a feminine body with curves. But with her, she didn't want the man's cut like Bianca Jagger. We had to cut in the darts. It was more tailored to her. Bianca wanted to look absolutely flat.'

Nutter often attended Beatles sessions with Peter. 'I remember them playing me "Strawberry Fields Forever". I think I was one of the first people to hear it. I thought it was marvellous. I was thrilled with it.'

Were John and Yoko disruptive during those recording sessions?

Brian Southall's authorized exposé of EMI during the Beatles days conjures up a picture of life at a recording studio which by current standards sounds extreme – all-night sessions, or sessions without interruption for weeks at a time; beds in the studios; the unauthorized presence of pot and LSD; and session musicians kept waiting for hours. And whilst some of the sessions will be discussed in depth later, for now let us concern ourselves with whether John and Yoko were disruptive influences.

Elgar Howarth and David Mason are session musicians who played on several Beatles recordings including 'Penny Lane', 'Magical Mystery Tour', 'A Day in the Life' and 'All You Need Is Love'. Mason's piccolo trumpet, unique at the time, accounts for much of the distinctive sound on 'Penny Lane' and 'All You Need Is Love'.

Having arrived at 1 p.m., the musicians waited until 5 p.m. when the Beatles appeared. Recalls Howarth, whose wife hails from Liverpool and who considers them the funniest people in the world: 'John was the most friendly and approachable and he did come talking. To me he was a typical Liverpool fellow – with an abrasive quick wit. A wonderful turn of phrase. Liverpool is the funniest town I have ever been in my life. There is a mixture of culture there. The Irish have a strong influence – gift of the gab or blarney. The place has always produced artists – singers, conductors and comedians. It is a seaport with a great mixing of the nations.

'We got chatting about various things, and since we were brass players we started talking brass and I said, "Since you are having unusual musical things in your records, such as brass trumpet players and the string quartet in *Sergeant Pepper*, which nobody had dreamt of, why not have a brass band?" And he said, "Oh, that *is* a good idea."'

Observing in Lennon a preoccupation with fashion which Howarth found effeminate, he recalls, 'Lennon had one of the first men's handbags that I had seen. The British never did take to the men's handbag in a big way. The British male is slightly bothered by it. But John Lennon had one. I said to him: "What are you, a Scouser, doing with a lady's handbag?" He looked at me and laughed, and in his very warm Liverpool accent said, "It's these bloody trousers. They're very tight." And it was true.'

Musically illiterate, Lennon was not, according to Howarth, able to write music. When Howarth offered to write out a few bars of trumpet licks Lennon could not sing them until he simulated the position of the guitar player, crouching his left hand as if to hold the guitar across his chest, his right hand doing the movements for the guitar.

Dave Mason recalls at the 'All You Need Is Love' session asking John, dressed as he was in a funny cutaway dress coat, a pair of candy-striped trousers and a great big green tie, if he had come from a film set. '"No, mate. We always dress like this," he replied. I had put my foot in it straightaway,' says Mason.

Lennon, he recalls, was quiet and contemplative. 'He sat around, listened and made a few observations. He had a good sense of humour. I remember thinking at the time that he came out with some quite witty remarks. He was very relaxed. There was a lot of interplay between them all.'

Violinist and former Beatles booker Jack Fallon, playing on Ringo's 'Don't Pass Me By' (*White Album*), recalls that both John and Yoko were there lying on the floor. 'She was there all afternoon, and during the breaks she came up and asked me where I came from. Paul did most of the work in the studio. He was in the box.'

Jon Hague confirms: 'Yoko was causing friction, but she wasn't intrusive. She was meek and mild. She didn't put in her opinions.

She was very much in the background. John was always sitting with her in the corner.'

Whereas Ono says there was no carnal knowledge between them until the night in May 1968 when they recorded *Two Virgins* while Cynthia was on holiday in Rimini, she admits that Lennon had tried to seduce her on any number of previous occasions. 'I was feeling tired,' she told a reporter, 'so John suggested that I lie down. He took me to a flat that I think belonged to one of the roadies.' Apparently he made a pass, but was rebuffed. 'It was so crude, so coarse. I said I didn't want to have sex but just to lie down.'

According to Leslie Anthony, however, it took place before May 1968, some time prior to the show which John sponsored on Yoko's behalf at London's Lisson Gallery in October and November 1967. It was originally entitled *Half a Wind*, but to honour John Yoko changed the name to *Yoko Plus Me*. Lennon, however, shy about his sponsorship, was absent from the opening. (It has been hinted that John felt guilty about hurting Tony Cox.)

Wrote Anthony in the *News of the World*: 'One day Cynthia went up north. Yoko arrived at their home to talk to John about him sponsoring some art exhibition. It was supposed to be a business meeting. But she didn't go back until the morning and after that John couldn't leave her alone.'

Yoko herself admits that for a while they believed she would occupy a role as his mistress, and that they were looking for a London flat where they could be together. That is until the famous *Two Virgins* night they spent together in May 1968, after which John decided to leave his wife and to marry Ono. While still married to others they went public in June, appearing together at the opening night of John's play at the National and at other events such as Coventry Cathedral's National Sculpture Exhibition.

Jon Hague was also John's artistic protégé at this time. Having seen Yoko at Apple sorting out finances with the accountant, and again at EMI, it was not until the break-up with Cynthia and John's move into Ringo's Montagu Square pied-á-terre in London (prior to the drug bust) that Jon got to know her well.

Was he surprised by the divorce announcement?

'I had heard the gossip that he was getting divorced from Cynthia. I asked him and he said Yes. He must have been seeing Yoko on the side. But I didn't know. I was surprised that he chose Yoko. She wasn't the most glamorous woman in the world. He could have had the most glamorous woman.

'I seem to remember asking him at his house in Kenwood the question: Why Yoko? So he might have been seeing Yoko prior to the weekend when Cynthia was away.' He told me why – 'Yoko was "the artist" and Cynthia was "a suburban housewife"'. In my interview with him, too, John said that paramount in his love of Yoko was that she was someone he could jam with and who also could stroke his head in bed.

Spending a week with them in London gave Hague ample chance to discover the origin of the attraction. 'I was in a little room next to their bedroom. I was seeing them in intimate terms – without make-up. She didn't strike me as glamorous or having a nice body. She chummed up with me, because she said that of all John's friends I was the only one who knew about artists. That is why she liked me to be around. That is why I was there at the time.'

And John's view?

'He thought she was wonderful. He was with her every second, their arms around each other all the time. I'm saying that I didn't fancy her. But he was completely bowled over by her.'

Did he know she came from a moneyed background?

'John knew that she was wealthy. I presumed that he knew she was from a banking family. I think I knew. So he must have told me.

'Yoko lived a sort of poverty in New York, so she obviously wasn't being supported by her family. But she led the glamour life with John. When she was with him she spent lots of money on clothes – his money. She transformed herself into his White Goddess.'

Whether out of guilt or conviction, Lennon pledged both soul and money to promote Yoko's art, films and music. During our September 1972 interview Ono talked at length about the problems of discrimination and sexism facing women.

Having just done the *One to One* Madison Square Garden concert on 30 August to aid retarded children, Ono complained about the old problem of censorship. Whilst there was no outcry against John's use of four-letter words in 'Working-Class Hero' or 'Give Me Some Truth', Yoko's articulation of words such as 'legs' or 'box' elicited antipathy. 'Why do people object to me being myself when they don't object to John being himself? Somebody asked me later, "Why did you say that?" The reason is because "Open

Your Box" has lines like "Open your legs and thighs". For men
to say legs, thighs or whatever is okay. People take it lightly. If
a woman says it – Well, what is this? – they want to know? The
reason is that they have seen women through their mothers. If a
woman asserts herself it is a father image.'

The belief that Yoko tailgated on John's success, although
wrong, prevails; and whilst one only has to look at monster hits
such as 'Give Peace a Chance' (the peace movement anthem) and
'Happy Xmas' (a seasonal perennial) to see that Yoko is an equal
if not superior partner, the myth remains. 'I think I have done
as much work as Stockhausen or John Cage, but I was mainly
an artist's artist until I met John.'

Added Lennon, 'I couldn't believe all the things that Yoko
would tell me were going on in the art world then. We were
doing this and that and at the end of the night the description of
the concert would be about these four guys, mentioning paren-
thetically that it was Yoko's loft and she was there. I thought
she was paranoid and argued that she must be doing something
wrong for all that to be happening – for people to be treating her
like that. I was looking for bad breath for three years.'

Veterans of media assassinations, the Lennons compared treatment by the press; Yoko noted the discomfort she felt at being
present in a situation where she had been asked to discuss her
work. 'There is the feeling that you shouldn't be sitting there,
the feeling that they would rather you didn't say anything. From
the audience. From the reporters. And that alone discourages my
inspiration. And those little things which you can't describe in
words, that if I do describe people say that I am paranoid, are
detrimental to the female spirit.'

John confirmed: 'On any TV show they always set the lighting
– even stills photographers – for me, and Yoko comes out looking
not even like herself, even. A camera angle on a TV show when
she is singing is a snap – just like that – whereas they spend half an
hour to make sure it is right for me.' In person Yoko is probably
better-looking than John, who suffered from a bad squint, poor
teeth, a receding chin and a flat nose.

Said Ono, 'I don't want to go into it but the art world is just as
filthy as any other world. I was brought up in the same conditions
as you were. I had no choice but to love, adore and respect people
who hate me. This is true even now. Most of these people who are
interesting and are male happen to despise and hate women. So I
can see their good points but they can't see mine. So whenever I

encounter somebody like that I say, I shall allow you to be yourself. I understand what you are. All I am asking is for you to understand as much about me. But they never do that. Everybody that I can understand seems to be woman-haters.'

Had it made her anti-man?

'I always had an obsession about my work and all that. Whatever came in the way of a relationship or whatever was always secondary. I despised men 'cause I had never met anybody I felt was intelligent. I was that arrogant. . . . Most men impressed me as being conservative in thinking. They had an incessant professionalism about them that is limiting. Even an avant-garde composer who is supposed to be far-out is limited and narrow in the sense that they believe so much in what they are doing that they lose a sense of humour about it.'

Had she over-reacted?

'I couldn't play it any other way. Otherwise I would have been killed. I was in so much pain. I retreated from the world. I think I can compare my situation vaguely with the black male's. The black male takes so much from the world. They can't possibly think about the black female. They become determinately masculine. I was like that. I didn't really know what men's troubles or sufferings were. I met John and was surprised that he was very versatile for a man. He is not narrow in that way. He has tremendous versatility and I thought: very admirable. I started to have a relationship for the first time in that sense. But', she hastened to add, 'if John and I have a fight about how I should express myself, the world is on his side.'

Trotting out the Trojan horse, the Lennons declared: 'What we are saying is – Be naked. It is nicer and easier if we weren't and we might prolong whatever is going on longer if we don't reveal ourselves. But whatever is going in, it is time to be completely naked and to run the risk.'

Coping with problems not only of sexism but racism too elicited a pragmatic reaction from Ono. 'There is no difference between Oriental and western women. In Tokyo in every little town, there is at least one discotheque where women can go and pick a man and pay him to dance with her. That shows a lot and not that a woman is not Mrs So-and-So because a man wouldn't bed her but it is a woman with independent financial means who goes to pick up men.'

Yoko admitted that her sense of betrayal was so keen that at the first hint of disharmony she would leave. While she had until Lennon only been married twice, giving birth to a daughter, Kyoko, by Tony Cox, it appeared that, certainly in the case of her marriage to Cox, if anyone was oppressed it was he.

'He was a liberated guy in a sense, but I don't think there was any problem except that the social pressure was a lot and there was an individual difference. He was taking care of management, like most wives do. I paid the rent. I was lecturing a lot. It went down from being a waitress to lecturing – odd jobs, like any other artist. I was the breadwinner.'

Although both Cox and Ono were artists and film-makers, it was Cox who was referred to as the film-maker in newspaper accounts of their divorce. John argued, 'When the press reported our marriage, Yoko was referred to as the Japanese film actress married to film-maker Tony Cox. Now when she makes her independent art or films, we get into a Gloria Vanderbilt scene where Mrs Lennon puts on her little knitting show backed by Mr Lennon's vast resources.'

Confirmed Yoko, 'When I used to make films I used to make them cheaply which was part of my pride. Now I can't do that because I am Yoko Ono or Mrs Lennon, and people expect more. They spend on cab fares, throw a party and spend $80,000. It is against my principles and all that. So I get less encouraged to make a film.'

John interrupted, 'The other option is to con Apple into giving us some money for a film they don't want to make because they know it won't be a commercial film. Nobody is interested in anything that won't make twenty hundred million dollars. Distributors think, "Oh, it has Beatles. Therefore it will make money." And they see a film that has nothing to do with anything. And they tell us to go underground.'

The feeling is, however, that Cox was the long-suffering partner. 'I am Yoko's favourite husband,' joked John. 'But Tony has a genius, and this is a nasty word, to manoeuvre so that she could make films. They could fix it so that she could do her work. Tony Cox was an artist who came to her and said, "I will give you my art because I believe in yours." He suffered from it and I think it shows.'

Argued Ono, 'But if a woman was in the situation she would have stayed without questioning it. All wives sacrifice their art for their husbands. Most women, because they have no confidence in their talent, use their husbands as an excuse. And they say, if it wasn't for him, I would do this and that.'

Whether the affair was platonic or not, until May 1968 there were definite tremors perceptible in the Cox marriage. When Ono mounted her Lisson Gallery show in October 1967 with Lennon's generous support, an observer noted that 'Yoko and Cox were reliant upon each other but were splitting up. It was a very unhappy time for them both. And for [their daughter] Kyoko. Both he and Yoko tried to get people involved in the splitting up – to get them to take sides. It was difficult and complicated, since it involved Yoko, Tony and John.'

Original, intellectual, Ono is also feminine. The letter inviting the Lisson Gallery director for tea to discuss the exhibition, reprinted in *Grapefruit*, conveyed a sense of the ridiculously sublime as she directed him to their Regent's Park flat: a big Edwardian place of about ten rooms with high ceilings, very little furniture and painted, typically, in white. Ironically, it would be houses of this type – empty, pristine – in which Lennon would find himself in later years during his incarnation as Ono's 'toy boy'. But at the time, in view of the threat by bailiffs to take possession, Lennon's financial support saw Ono and Cox through.

Yoko's note read: 'It is only a five minutes' walk from your place. First you make a left turn at the end of your street on the right and go about 50 foot and turn right (you will see a sign saying one way that is where you turn) and go until you see a coffee bar (not clean) on the left with a sign saying "closed". . . .'

At the time of the show Ono was already a cause célèbre in London, *Bottoms* having been a renowned and controversial art world social event. But since at least two of the 'bottoms' have since died of Aids – Robert Fraser, the gallery owner, and Mario Amaya, an American art critic living in London, one wonders about Ono's vocal protest against the gay art Mafia.

Known at the time as a demanding, precise and tireless perfectionist, Ono insisted she be allowed to make structural changes to the building to accomodate her ideas for half a door, half a window and so on, and when frustrated by lack of funds she satisfied herself with creating the illusion by severing a bed, a chair and a chest of drawers into two. These artefacts were later dotted about Kenwood with nonchalance.

It is, I think, an exact observation that when Yoko married John she ceased to occupy her place as an important member of the post-war Western art movement. Perhaps the gestation was too quick, for while the songs have increased her popularity the celebrity has quelled her motivation to create new pieces. The recent Whitney Museum show in New York exhibited old work from her Fluxus days in a renewed (but moribund) bronze setting. I read somewhere that she cried when her new boyfriend, Sam Havadtoy, suggested the idea, but proceeded as much out of resignation as despair.

But the winds of change did not augur well for Lennon and Ono. Following their exclusion on 15 June 1968 from a piece of consecrated ground at Coventry Cathedral where they proposed to plant two acorns as part of their first public 'event', they were charged with possession of cannabis resin on 18 October 1968 at Ringo's Montagu Square, London flat, for which Lennon took full responsibility. It is curious, following Mick Jagger's arrest which Brian Epstein objected was badly handled, and in view of the public outcry about stiff sentences for 'users', that Lennon was prosecuted and convicted.

Don Short, the *Mirror* newsman who followed Lennon's career as a sort of Father Confessor after breaking the 1963 story about John's pugilistic encounter with a Liverpool disc jockey who called him 'a queer',* tells me that on any number of occasions 'there was a lot of drugs around. I tipped off John about a possible bust. I tipped them off about three or four times, 'cause our paper had good police contracts. I was concerned.

'I remember that second tour of the States and Peter Fonda was there. They wanted to get rid of me, 'cause I was staying at the house with them. They didn't want to tell me that they were taking acid. I was into booze and not drugs. Neil Aspinall was the conduit to ensure that I wasn't around. He took me down to the lower ground level, the basement or swimming pool level, to play a game of pool. I thought that Neil was trying to divert my attention but he played a brilliant game of pool. Every ball went down.

Despite rock's *laissez-faire* attitude toward drugs, the political attitude remained status quo, and Short bemoaned the prosecutions which resulted. 'The Stones got busted. Everyone got busted. John called Sir Joseph Lockwood (EMI chairman), thinking he would help him to get out of it – he thought he could pull

* *Daily Mirror*, 21 June 1963 – buried in the last page but still national news coverage.

a string or two. He couldn't, because it had passed the process of law once it had been booked in. They wanted to nail
him.'★

And yet, four years later, when I talked to John about drugs, he
was unrepentant. 'They used to say that "religion is the opiate of
the people". But opium is the religion of the people now. That is
what happened to our drug scene. It is like somebody put poison in
the food. I still don't believe the stories I heard about acid because I
do not know anybody who went through those things. The actual
bad trip is when the drugs were tampered with by whoever sold
them to us – whether it be the Mafia or the CIA.

'The *drugs* are not the problem. The problem is why everyone
in society is taking drugs from alcohol to heroin. It has nothing
to do with taking or not taking drugs or if they are going to arrest
a few more pushers on the street. Who is making the drugs? Who
is bringing them in? Who is allowing it? And why do we keep
talking about junkies? Who is manufacturing all those pep pills
and sleepers? Every drug house is making 20 million more than
is necessary.'

While it is often joked about that Paul McCartney upstaged
Lennon in his marriage to Linda, it is true that John wanted to
marry Ono first. Chauffeur Leslie Anthony recounts that, on
a visit to his aunt in Poole, Lennon asked him to see if they
could marry that very day on a cross-Channel ferry. 'I went
to Southampton and talked to the skipper, who decided they
couldn't since marriages are no longer performed aboard ferries.
He said they could marry on a Cunard ocean liner and that there
was a round-the-world cruise departing that very day. I rang up
John. But he had second thoughts.'

Since Yoko had a passport problem and could not get to
Paris the plan was put aside until 20 March 1969 when, in
view both of their rejection by the Archbishop of Canterbury
since the Church of England did not then marry divorced
people, and of waiting requirements for licences in several
other countries, Lennon and Yoko settled for Gibraltar as the
scene of a three-minute ceremony which Lennon said afterwards
was 'quick, efficient and British'.

★ See *Times* marijuana advert 24 July 1967, signed by several names including Tom
Maschler, George Melly, Dr Jonathan Miller, Brian Epstein, David Hockney, Kenneth
Tynan and the four Beatles including John Lennon – singular in being the only MBEs
to sign.

Five days later they were in Amsterdam, on honeymoon in Room 902 at the Hilton Hotel, where they stayed in bed for seven days talking about peace with newsmen and photographers. Don Short was present at the famous Amsterdam Bed-in where the couple jumped in and out between the sheets, failing to perform, but talking at length about peace and love. Neither naked nor carnal, the Lennons were disappointing – John pleaded that the latter was 'too private'. There was also talk of a vice bust which didn't occur, although I never did discover if they were smoking pot.

Short also travelled with them to Majorca where they had gone to see Yoko's daughter Kyoko, who was living there with her father, Tony Cox.

Whilst everyone believes that Bagism was an idea original to Yoko, Short points out that John was hip to the idea when they toured in Spain before his marriage to Yoko. 'John and I were in his suite one night, just he and I. The clothes which had been dry cleaned came back in a huge plastic bag. We took out the clothes. John climbed into this huge plastic bag. He sealed it. He pushed the button for the waiter to place an order for drinks. I sat in the corner as if I were some sort of stooge. I pressed the bell, and when the waiter came in he almost dropped the tray when he saw John wrapped in a huge, green plastic bag, trying to give him an order. Then he looked at me and I kept silent, reading a book as if I was not party to it, sipping my gin and tonic. The waiter gave up at the end.'

Having visited John at Kenwood many times during his marriage to Cynthia, Short describes him as a fragmented personality projected in the general disarray of the house. 'It was a jumble. He had a traditional piece with something modern or something he picked up somewhere else. John was full of good intentions about the furnishing of the home, but they travelled so much and bought this which didn't go with that that they never got round to designing the place. There were fabulous pieces of artefacts and furniture, but none complementing the other.'

What was Lennon really like?

'John was a man of moods. He would sleep in any room. He would kip down on the floor – on the sofa. He was a nocturnal person. Sometimes he would sleep right through the day and get up at night.

'He was a nice guy but he had a nasty side, a black mood which emerged. He would fly into dark rages – shout and scream about

85

anything which would upset him. He would slam the door and say, "Fuck off." When John was in a bad mood he would lock himself away. I don't think it would be beyond him to be spiteful and malicious and to seek revenge. He would write a sour note. He would get his own back. He would make that person feel as if they had to issue an apology.'

The handling of the divorce is an example of John's darker side, with Lennon trying initially to get Cynthia to allow him to sue her for adultery, although groundless, and hiring a slick London divorce lawyer to con her into accepting a paltry £100,000 settlement. Not only did Cynthia *have* to work again, but she worked herself into the situation of promoting Lennon's name in a night-club and then quitting when it all became too much.

'I was shattered when John broke from Cynthia. I couldn't believe that John had gone with Yoko,' recalls Short. 'But he was always fascinated by unusual things or challenges. She always had this great influence over him. She almost knew how his mind worked. He was spellbound by this.

'John wanted to sue Cynthia for adultery, although she was blameless. And she behaved properly. John would lay blame and walk away from it. Perhaps he was angry that day. There was a bit of a black mood situation with John. If he was in a black mood he would pass the buck. There was a little hurt pride there. He felt like all men with double standards. It is all right for the man to fool around, but when it comes to your wife doing it – no way. I'm sure she behaved properly, but when she told him off he knew he couldn't keep all women around without them considering doing likewise. But your wife is not allowed to do that, although she is estranged from you. You still want the power over them. I think John felt that his power had been usurped.'

Whereas Lennon in later years decried the press's intrusion into his lifestyle, he openly courted its presence at the height of Beatlemania by allowing Short, among other favourites, to pry into family secrets.

On the famous night that Lennon brought Yoko into the house when Cynthia was in Rimini, Short says, 'I gave him a dressing down for it. I said that he ought to treat Cynthia with a little bit more respect. He told me to get knotted.' Of course, Short acknowledges that the marriage was actually over when John and Cynthia were in India with the Maharishi, and Lennon was writing to Ono back in London.

Tight with Cynthia, how did he cope with Ono?

1. John's Aunt Mimi's solidly middle-class values set him at odds with the Establishment early on. She took him in after he had been deserted by his parents.

2. Diamonds in Dirt. John, ragged and unkept, with Cynthia, amid the Liverpool slums. Cynthia lived with Aunt Mimi, until her pregnancy became visible.

3. The Beatles *after* the cool hand of Brian Epstein subdued Teddy Boy appeal promoting instead the image of 'repressed sex'. Suits, ties and Cuban heels.

4. Brian's unrequited love for Cilla Black disturbed his life. The *only* girl in his stable.

ʋove left: Part of Robert Whitaker's controversial and later withdrawn Butcher's Sleeve cover of the Beatles 'Yesterday . . . and Today' album. An early insight into John's penchant to shock.
ʋove right: 24 Chapel Street, Brian's posh Belgravia townhouse, where he lived and died. The verdict was suicide, but couldn't a murderer have got in by way of the Georgian sash windows?
ʋlow: Business partner and confidante Peter Brown en route to the inquest following Brian's death. Police testimony confirmed rumours of an unstable private life.

8. John's crush on teen girl star headliner Helen Shapiro. But he got her bad press when they were asked to leave a Carlisle hotel dance. Began 1963 Tour as a supporting act, finished up as headliners when 'Please Please Me' went to number one.

9. A classic Robert Whitaker photo, circa 1960s, of John and Cynthia attired in Carnaby Street gear, within the confines of their Kenwood (Surrey) estate garden.

byles luncheon
n of John's first
k, *In His Own
e*, which Brian
scouraged.

11. Adaptation of *In His
Own Write* as a play at the
National Theatre. John's
vision of Liverpool street
fe. Gratuitous racism and
nti-Semitism demean the
prose.

2. The Beatles as symbols
of British working-class
nobility get awards from
Prime Minister Harold
Wilson.

13. A rare charity event appearance in America. John normally declined invitations to fund-raising events.

14. John in conversation with Walter Shenson, producer of *A Hard Day's Night* and *Help*, with a view to starting his own film career. Paul was the natural, while Ringo has since become the film star.

15. Eleanor Bron with the boys filming *Help*.

16. *Magical Mystery Tour* – the Beatles produced, directed and filmed it. Profoundly anti-social, it makes the point about John's anger at prostitution of fame.

17. 'Let It Be', with Yok[
in the background.
Lennon, fed up with
mainstream crap, decid[
to go underground.

18. Cynthia misses trai[
to Bangor for Maharish[
seminar in Wales.
Security police delay
passage – are
unconvinced that she i[
'Mrs Lennon'. Console[
by Neil Aspinall and
Peter Brown.

'All new wives don't like their husband's old friends or cronies,' he replies. 'I don't think she liked Paul. I think Paul was ready to like Yoko. Maybe she saw Paul as a threat. It was a partnership. The partnership should have been John and Yoko, not John and Paul. I am not saying it was a deliberate process, but it was a natural process. John had a new partner: she. Yoko Ono. It was going to be John and Yoko's songs and not Paul and John's songs.'

Did Short endorse the direction John took with Yoko?

'John sent me a copy of *Two Virgins* with a doodle on it. There was an earlier scandalous album which they had done which Brian withdrew – butchers on it. Brian thought the cover was in bad taste. He sent it to me and asked me for my opinion and I didn't like it very much and said so. The next thing I knew he had destroyed the whole bloody stock that had been printed.'

And *Two Virgins*?

'I think we all saw it as a detour. I wondered how long it would last. When I heard that John had gone off with May Pang, I had the feeling at that stage that John wouldn't return to Yoko – but he did. Yoko had tremendous influence. Even though he went off with May, it still seemed to me Yoko was pulling the string.'

He pauses. 'I find their relationship sad in many ways, 'cause I knew John Lennon when he was his own man. When he got himself into Yoko's jetstream he couldn't shake free from it. And I think she could have helped him to do things of his own design and creative ability without saying, "You have to do them with me." She seemed to restrict him in his thinking and what he was doing. That might be a hard thing to say, 'cause I have no axe to grind so far as Yoko is concerned.' While others thought John made a change for the better, Short disagrees. 'Maybe some talent was lost there. He did write one or two nice songs, but I think there was so much more talent there that went adrift.'

Of Yoko's own work, Short is ambivalent. Having attended her show at Indica and seen the various exhibits of conceptual art, he says: 'She had some interesting theories and ideas. I think that is what fascinated John. She wanted to do things. She wanted to raise people's consciousness. I think this is what inspired John. But at some stage he seemed to lose his way. We have a sad figure at the end, almost a Howard Hughes-type figure. She provided him with his needs, if he wanted to eat food of this or that quality. If he wanted a book to read, she'd send out for it. If he wanted someone to talk to, she'd write the person to come in. Anything to make John happy. That was eroding his talent. You ask at the end of the day, "Was Yoko good for him?" And I wonder about that.'

Short's favourite impression of the boys is of them at the height of Beatlemania. 'They were their own best PR. They made themselves with their attitudes, their expressions. They didn't say much, but their off-the-cuff remarks, their Liverpool bluff answers to questions, their disregard for accepted things created for them a very special niche in the heart not only of the British public, but the world public. When they got their MBEs they didn't know what to do with the bloody medals – John gave his to aunt Mimi who kept it on top of the TV.

'They couldn't care if it was duchesses or ladies of the land. It was all the same: "Hello, luv." They would not curtsey or bow down. They'd give them a nudge or a wink and treat them like an ordinary person. And they'd get away with it. If I did that, I'd get thrown out.'

The Lennons have always had problems with their kids – when I talked to John in 1972 he said he hadn't seen his son Julian since arriving in the States in 1971 because of immigration laws which would prevent him from returning if he left the country. But even when he lived in England Lennon rarely saw Julian, and when he made time to take him on a Scottish holiday the episode ended in the famous car crash.

Doubtless what Ono wanted was a happy domestic life, safe in the knowledge that her daughter was living with them. Her devotion to her own mother borders on reverential, although from all accounts they had the normal mother–daughter quarrels. So it must have been doubly heartbreaking to find herself chasing around the world for custody of her own child. The reality, of course, may be that the girl preferred to remain with her father. Since our interview Ono's contact with Kyoko has appeared to be touch and go. And whilst the relationship might have since improved, when Lennon died Kyoko, by then a young woman, expressed her sorrow to Yoko by despatching a consolatory telegram.

In April 1971 John and Yoko tracked down Cox and Kyoko in Majorca, where Yoko tried to regain custody of her child. In an attempt to secure the child, John and Yoko were detained by the police before being despatched to Paris. Kyoko was handed back to her father. In March 1972, five months before we talked, the

Houston courts had awarded Yoko custody. But by then the child had been taken elsewhere.

Said Lennon, 'We would like to get in touch with Tony, Melinda [then Tony's wife] and Kyoko. We'd like to stop the war whatever it is and be sensible about it, without detectives and FBI and guns and people jumping on them in the middle of the night. We have been through all that. They think we are going to take Kyoko away and they are never going to see her again. We want a mutual agreement between the two of us irrespective of court cases. It is like a divorce. It is as if war has been declared. It gets unreal. Particularly with a child. It should happen friendly and mutually without lawyers, courts, agents and detectives. We have information given to us all the time that they have taken her here, there and everywhere. We have taken plane trips and sent people but they are not where they said they were.'

Yoko added, 'I hope that she is well. I hope that they love her. And I hope that is the reason why they have taken her away from me. And I hope that they will start to understand that there is no reason for them to keep the child away from me.'

It was during the famous Bed-in honeymoon in Amsterdam in March 1969 that Lennon got wind of ATV's takeover bid for Northern Songs, catapulting him into a protracted involvement which ended with defeat in May 1969.

City correspondent Edward Connolly rang Lennon in Amsterdam with the bad news, reporting that John was 'shocked' when he heard about Sir Lew Grade's bid and appalled by Dick James's negotiations behind his back. Said John, 'They are my shares and my songs and I want to keep a bit of the end product. I didn't have to ring Paul. I know damn well he feels the same as I do.'

The irony is, of course, that John and Paul did not get control, and when ATV sold off its Northern Songs catalogue in the eighties, the list, containing all the Beatles classics along with some Tin Pan Alley standards, went to Michael Jackson. But at the time the dreadful thing was that, whilst the Beatles turned out hit after hit, responsible as they were for 50 per cent of Capitol Records revenue, they were unable to convince stockholders to back them in the shares fight.

When Northern Songs was formed in 1963, going public in 1965, it allowed Lennon and McCartney to realize a bit of money because of the capital gains sale. Offering some shares to the public, the company kept the rest for itself, split among Dick James (music publisher) and Charles Silver (accountant) on the one hand, and John Lennon and Paul McCartney on the other, with Triumph Investments (via NEMS purchase) holding 5 per cent.

Replying to Lennon's comment about being 'sold down the river', Dick James (now deceased) said at the time, 'I really thought I was acting for them. The deal would have been worth similar amounts to each of the two Beatles had they accepted.'

Whilst Northern Songs was the first music company to be quoted on the London Stock Exchange, there was sustained disbelief that the shares would ever be worth anything, and in spite of monster hits such as 'Michelle', 'Yesterday' and 'Eleanor Rigby' the public remained sceptical, running scared when offered hard cash by Sir Lew Grade.

Forgetting acorns and peace, Lennon determined to wage war for control. He summoned back from holiday Allen Klein, who a month previously had joined Apple as financial adviser. Klein put Lennon and McCartney in touch with bankers Ansbacher and Co., and together they conspired to map out a deal for control. The whole thing, consummated in haste, left the Beatles unable to rally shares held by fans in diverse places around the globe. But at the time they made an effort to woo the consortium of 'uncommitted' stockholders, consisting of investment bankers, brokers and others.

Lennon and McCartney's bid to the suit-and-tie cartel consisted of newspaper adverts to convince everyone that their shares were sound and would increase in value, since the Beatles were capable of and willing to renew their contract with Northern Songs, which meant a profusion of Lennon–McCartney hits.

What appeared in the *Times* of 30 April 1969 was an entreaty from the Beatles via their bankers to the stockholders to sit tight. The proposal made several points: among them, that neither the Beatles nor Allen Klein intended to sit on the Northern Songs board, content as they were to leave its running to businessmen; that the boys intended to renew their Northern Songs contract for an additional two years; that the position of minority shareholders would not change under the Beatles' control; that James and Silver had made the offer without consulting the Beatles, and that by accepting the Beatles' offer shareholders would obtain a higher price. The final plea entreated those who had profited from a stake in the Beatles' past compositions that, if they wanted to ensure further profits for Northern Songs, they should reject the

ATV offer and accept the Beatles' offer in respect of their entire shareholdings.

But the Dream was over, and nowhere was this more perceptible than in the loss-of-confidence vote. The Beatles follies – *Magical Mystery Tour*, Apple, and Lennon's personal shenanigans – convinced the shareholders to go their own way.

But why did James sell out? An observer confides: 'When the Beatles were falling apart after Brian's death, James discussed it with advisers that the Beatles looked very much as though they were going to break up and go their separate ways. It was felt by the advisers that the City would not understand that Northern Songs could continue to earn large sums of money even *after* the Beatles had broken up. They felt that the City would regard it as a serious matter and the shares would plummet. So before the City got wind of this, James wanted to sell Northern Songs.'

Since it was widely known around the music industry that James wanted to sell, it was not surprising that he received an offer from his one-time artist's representative, Lew Grade, chairman of ATV. Says my source, 'Grade told him basically that he thought this was the time for Northern Songs to be sold as he was aware that the Beatles were in trouble relationship-wise.' Apart from James's and Silver's shares, Grade also acquired public shares, putting him in a formidable position to combat the Beatles' bid.

It is not commonly known, but James openly told Lennon and McCartney that it was in their best interests to sell. He didn't have faith that the City was going to understand. McCartney was annoyed that James was considering selling and not standing by them. John went along with Paul, got very annoyed and left James out on his own. James felt that what he was doing wasn't only in his own best interest but in the best interest of the Beatles, and at the end of the day they might thank him for, as minority shareholders, they would get top money for shares which he felt would slide drastically.

It is Dick James who held the key to the Beatles' musicianship. Isn't it odd that a man who made millions from his top songwriters should suddenly run scared when the manager died, even though the very songwriters agreed to extend their contract with the company? Didn't he have faith in their sustained talents? And if not, why not? Did he know, perhaps, that while McCartney was capable, Lennon couldn't write a hit, and that it would not be until after his death that his solo songs regularly reached the number one position?

Nevertheless, Lennon and McCartney sat tight, appealing to the consortium of suit-and-tie men via their financial advisers 'Sergeant' Bruce Ormrod and 'Captain' Allen Klein. They had almost succeeded in closing the deal when Lennon's prejudices got the better. According to witnesses, Lennon was coping with the investors when a problem emerged over which they disagreed. 'I won't be dictated to by men in suits sitting on their fat arses in the City,' railed Lennon. It remained for the Beatles to make an independent bid, which failed. Allen Klein pledged MGM shares, but even so the deal failed and ATV got the control it wanted. Because Sir Lew Grade wanted the collateral of Beatles stock within the company the boys had to get a City takeover panel to demand that the same cash offer of sale be made to them. Holding firm, ATV conceded to make a loan stock offer only.

When Mama Cass heard that the Beatles had formed Apple, she exclaimed, 'My God! You're a corporation!' The company was formed for ten years in April 1967, four months before Brian's death, as a way of giving the boys greater control over their songs and films, since it was well known that Lennon was becoming increasingly distressed with his work being credited to George Martin (musical producer) and Richard Lester (director). It evolved, moreover, said Lennon, to help other artists so that they might be spared the indignity of going down on their knees in some businessman's office.

Whilst the company scored with such monster hits as 'Hey Jude', its standard product was middle-of-the-road. Artists included Mary Hopkin, Billy Preston, James Taylor – people who could make it anywhere, and did. Apple, waving the banner of co-operative capitalism, fell short of its objective; James Taylor became involved in prospective litigation which resolved itself out of court. But its aims were high – its interests included electronics, films, publishing, retailing and records, with offices in many different countries.

The company produced one successful film, *Let It Be*, a couple of hit records and a few mainstream artists whilst subsidizing the ventures of friends and united underground artists. One, Jon Hague, quit the business and the other, Yoko Ono, married the boss.

The whole thing wound down when they discovered their essential individual differences, all four wanting separation from each other. In December 1970 McCartney filed for divorce, although the end had been coming since inception. The final decree was granted in January 1975, four years after Lennon had moved to New York. (It is ironic that his divorce from the Beatles was more complicated and prolonged than that from Cynthia.)

Apple, whose offices originated in Wigmore Street, then moved to Baker Street where the Fool, a Dutch design firm, painted the building in psychedelia (which Westminster Council required be effaced). They finally settled at Number 3 in smart Savile Row, in what appeared to be an embassy or the head office of a building society – a lovely Georgian edifice with classical portals, the interiors boasting moulded ceilings and fireplaces that were kept lit with real fires. The site was immortalized in the *Let It Be* film, with its famous traffic-stopping jam on the roof.

There was plenty of liquor and pot, and there were cordon bleu cooks. Nevertheless staff morale was low, particularly when Lennon started bad-mouthing about overspending, and hiring Allen Klein as financial adviser to streamline the company. Ron Kass and Alistair Taylor left in the wake of Klein's arrival, and a squatting tenant was also asked to leave, much to the dismay of the Apple staff.

So what was it like at Apple, then?

Alison Tilley, one of the cordon bleu chefs employed to prepare simple food, dispels the image which prevails of the office being infested with sex-crazed, pot-smoking tarts, the kind whom Lennon characterized as rude to Yoko and muttering 'bitch' behind her back. In fact, whilst the executives comprised mainly working-class Liverpudlians, the cooks and secretaries were ex-public school girls.

Tilley, then a deb, now a wife and a mother, recalls her days at Apple with pleasure: 'Paul was at Apple the most. He was recording, playing it back and listening to it with Linda with him quite a lot. Paul held court. You would be aware that he wanted something – coffee, lunch. Whereas George would just ring up and then ring back and say, "I'm off. So don't bother to bring it." George was a tea drinker. He drank endless cups of tea. Ringo was always very happy. But George had the best manners. Paul was going through a bad patch with Allen Klein and Linda was very pregnant.'

The outsiders, predictably, were Klein and Ono. 'No one wanted Allen Klein in the end. John and he had been quite good friends at the start. But I seem to remember the whole thing ending in tears. I think Allen was resented by the staff too.

'I met Yoko when she first came to Apple when the bust-up happened and all the Beatles were fighting and Linda was with Paul. Yoko was a presence nobody seemed to welcome. There was major friction between Yoko and Allen Klein and the other Beatles. She had her views and persisted in them.'

About the antipathy with Klein, John was to comment that Allen simply didn't understand Yoko. 'He tries, but he is unable to grasp the complexity of her mind.' Bitter about the Beatles, John said, 'They are rude to us and do not apologise.'

Characterizing the atmosphere at Apple as one which heaped blame upon Ono, Tilley says, 'I was aware at the time of Yoko being disruptive and that the Beatles blamed her a lot. She wanted to know what John was doing all the time. He was mesmerized by her. Their other halves had always stayed in the background, or like Linda had been very supportive. Yoko's presence certainly was not welcome there. I think Yoko would have liked to represent them. She is a very ambitious woman.'

Was it known at Apple that she was a Japanese heiress?

'We knew that she was a banker's daughter. I think people thought Cox was wealthier than he is. No doubt about it. We were made aware that she came from a good background. She might have been an impoverished artist, but she made it clear that she came from no ordinary background. John certainly knew. That was the impression she gave around the place – of a well-bred woman. Not just anybody. Certain people play it down. Yoko did not.'

Grapefruit publisher Peter Owen recounts his own visit to John and Yoko at Apple, where he had gone to discuss publicity for the upcoming British publication in 1970 of Yoko's book, which had previously been published in Japan and the USA.

I went to see them at Apple when they were in that posh building in Savile Row. She had her hat on and was eating caviar from Fortnum and Mason at £36 a jar. In the sixties that was very expensive. She didn't look glamorous or well-dressed. But she was eating this caviar out of the jar with a kitchen spoon, which gave her cachet. John wasn't eating – she was eating the caviar on her own – and she didn't offer us any food. She was interviewing us rather grandly.

'Lennon was very pleasant and did some sketches right then and there to use in the English version of the book.'

Apparently, however, the use of John's illustrations and introductions became an irritation to Ono, who was quoted in the press as saying that she believed they were used to promote the book for the wrong reasons.

Having done one printing, the book went into paperback and expired. Yoko's involvement became a nuisance towards the end. 'She would phone me up at the most inconvenient times until I stopped it,' says Owen. 'I said it was really inconvenient of her to pester me all the time. She wasn't being helpful.'

Whilst it has been reported that Lennon was stoned at business meetings and McCartney distracted himself by doodling, it is none the less true that on such occasions they were totally lucid.

Hy Smith, marketing man for United Artists which released *Let It Be*, produced by Apple and a financially successful film venture for the group, recalls the professionalism of the Beatles. He had been warned that, despite their hippie image, in business matters they were pros.

'I met with them in autumn 1968, since the release date for the film was spring 1969. I came into London and went over to Apple and had a meeting which ran a couple of hours. We didn't have lunch. I had two missions – one, to work on the possibility of getting some help and additional material which might be available, such as stills, and two, I had a young cousin through marriage who was a Beatles fan and had asked me to get an autograph. All the Beatles except Paul McCartney were at the meeting.'

Was he surprised by the posh Savile Row offices?

'I was told not to expect the expected – bohemia. They lived well, but they didn't throw money around. They liked to be comfortable. They were astute businessmen. They knew what they wanted.'

How did Lennon strike him?

'He was casual, wearing blue jeans. Presentable. One of the things I was told was that they were very casual. I remember getting out of the car and taking off my tie. My associate said, "Why are you doing that?" I said, "It makes me look less like a blue suit."'

For an observation about what it was like working for the Beatles as producers as opposed to performers I talked to Sheila Bromberg, the 'hippie harpist' who played on the Beatles' 'She's Leaving Home' and also on the McCartney-produced Mary Hopkin album.

'There were just two harpists in the studio on the Mary Hopkin album. She was one of Paul's protégés. The music was fiercely difficult and with just two harps. We were grumbling like crazy, "We've got to play this for £4. They must be up their trees." At this time the microphones had been set up, but we weren't aware that they had been connected up to the control box. Eventually we heard a pitter-patter down the stairs, and Paul McCartney came and looked over the top of the music stands and said, "Fifty quid apiece do ya?" So we got £50, which was a lot of money for a musician in those days.'

Following the Lennon car crash in Golspie, Scotland in July 1969, Apple girls Alison Tilley and Alexandra Palmer were despatched to Kenwood to look after the couple as cooks-housekeepers.

The Scottish summer holiday was to have been a release for the couple after the Amsterdam and Montreal Bed-ins, and an opportunity for John to introduce his legion of aunts to the new bride. The excursion was also intended to give John and Yoko time with their respective children, Julian and Kyoko. Things progressed nicely at first, with the couple stopping to outfit the kids in tartans. And then, due either to nerves at being reunited with his son, or drugs, John lost control of the car, injuring himself, Yoko and Kyoko. Julian suffered shock.

In the Lawson Memorial Hospital in Golspie, Lennon received seventeen stitches in a facial wound, Yoko fourteen stitches and Kyoko four. Alex Palmer recalls the Lennons arriving home by helicopter, Yoko's head in a bandage, bringing with them a basket of bloodstained clothes 'which they asked me to send to the laundry'. Alison adds, 'I remember thinking: "Gasp. How awful. He's always going to look different."' Alex says, 'John was cut up very badly and had a lot of little scars on his face.' (I have written to the hospital enquiring about whether he had plastic surgery, but have not had a reply.)

Alex and Alison were transported to and from London every day by John's chauffeur in a posh white Rolls Royce fitted with a drinks cabinet and a TV aerial. They were sometimes assisted by someone to look after the child, but since John baulked against the idea of a nanny, more often Kyoko stayed alone.

Recounts Alex, 'I liked looking after Kyoko, their little girl. She was sweet. I felt a bit sorry for her. She was very lonely. She was aged three.* I used to take her shopping with me and buy her a few clothes and things occasionally.

'She was Catholic and had an altar set up in her room. One

---

* Kyoko was aged six in 1969.

day when she was saying her rosary down on her knees I asked her what she was praying for, and she said, "For Daddy to come and take me away." She was unhappy there, really.'

Alison Tilley disagrees: 'Yoko's very spoiled daughter Kyoko, was aged about nine.★ She was the rudest child I ever have met. The first time I met her she bolted into the kitchen demanding, "Are you the kitchen maid? Get me a plate of peas." No please or thank you. Yoko always said "Thank you". And she did say "Please". Her daughter Kyoko was charmless and had no manners. She treated us as if we were dirt. And she had this horrendous bedroom with a miniature four-poster bed and all those dolls.'

Circumstances seemed to conspire against any permanency to the union, for when the Lennons tried to send Kyoko to school at Hurst Lodge, Ascot, near where they intended to live at Tittenhurst, they were told that the school was full up. Julian, at Heath House primary school, and later at Ruthin in Wales, was absent for the summer holidays; his mother had removed him from hospital in Golspie without a word to Lennon.

Alison was impressed by the private estate's smart golf course, swimming pool and host of celebrity residents. 'St George's Hill, Weybridge, is very exclusive because of its proximity to London. There are lots of big houses with big gardens behind electric gates. The security is good. It is millionaire's row, with a private golf course for its residents, most of whom are celebrities. I think Cliff Richard still lives there. When we were there other residents included Tom Jones, Englebert Humperdinck and Peter Sellers.'

Although Lennon had been warned by doctors against intercourse during pregnancy, he lived incommunicado at Weybridge in bed all day – and who knows what by night? The girls were buoyed up by each other's company, although quite clearly they didn't know what was expected. 'We were told that John expected us to use the pool,' recounts Alison. 'The chauffeur told us that "No one swims with any clothes on around here." I don't think we used the pool. We had our eyes open wondering what was going to happen next.'

Life with the Lennons sounds like a horror movie, the girls fearful not that the man will make a pass but that he will involve them in perversion. Following the drug bust there were fears on the part of the girls' parents that they would be introduced to drugs and therefore become 'junkies'. But drugs were not the problem.

Lennon's sexual proclivities were bizarre, and he made the girls indirect parties to them. When Alison Tilley talks about it all twenty years later she still seems in shock.

'We were told never to knock but simply to enter their bedroom. When we arrived at 10 a.m. we'd go in and ask if they wanted something. We never saw them naked – they always had the covers over them. Often John was sitting up in bed strumming the guitar, or playing with a simple tape machine. There was not a lot of electronic gear about.

'We kept thinking we'd walk in on them when they were having sex. But we never did. But knowing John, he could do anything. He rather relished shocking people. I remember we used to stand there and rattle the tray to give them a minute. You had no idea what to expect.'

Their duties included cooking, shopping and feeding John's menagerie of cats which roamed around the house. Alison recalls, 'They were faddish on food. Yoko influenced John enormously on what they were to eat. I always thought he wanted steak and chips instead of jelly, jelly and more jelly.'

Into a meat-free, macrobiotic diet, the Lennons would breakfast on scrambled eggs, custard and jelly. Alison observed: 'The consistency of the jelly was most important. We had to put a bowl of jelly in the fridge at night. I remember Yoko, who was pregnant, would come down, and tell us what kind of jelly they would like for the next day. It seems ridiculous, but her main worry was that the jelly wouldn't set.'

Later in the day the girls would prepare a hot meal, consisting of boil-in-the-bag fish, vegetables and more jelly. 'We were not allowed to put butter on the vegetables,' recalls Alison. 'Yoko would say she was afraid they would put on weight. They appeared not to mind that the fish was brought frozen from a shop in Weybridge.'

The girls were also required to clean the bedroom on the one occasion the couple removed themselves from bed during the day. Recounts Alison, 'I remember that the room was messy – cigarette butts stubbed out on a lovely white carpet. After we changed the sheets (which were something else!) we were asked to empty their potty. They always had a potty by their bed, preferring it to using the loo.'

Alex recalls, 'I remember being surprised by their non-literary reading tastes. I expected them to read love poetry to each other, but instead they spent their time reading magazines such as *Woman's Own* or *Private Eye*.'

She continues, 'He used to keep money under the bed. I remember one day he gave me a fistful of five-pound notes and asked me to bring with me the following day an outfit which he and Yoko had seen advertised in some magazine from a shop on the King's Road.'

Her impressions of Yoko?

Alex says, 'She impressed me as being fragile. Didn't seem that well. And John was always very protective towards her. He seemed to do most of the talking.'

Alison disagrees. 'Yoko was very original and highly ambitious. She was pulling strings and he was jumping when we were there. He seemed to hang on her every word.'

And Lennon?

Alison reflects, 'He could be devious, snubbing people he had arranged to see and wouldn't show. He just wouldn't get out of bed. Calls from people they didn't want put through. There were a lot of business disputes.' She pouts. 'I remember one time a problem with the Ferrari that he had ordered. It was a wonderful blue Ferrari with fittings, fixtures and extras. I went up and told John it had arrived. He said, "Tell him I don't want to look at it." He didn't get out of bed. He didn't apologise. I don't know what happened. I hope they sent him a large bill.'

Adds Alex, 'I remember him being preoccupied with big business. Allen Klein rang a lot. And Paul McCartney. There were heavy, preoccupying consultations, since Paul wanted the Eastmans [Linda's family] and John was keen on Klein.'

On 3 September 1971 Lennon left Britain to live in the United States, never again to return to the country where he had become an international idol and a multi-millionaire. His lavish Ascot mansion was sold in September 1973 to Ringo Starr.

As time progressed and his political vernacular became increasingly philanthropic, Lennon's personal sense of acquisition reached Howard Hughes proportions.

But back in the days when he was plain John Beatle, what was he like? The ensuing chapters reveal the origins of Lennon's darker side.

6

School Kids

The magical, mythical never-never land glorified by the Beatles is an idealization of one place – Liverpool and the surrounding countryside of Woolton and Allerton where the boys grew up. Though now a second-rate port, in the Victorian era, Liverpool was a portentous place despatching cargo ships around the world. The dowager Adelphi Hotel is a lone reminder of the grand age – crystal chandeliers limning the salon ceiling, English oak panelling girding the hallways – whilst the city's Victorian mansions that once belonged to cotton and grain kings have become schools or charitable institutions.

Still rich in parks, the city had far less industry and housing when Lennon was growing up, and the area around his Menlove Avenue home in Woolton, the suburb south of Liverpool – now full of apartment blocks and housing estates – was then mostly farmland and parkland. John's uncle George was a dairy farmer who until he died used to deliver milk in a horse and cart.

Raymond Feather recalls: 'Woolton was very different in those days – much more open land. Not only the golf links, but next to my house there was a twenty-acre field. At the back there was a large pond which we made rafts on. There are now new housing estates. Next to John's house was an open field. Next to that was an old farmhouse – which had become a remand home for juvenile delinquents. Another was Strawberry Field, which was a Salvation Army orphanage. These big old houses which had belonged to the nineteenth-century shipping barons had fallen into disuse and been converted to other uses. The golf club, which is municipal, had been the home of a shipping magnate. And the clubhouse is still like that. Liverpool was the

School Kids

New York of the nineteenth century, and up until the war it was a very important port.'

That municipal golf course where John used to play or stroll with his first girlfriend remains, as does the perilous dual carriageway where his mother was killed whilst crossing the street.

A visit to the sacred shrine inspires, and whilst Shakespeare and the Brontës are reckoned to attract greater numbers of tourists, it is estimated that Liverpool is visited by a hundred thousand people a year with the intention of visiting Beatles sites. To arrive at the places mentioned in the songs and to visit the sites associated with the Beatles, notably with John Lennon, is a profound experience.

Whilst the demise of the port has left in its wake unemployment and lower living standards, the town centre is alive with shopkeepers and small businesses bustling to survive. Victorian architecture pleases the eye in the form of the Walker Art Gallery and City Library, but there are modern shopping arcades dotted around the city, which, whilst obtrusive, reassure one that the city is not totally at odds with the twentieth century.

Cobbled thoroughfares have given way to tarmac, and Brian Epstein's Whitechapel NEMS record store is now an electrical appliance shop in a pedestrian precinct. Liverpool docks, once thriving, then moribund, have been tarted up and converted into expensive flats, offices and arts complexes.

A meander around the city reveals things which remain – the old yards from which John used to pinch coal for heating are now used as storage spaces for woodworkers, booksellers, ironmongers and so on. The lovely terrace of late Georgian houses in which John occupied a flat whilst at art school with Stuart Sutcliffe and Rod Murray has not been altered. Still standing is the pied-à-terre which Brian let and which he gave to John and Cynthia when they married. But gone are the hundreds of sixties' coffee bars and rock clubs that popularized the Mersey sound; those that remain are expensively refurbished nightclubs. The famous Cavern, originally an old warehouse converted into a fetid coffee bar where the Beatles played 292 gigs, is now part of an upmarket shopping mall closed to traffic, with a bronze statue of the four Beatles in the courtyard. The Grapes, an old pub, authentic as ever, is what remains of the original street. But the Blue Angel, a nightclub owned by Beryl and Allan Williams, the boys' first proper manager and responsible for their Hamburg gigs, has become an expensive showplace.

The art college is still there though the Liverpool Institute survives only as a building, now part of the art polytechnic. The pubs where Lennon and his chums used to drink remain. Ye Cracke, his favourite watering hole, around the corner from the college, triumphs in having survived the eighties without being tarted up. It remains a grubby nineteenth-century pub, plastered with historical newspaper cuttings and period posters. The locals who remember Lennon as a schoolboy are eager to natter, regaling you with stories about the goofy things he would get up to. For instance, one time he lay down on the floor, moaning that he was drowning. 'If you're drowning, swim,' joked a local. John flapped his arms with the vitality of a seal. 'I'm swimming as fast as I can!' he rebutted, leaving the man in peals of laughter. The Philharmonic pub, with its marble men's lavatory, remains a magnificent specimen of Victorian architecture. A wander inside for a pint recalls memories of where Lennon got pissed, became abusive and was ejected.

The Mount Pleasant registry office, where Cynthia and John were married, remains, though as an adult education centre. But the stalwart red brick hospital in Oxford Street where John was born, purportedly the site of an air raid on the day of his birth, is still in business.

Woolton itself, a villagey suburb south of the centre, has its obligatory high street and hedgerow of shops: ironmonger, butcher, grocer, fishmonger and so on. Up the hill is St Peter's parish church, where for a short time John was a choirboy and where he briefly received religious instruction though he was not confirmed. The verger, the same man who tutored John, kindly showed me round the churchyard where gravestones engraved with local names like Rigby and McKenzie evoke memories of Beatles tunes. He took me to the field where John played at the famous church fete where he met Paul, a friend of a member of John's Quarry Men skiffle group, Ivan Vaughan. We wandered over to the church hall where John and the group used to perform regularly at Saturday night church dances, playing above the crowd on a proper stage. We also visited the small rehearsal room where John would practise on the piano.

Still a source of paternalism, the verger remains involved in the religious instruction of Woolton youth. Recalling John as a youth with both pride and concern, he talks about what the press has termed 'his impoverished background' but which in reality was the stigma of having been the product of a 'broken home' – deserted by his father, his mother living unmarried with another man without demonstrating any intention to reclaim her son.

In much the same way that Brian Epstein was a boy marked by the circumstance of having been chucked out of several preparatory schools, Lennon was ostracized as unacceptable on account of his social background. And whilst in later years the pace of his life compensated for this lack, when he was a youth he was very much victim of social forces – an outcast.

Fortunate to gain an interview with John's Quarry Bank head-master, William Pobjoy, I also got him to come back to the school where one warm spring afternoon we sat on the green and talked about John, whom the headmaster recalls alternately as contentious and desolate, characteristics ascribed to the instability of his background but which seem to have been aggravated by the insensitivity of the staff. The school itself remains a testament to the splendid Victorian age, with a warren of outbuildings subsidiary to the main building which is a surpreme example of Victoriana – oak-panelled rooms, turrets, bays and lovely stained glass windows.

Pobjoy and I head back to town on the local bus, sitting cheek by jowl with the boys. We travel down Allerton Road to the Penny Lane junction, all of which has seen an increase in shops and such since Lennon's time. The Beatles have been absorbed into the culture with typical British understatement and taste, so as not to obtrude but merely assimilate into the environment. At the Penny Lane roundabout there is a café, a coffee and doughnut place, with bits and bobs of Beatles memorabilia; whilst down the road is a Beatles wine bar, with a replica of John's acoustic guitar and other mementoes, dispensing tasty 'fish and finger pies' ('Penny Lane') along with other hot pies.

Most of the Mersey groups have left Liverpool long ago – McCartney keeps the family house for sentimental reasons. Happily the others' old homes, although owned by newcomers, have been neither altered nor demolished: John's Menlove Avenue semi remains, near to the Strawberry Field orphanage where at summer fetes John would sneak through the fence to pinch the strawberries.

The circumstances of John's background have been mooted in mystery, but it appears as if his father's desertion and confine-ment during the war at Ellis Island, New York prompted his mother's promiscuous behaviour with various men, several of which relationships produced offspring. There is a letter in the Hunter Davies collection in the British Museum, in which John asks the Beatles biographer please not to mention the part about the Norwegian seaman in the text. According to Bill Harry's *The Book of Lennon* (a Lennon A–Z), Julia had an affair with a Norwegian sailor which produced a child whom she placed in the care of a Norwegian couple. Whilst the origins of 'Norwegian Wood' have always been mooted to be a secret affair that John had with some woman journalist, I have always thought that they probably had to do with a more painful reality. Julia's affair with 'Twitchy' Dykins, a Liverpool waiter, produced two half-sisters, Julia and Jackie, recalled by John as referring to him as 'Stinker'.

The background to the romance between Julia Stanley and Alfred Lennon, rife with orphans and Stanleys, sounds like the libretto from *The Pirates of Penzance*. A former inmate of Liverpool's Blewcoat Orphanage (now extinct), Alfred Lennon knew all the Stanley sisters for years, but took a fancy to Julia whom he married after a ten-year courtship.

Whilst the press makes out that Julia willingly despatched her son into her sister Mimi's (pronounced Mamie, as in Eisenhower) custody, in reality there was a struggle, with Mimi getting what she wanted only when social workers ganged up on Julia, removing her boy John to a proper home. The definition of 'proper', as conventional and conformist, would be a source of continual friction between Mimi and John, resulting in feelings of self-alienation and need for self-justification which were formulated in his youth and exhibited for the rest of his life.

Neighbour Raymond Feather recalls, 'John was not interested in being *respectable*. He did not worry about how he was going to qualify to be an orthodox anything. He was idealistic in a way. He was revolting against ordinariness.'

He continues, 'His father had left the family and his mum was living down the street with some other guy. I would say that John was always insecure. He was intense. His music was very emotional, always. He wasn't interested in analyzing arpeggios. He was interested in warmth, sorrow and emotion in music. He was a very emotional person, always.

'The aunt dominated him more than a little bit. I won't say that it was hostile, but it wasn't the easy, warm or loving relationship that I had with my aunts or my mom. And I was surprised when he bought her that house.

'His aunt once said to me when I was aged eighteen and John was roughly the same age: "I don't know what I can do with my John. He will never be anything. Him and his bloody music." I was a first-year law student and a middle-class respectable person, and John was into clubs and not a respectable profession. The Cavern was never a respectable place. It was a place for working-class girls to go in their lunchtime.'

Stories about John's lack of music encouragement are legendary – rehearsal space was always the main worry. Lennon darted from place to place so as not to intrude or offend. His aunt's sun room, McCartney's family home, college digs, his mother's lover's house – all at one time or another served a purpose.

'Don't tell Mimi' was by then a byword, for it was well known among his friends that John's aunt was against his becoming a performer. Legend has it that she strode into the Cavern one afternoon, having heard (not been told) that they were playing, and threatened to remove John from the premises.

In short, Mimi was determined that John would amount to something more than his father (a waiter). In this endeavour she had always been anxious for him to go at the age of eleven to Quarry Bank, a grammar school, where she hoped he would meet and associate with a better class of boy and perhaps be encouraged to forget music and to pursue a proper profession. But John's friendships there with boys whom Mimi considered to be as rebellious as her nephew were disturbing, and his formation of a skiffle group called the Quarry Men whilst at the school was downright alarming.

It is therefore ridiculous to imagine that Mimi Smith bought John his first guitar. Accounts credit the purchase to Mimi or Julia. However, since Mimi wouldn't and Julia couldn't care, it is credible that John bought it himself. An account in the *Daily Mirror* file confirms that John bought it from his earnings as a construction worker one summer in Hanover, Germany (years before the Beatles ever set foot on foreign soil).

Controversy with Mimi was unabating. Paul McCartney recalled that, when he first met John at the St Peter's church social, he smelled of beer. John began drinking at an early age; its origins had a lot to do with the friction he encountered at home, at school and in church.

Undeterred, Lennon pursued his passion with clandestine intrigue, scribbling, writing or listening to records alone in his bedroom. Feather recalls, 'John liked American rock 'n' roll

– Chuck Berry and Gene Vincent. But he would also listen to classical blues – Muddy Waters and people like that.'

McCartney tells the tale that he and Lennon, unable to purchase records which had no European distributor, got hold of Sun or other small US labels by buying them off the dockers or by travelling miles to obtain copies or to crib the tunes. Paul told the BBC, 'You'd take the bus to the roundabout, change for another which would take you so far and then change again before you'd get to where you'd change one last time.'

Translating American blues into their own idiom produced a sound so unique, so exotic that it acquired its own name – the Mersey Sound, distinguished not only in Great Britain but throughout the world. Not since the imperial age of merchant shipping had Liverpool enjoyed so great a respectability. And whilst other Liverpool groups embraced the same tradition – some continuing long after the Beatles retired from performing – it must be said that the Beatles were in the vanguard of establishing an international reputation for an essentially local sound.

'The Beatles as a pop group were very different to anything which had been before as idols of the teenager – Sinatra or any of them,' recalls Feather. 'They were working-class, purposefully not respectable and slightly anti-Establishment. Slightly James Dean.'

An amateur drummer passed over by Lennon – having abandoned skiffle for rock – when recruiting percussion, Feather is well aware of the changes he helped to make in a Liverpool music scene committed to jazz. The enormity of their protest against status quo musicianship exhibited by having gained even a lunchtime showcase at the Cavern, then a jazz club housed in a damp, dark warehouse in the centre of town, cannot be under-rated. Before long they dominated the scene with their rock 'n' roll music. But, as George Melly recalls of their early encounters, the Beatles were on occasion even barred from entering by the bouncer for not wearing jackets and ties.

Footage of the early Cavern sessions reveals the group's crude musicianship, untutored vocal talents and minimal stage presence, which should have rendered them hopeless but did not. There was something fresh about the jiving, rocking and offbeat stage remarks, uttered mostly by John, which, whilst awkward in part, together made a captivating whole.

Even by rock standards the Beatles were brassy, uncivilized and unpredictable, and when a young staff reporter from the *Liverpool*

Echo, Vincent Kelly, now managing editor, made his way to the Cavern to conduct the group's first major interview he was made to feel so ridiculous by the encounter that he never filed the story. Years after the enormity of the group's international success, Kelly still sounds bitter as he recalls being made the object of John Lennon's sarcasm. 'Lennon started it, I recall' he says, talking to me in his office. 'If I asked a simple question such as how they got started he'd parody it by slapping the side of the table and mouthing the words, "How did we get started? How did we get started?" The other fellas would pick it up and it became a chant. The same thing with anything I asked. They simply wouldn't take it seriously. I got so fed up I left in disgust.'

It was not uncommon for Lennon to make off-colour remarks to female audience members, telling one girl to move her arse when she got in the way, or calling another a 'fat cow' for some perverse reason.

History seems to suggest that they were immediately taken to the public heart, but that is not entirely true. Phyllis McKenzie, now Fearon, knew John first at St Peter's, Woolton, and then at art college. Her father lived in a flat in the same house as John's maternal grandparents, the Stanleys. One of the few who can claim to have actually been there at the St Peter's fete where John met Paul, Phyllis also saw John at the Cavern when he had re-formed the Quarry Men into the Beatles. 'They looked scruffy – like Teddy rebels. They dressed to shock. I don't remember the music. I was listening to Chuck Berry. Buddy Holly was my hero. I wasn't into Elvis.'

Ray Feather reflects, 'Presley would appeal to John, because he could identify with him. Music of the "underclass". If you look at the early Beatles in their black leather jackets, they were Mods and Rockers. They were aggressively anti-. They weren't sure what they were against, but they were against it.'

An early witness to Beatlemania, Phyllis recalls the trepidation of arriving with Cynthia in the midst of John's adoring female fans. 'Girls would pull her hair, push her slightly. Women were crackers about him and they preferred it if the boys were free.'

Confirming the distinct lack of encouragement for the boys when they began, Phyllis says, 'Most parents like kids to go to grammar school and get a job. They don't like them fooling around. Thirty years ago not a lot of musicians were making it. Performing was a precarious life. Nobody thought they'd make it.'

Ray Feather agrees, 'It was very courageous of John to resist his auntie and go his own way. For a boy of twenty to go to Hamburg with other pop people you have to be able and determined to break your family ties and go to a dirty, filthy port because you want to play music. And they were very emotionally involved from the age of fourteen or fifteen and serious about their music.'

Another school chum of John's recalls occasional visits to the Menlove Avenue house when they were practising. 'Even then they had that marvellous blend of their music together, even though they were childish and infantile. John had a very creative lyric brain. But he was always playing music and skiving away from school. They didn't work.'

Her memories of John's indomitable aunt confirm the general view: 'When Mimi came into the house and they were playing their music she would chase everybody out again. She didn't want John to be a musician. He was always moaning about Mimi – "Mimi will bloody have a wobbler. Mimi will go mad. Don't tell Mimi."

'She wanted him to do more straightforward things in life. She wanted John to have a career. She adored him. She wanted him to do something *boring*. She wanted him to have stability more than anything else. His aggression is due to that, really.'

But while aggression and soul are elements in the conception of Beatles music, it is indisputable that a singular distinction is its 'villagey' sensibility. Not since the Elizabethan balladeers has the country produced such a band of troubadours. And it must be said that a great deal of this love of countryside and landscape derives from the bucolic atmosphere in which John grew up.

Remembers Feather, 'Woolton is a yuppie suburb now. It has been Chelsea-ized. But then it was a community of its own, with its own council housing and swimming pool. Few people moved out to Woolton, the way people moved to Childwall or places closer to the city. Woolton was always a place of its own, with Woolton people.

'When you came home from school, you'd do a little bit of homework, listen to records, and when dinner was over you'd go out to play. You'd look for balls on the golf links or go and climb trees or go swimming. Away from Liverpool, Woolton had its own identity.'

Whilst it is generally believed that Cynthia was John's childhood sweetheart, whom he met and married after a mild flirtation with other girls, before meeting her John had had an intense relationship with an older girl from Quarry Bank's sister school, Calder High. Now married and living in the Wirral, she refuses to discuss her relationship with John Lennon. Although photos characterize her as a leggy girl with big boobs, the girlfriend whom Feather recalls 'tagging along' on their excursions was a diminutive lass with sandy brown hair dressed in a brown school blazer. 'She used to come to John's house, and she knocked around and played with the boys. She'd sit at the side of the football field if we were playing football. When we went on the rafts, she would come on the rafts too. They would go off together. It was not a matter of going off to the woods, because the whole area was semi-rural.'

Recounting the circumstances of John's distress over the girl, Feather says, 'He didn't talk about her, but I can remember them becoming antagonistic to each other and John becoming upset – the kind of thing which happens when you are eighteen. There were terrible emotions. Intense emotions. He'd get cut up if they had an argument once or twice.'

Although Feather suggests that the relationship was part of John's adolescence and a prelude to his love affair with Cynthia, another source reckons that John was dating the girl whilst at art college, and that the friendship was terminated only after his romance with Cynthia had resulted in her becoming pregnant. 'He had a girlfriend at college – a girl whom he had been seeing for a number of years', says a friend. 'Big boobs – the kind of girl who looked as if she went all the way. He was always talking about her. And maybe she wasn't like that at all for all we know. He was still seeing her until he became friendly with Cyn, and that finished all that.'

If John's interactions in later life were formulated when he was a student, it is important to understand what made him the way he was. Pursuit of childhood and scholastic influences had taken me to his grammar school, Quarry Bank, which he entered in 1952 – about five years after it became a grammar school, having originally been endowed by a wealthy Victorian merchant and boasting among its old boys a couple of Members of Parliament. Although John passed the entrance exam (some say he crammed), he left in 1957 having failed his O-levels. This was the same year in which he set up the Quarry Men.

Advertising genius Michael Issacson, another Quarry Bank old boy, was also at Dovedale Primary with John and recalls their schooldays. 'When he got to Quarry Bank he determined that he was going to make up his own rules. He had a kind of magic, even as a kid, and was able to get people around him – usually people he could control.'

Outcast or loner? Whether John determined he was going to make the rules, or whether he meant that he was no longer going to allow himself to be defeated by rules which diminished a boy from a broken home, he failed to conform to the Quarry Bank profile as an academic or an athelete, bidding for attention instead as a prankster.

The Quarry Bank records chronicle Lennon's misbehaviour on any number of occasions, varying from gambling on the school cricket field during a house match, throwing blackboard cleaners through a window, and disturbing the headmaster's concentration by playing the guitar when he was bowling during a cricket match.

Headmaster William Pobjoy had interviews with Mimi Smith on any number of occasions in respect of John's misbehaviour. 'I saw Mrs Smith quite a number of times because John and his friend were described to me when I took over the school as "two of the problem boys". I do not know of any single heinous action which any of them carried out, but a succession of acts of mischief. He was first brought to me having done something which I have long since forgotten. When he was next brought to me I realized that it [spanking] had not done him any good, and it was no good repeating the dose.

'I had two things I could do to get John to behave badly less often – put him on daily report, which meant that at the end of each lesson the subject master had to write a note on his behaviour, and each day John had to bring me his notebook with all his subject reports so that I would know if he was misbehaving and moreover so that he would know that if he misbehaved I would know too. In the end he did misbehave. The other option was to talk to his guardian to see if together we might bring about some improvement. And that is why Mrs Smith used to come to see me. She was a model of courtesy, propriety and concern. She was not despairing. She was persevering and she was determined to do her best for John. She also wanted to keep him in line as far as possible.

'Mrs Smith intimated that John had problems at home with his father and his mother.' He pauses. 'I met her the week before she moved into the house which John had bought for her in Poole. She mentioned a sum which to me at that time seemed very large. She went on to tell me that John had bought a supermarket for Peter Shotton in Hayling Island. She said that he very much would like to come back to school, but that he was nervous of doing so, and I think at the time I wrote and said, "If you feel like coming, come!" And he did. He came back with Yoko Ono. I didn't meet him. I was in the other building. He didn't seek me out. They were just paying a flying visit. They looked around and left.

'One or two old boys who had been in New York said that he actually was wearing the school tie on the day of his death. . . .

'When I considered what John might best do, I asked him to tell me what his interests were. He said that what he enjoyed most, in his order of priority, were salmon fishing, writing poetry, painting, drawing, poster design and skiffle.'

Was John rebellious? Only moderately so, Pobjoy relates.

'He would come to me and ask if he could have permission to play at the sixth form dance. John wasn't in the sixth form – he was in the fifth form. And I would say, "I'll think about it. Come and see me tomorrow." And I would go through the motions of thinking about it and I would say, "Yes!" There was no question of the boys ever asking for payment. I do not think that money even entered John's head.

'And he would go into the park and have a smoke behind the bushes.'

Was he a practical joker?

'I recall one incident during the October half-term where John brought his friends from the Liverpool Institute, George Harrison and Paul McCartney, into the art class. And the senior art master, a very distinguished man, was told by John that they were two new boys. And the master entered them on his form list. It was a joke. When it was discovered the master was furious. And I remember when Lennon was brought to me what my attitude was: "What an amazing waste of half-term. What a fantastic thing to come into somebody else's school and waste your time!" I couldn't see the point of it. I didn't mind in the least. I thought: "More fool you if that is where you want to spend your half-term." As far as I remember I said, "What a silly ass!" . . . I have never known John to be rude, except maybe when he was in trouble. But having been detected in some mischief, he was always contrite. There was no question of defiance.'

As to his future, at the time when John was taking his GCEs Pobjoy recalls, 'I suggested that with talents in poster design, drawing and painting he might go to the college of art. So I wrote to the principal on 17 July, the last day of term, asking him to consider admitting John. It wasn't until five weeks later that the examination results came out and John had failed by the narrowest margin each one of his seven or eight subjects. And so John went off to art school.' The alternative – returning to school to do the previous year's work again – would have been too demoralizing for John.

Another Quarry Bank contemporary of John's was Gordon Cameron, the good boy to John's baddie. Currently Master of Fitzwilliam College, Cambridge, where he is an economics professor, at Quarry Bank he was head boy. He recalls, 'The BBC documentary about John which I saw shows him in Calderstones Park with his pals. He was breaking the rules. One of the things a prefect had to do was to go into the park, see if he was there and report them. The prefects had the power to detain after school or ultimately to hit offenders with a slipper. It was quite common, but it was a power which I refused to let prefects use.'

Cameron remembers Lennon as a misfit who wouldn't match the school's ethos. 'He was artistic. He was iconoclastic. He was anti-social in the social norm of the time. He just wouldn't have fitted.' Admitting that his personal encounters with John were few, he recalls, 'I cannot say that I ever met John Lennon except to take away his guitar. It didn't bother me that he was playing by the boundary. Who cares? But I was ordered by the headmaster, who was concentrating on his cricket, to confiscate the guitar. He was a keen cricketer and this was annoying him. I went over to Lennon and asked him to please stop playing the guitar. He stopped for a bit and then started again. Then I was told: "Confiscate the guitar." I do not remember if I kept it for a day or a week. I do remember taking the guitar away from him. It had no significance for me, because he wasn't a famous guitarist – he was simply a boy annoying the headmaster. The captain of the ship told me to do something, and I did it.'

The general feeling about Lennon's musicianship at Quarry Bank was less than enthusiastic. Both teachers and boys were unimpressed by his display of ability at dances or socials.

'We thought that another student, a Jewish boy, would become the star, since he was in the tradition of Frankie Vaughan. He was the star of the school. If we had a school dance this chap would deign to come and sing for us – he was earning £20 to sing. John Lennon didn't do very much within the school. He used to play this guitar on the sidelines and was obviously guitar-mad. He would have formed the Quarry Men by then.

'I remember Peter Shotton's face – very blond, sharp features, long and thin face. He was sometimes in trouble. He was quick and sharp. Lennon was more dour. Probably more articulate on paper than verbally. Shotton was very quick, very abrasive – tremendously anti-authority of any kind.'

Recalling John as a distinct bully, Cameron mentions an incident involving him beating up some younger boys. 'We used to have in the school a great long corridor which joined the senior to the junior school. The masters would stay in their rooms and the boys would move between periods. And that meant there was enormous to-ing and fro-ing every forty-five minutes, modified by rules about moving up and down to minimize the chances of a real scrimmage. The bigger ones would go down the middle, while the little ones would go against the wall.

'Archie Evans, prefect of Allerton, John's house, came to me and said that when John, an older boy, went up and down the centre, he hit the littler boys. I remember him saying, "He just has to be slippered. Because he punches them."'

Cameron pauses. 'The truth is that I can't stand Archie Evans from that day to this. I query the credibility of this story, whether rightly or wrongly.'

Cameron's memories of Quarry Bank, vastly different from Lennon's, evoke an atmosphere of nurture and civilized behaviour. Ironically, Cameron's former secretary's grandparents were the school's original owners – wealthy Victorian seed merchants who had the house built for them. 'It was a lovely place,' he reflects. 'There was a huge field. Maybe they have built on it, but at the time they had an enormous field.' He adds, 'The school was a very gracious environment. For its time it was an extremely tolerant environment. I have a strong memory of being at the school and being happy for much of the time. The masters were caring and committed and very civil.'

Whilst Pobjoy became headmaster for John's last year at Quarry Bank, effecting that important entrance into art school on his behalf, it was E. R. Taylor who set the school tone in the preceding years. 'Under Taylor you wouldn't dare to have rows,' recalls Cameron. 'He wouldn't have them. His was a caring environment of dedicated teachers mainly orientated to academic achievement or sport.'

A tremendous presence, Taylor was a remote, isolated figure

in the grand headmaster tradition. Upper middle-class and of independent means, he conducted himself with the assurance of someone who knew where he belonged. 'You couldn't warm to him, but when he came into a room you were impressed by him. The place was silent. He wasn't popular with the staff because he didn't come into the staff room. He stayed in his own room. Aloof, scholarly, he set high academic standards.'

Cameron repeats, 'It was a good environment – a happy school. But if you were artistic or a bit oddball and a bit anti-authoritarian, which I suspect Lennon was, you wouldn't get the support that you needed.'

It wasn't until Lennon enrolled at the art college and formed an alliance with his painting tutor, Arthur Ballard, that he won any appreciation of his talents on his own terms. Ballard, an ex-boxer, was also an outstanding local painter whose works are today on exhibition at Liverpool's Walker Art Gallery. It is not insignificant that Ballard is portrayed in plays about John as a father figure, so enveloping was his influence over and affection for John. He is also the subject of Lennon's own oils, sketches and drawings, peering out of the canvas as a silly, shy, self-conscious figure with bald head, pug nose and beady eyes.

Perceiving in John a talented but eccentric personality, Ballard laboured to get him accepted into the department of illustration, to which his flair for sketching and drawing would be better adapted. 'But they wouldn't have anything to do with him. Mainly on moral grounds, because he was an "outsider" and all this kind of thing. I couldn't persuade the chap who was in charge and a new chap who was head of the school. I argued with them for ages, and I got him to bring his illustrations – which were very good, I thought. But they wouldn't have anything to do with him at all.

'After arguing with these people for over an hour, I said, "Look, you shouldn't be teaching in an art school but a bloody Sunday school if you cannot accept characters." And this new head of department turned round to me and said, "As a matter of fact I do teach in a Sunday school, but I do not see what that has to do with it."'

Tutor of Lennon, Stuart Sutcliffe and Jon Hague, Ballard talks authoritatively about their relative talents. Believing John to be a stronger artist than musician, he says regretfully: 'If I had had my way there probably wouldn't have been any Beatles. John didn't take himself seriously, or the sketches either. I just discovered these sketches when I was standing around the desks where people were working, and picked up a book of John Lennon's caricatures. They were very witty and bright.'

Students regularly exhibited their paintings for criticism, and Ballard recalls: 'We got to John Lennon's work. It was appalling. So I opened the sketchbook. I said, "This is what you should be doing. This is what you want to do." He was so relieved that he was able to do these bright things. I knew he was never going to become a painter.'

About Hague he is unimpressed. 'I do not like Hague's work. John helped to finance an exhibition. He was good to him.' The shining light undoubtedly is Stuart Sutcliffe. 'Stuart refused to come into the studios, so I would go to his house for tutorials. Stuart, short in stature, was painting six-foot canvases and leaping to the top of the canvas. When I looked at his huge abstract at the Walker it amazed me, because it was so like my own painting.

'I was furious about the German thing, because Stuart Sutcliffe went with them. Stuart was a very good painter, a very good student. The chap who organized it is Allan Williams. I put it around that I was going to do this guy the next time I saw him for interfering with Stuart's career. So I get a telephone call from this guy saying it had nothing to do with him at all, saying he just took this group over and organized them. He gave them away.'

He adds: 'He used the John Moore award to buy a guitar. They took the school amplifier with them to Hamburg which was never returned and was why Sutcliffe couldn't come back.

'Stuart used to write to me often – his last letter came about four months before he died. Paolozzi [the painter] had fixed up an exhibition in Paris and he was excited about this. John got his education from him about surrealists and Dadaists. A lot of John's work was influenced by Stuart. His behaviour pattern was very Dadaist, surrealist.'

A self-conscious and ambling man, Ballard nevertheless perceives with unexpected clarity the withdrawn and troubled personality beneath Lennon's bravura. 'It was nothing to do with his family background,' he protests, 'but just that he was a disruptive character. I never had any problems with him myself. Other people knew he was "a naughty boy". He had these two pals and they were always in trouble.

'My experience of John was that he was a loner and looked after by the rest of the group. They were gentle about him, covered up for him and so on. He was very reticent.'

Encountering John in July 1958, the day his mother died after being run over by a police car whilst crossing the Menlove Avenue dual carriageway, Ballard recalls seeing John sitting in the window at the top of the stairs crying. 'He had just learnt that day that his mother had been killed. Tears were rolling down his cheeks. I went to find Geoff Mohammed and gave him ten bob and said, "Take John out for a drink." He was terribly upset.'

According to Ballard, Lennon went off on occasional binges – often drinking to forget some family or scholastic problem. 'He used to get terribly drunk and come back with these two other guys and disrupt everything that was going on. He used to drink at Ye Cracke in the room they called "the War Office" because during the Boer War all the old men used to sit in there and discuss tactics.'

Ballard remembers him as inward-looking and quiet, but concedes that on occasion the repressed pathology could erupt. He cited one instance where he observed John 'urinating from the stairwell. No official action was taken. Everyone knew about it. It would have been a suspension job.'

Witness to the evolving romance with Cynthia Powell, a shy, self-conscious art student from Hoylake near Ballard's own home, he scotches accounts of her being a gregarious, confident blonde and conjures up an altogether different image. 'Cynthia was a mousy girl and wore spectacles. [So did John.] He persuaded her to dye her hair and then she was a very attractive girl. Retiring. So was he. She reminded me of a librarian. Not gregarious. Very plain. Not Bardot from the start. He made her into a good-looking blonde.'

A good student?

'Diligent. But she failed her teachers' exam because she was pregnant and John came back from Hamburg the night before the exam.' He pauses. 'I remember Jon Hague's exhibition was attended by the man who failed Cynthia. John stalked up to him and bellowed, "You bastard. You failed my wife!" He was head of ATD – Art Teachers' Diploma. Cynthia wasn't there. The chap probably didn't remember he failed the wife. John remembered.'

Recalling Lennon as a man of jealous moods, Ballard talks about his possessiveness towards Cynthia. 'We had a showdown at a farewell party I gave at college for my students. I used to live in Hoylake, which is where Cynthia lived. About twelve midnight it was time for me to go home. I found Cynthia and said, "Do you want a lift home?" She wasn't married then. She said, "Yes, that would be nice. I'll go and tell John." She came back and said, "He won't let me come with you."'

Maintaining contact with Cynthia over the years has given Ballard special insight into her situation. 'She's had three bad trips – three times wed – and now she's living with her fourth. She rang me up when she got back from America [27 December 1974] – the last time she saw John.

'She had taken Julian, who had never known his father. It was a couple of years before John died. He was in a very bad state at the time, having recurrent trips on LSD from when he was younger. John had stopped taking LSD. He was depressed. All he did was to talk about Liverpool. I wrote quite a long letter. I never received a reply. Cynthia hinted that there was no longer anything between her and John. I just took it for granted that was the end of it. He was so completely removed from her.'

Comparing Cynthia with Yoko Ono, whom he recalls seeing at a Happening in Liverpool years before she showed at the Indica in 1966, Ballard recounts: 'It was before Lennon was a student of mine, which was in 1959. So it must have been before that. She and her husband did this performance. They got into this bag, took their clothes off and copulated. Or didn't. They got out, got dressed and walked out. Never said a word.

'She was younger then – in her early twenties. Although I didn't find her terribly attractive, it was apparent in her self-confidence that she came from an aristocratic background and so on. You need self-confidence to be able to do all that, and then society tried to put her down. The media. She is quite astonishing, really.'

Whilst the press tries to make out that John and Cynthia represent the attraction of opposites – working-class boy meets middle-class girl – the reality is that they were closer than people think. Phyllis McKenzie observes, 'John's background was similar to Cyn's. He came from a private semi in Woolton. He went to a grammar school. From what people say, you would think he had been raised in Liverpool.'

The difference, then, was not of class but of type. 'John was sarcastic, enigmatic but nice. A slob, with sideburns and longish hair. He'd slouch about, hands in his pockets. He'd make rude remarks. He was sarcastic about school, and in lettering class instead of doing it he'd strum his guitar. He used to try to get Cynthia to do it for him. I didn't think John was attractive. I didn't think he was Cyn's type. Her boyfriend before John was dark, good-looking and well-dressed. Your mother would like the other one. You couldn't take John home to meet mother.'

It was McKenzie who accompanied Cynthia to Sefton General when Julian was born while John was on tour in Hamburg in April 1963. She recalls, 'John was on tour in Germany and I was staying overnight with Cynthia at John's aunt's house. It was an unexpected birth. The baby wasn't due for a month or so later. But she started to go into labour. It was one or two in the morning. We called the ambulance. I had rollers in my hair and was wearing a nightie under my coat. I was walking down the road carrying her huge suitcase. I hailed a taxi and they thought I was running away from home.'

Jubilantly she recounts, 'John came rushing back from Germany as soon as he heard. He didn't like hospitals. He found them frightening. But he rushed back. He was so happy.'

Having missed their wedding by being away in Italy, McKenzie was there for the divorce. 'It was horrible. Cyn was loyal to John. He was to her. But he was worried about Yoko. Yoko did the running. He didn't want to hurt Cyn. He couldn't face telling her.' She pauses. 'She never thought he would leave her. She knew there would be girls on the road. But that is part of the pop scene.'

Continuing, she says, 'I used to visit them when they lived in London at Emperor's Gate. Cynthia couldn't walk out of the flat. Fans were waiting. They used to pull her hair. That's why they moved to Kenwood.

'I often went down when Cyn was on her own. We went to the pictures, around town and the shops. Or watched TV. She is very generous. Every Christmas she sent me a hamper from Harrods, and always brought flowers when she came to stay.'

Another of Cynthia's friends recalls being impressed by the chauffeur-driven Rolls with the bar in the back. 'Cyn and I used to go on Saturday shopping sprees in the Roller. It was fabulous.'

Confirming that the Kenwood experience was one of chaos, with John and Cyn holed up in the attic whilst the workmen renovated the main part of the house, the friend continues, 'It was a mock–Tudor house – Victorian. Beautiful, with large rooms. But it was strange, because Cyn was more or less living in a flat on the top floor with a kitchen. Cynthia saw so little of John – he was on tour so much. She was quite lonely during her married years to Lennon.

'Her mother lived with them for a while. She liked John, although they were always quarrelling and at daggers drawn. She knew too much about promiscuity and girls coming into the house. She knew it backwards what was going on. She was the fly on the wall through all of it.

'The divorce was sad. I think that Cynthia got a raw deal. He was obviously under an influence. Drugs. Besotted with Yoko. He couldn't see straight. Strange. I felt sorry for Cynthia throughout that.

'Cynthia will always love John and there will never be anybody quite like him. She has a nice man now, but the John thing is separate to all of that. She said, "I will never love anybody in quite the same way as I loved John."

'I met Cyn again in 1972 when she was splitting up from her second husband, Roberto. She went back up north and we saw a lot of each other. And I unfortunately introduced her to husband number three, John Twist, who had not long before split up with his wife. He rang and asked if I'd like to go to his company's annual dance. I was seeing Cyn that evening. We went to this dance in Liverpool. They instantly liked one another. He fitted the bill at the time, because Cynthia was so fed up with playboys.'

Her friend's description of Cynthia as a stoical, accepting person seems accurate, since her willingness to grant John a divorce has always seemed to me curiously compliant. 'When she talks about Yoko, she says, "I realize now that Yoko was right for him. I had him at a time when he was right for me and I was right for him." What will be will be – that is her philosophy. If John is not meant for her, he will have Yoko and that is that. She accepts things. She believes everything is meant. She is a deep thinker.'

When Lennon left Ono for that fourteen-month Lost Weekend with May Pang, Cynthia travelled to America to reunite her son with John. 'I remember Cynthia going on that trip. She and John flew together on the same plane to Los Angeles. But they didn't speak to each other. John just stayed in his seat for the whole journey and Cyn was really upset. She thought John was most peculiar with her. That was the trip with May Pang. When they went to Disneyland, Cynthia was left by herself a lot. She thought that by going with them she could have achieved a rapport with John, but it was not to be. Sad!'

That John, for whatever reasons, wanted a complete break with his past was hardest on their son. 'Julian adored John. He was always ringing him up and asking to come and see him. Yoko was not interested. Cyn used to be concerned about it, and wanted John to take him to the States. But John was engrossed in another life.'

On one occasion when John rang Julian in Hoylake (about the time Cynthia met John Twist) the friend recalls his nostalgia for England and things English. '"You have no idea how much I miss England," he said. "I'll be coming back soon, 'cause I've nearly got my Green Card now. In the meantime see if you can get hold of an art school scarf for me and a string of black puddings." I said I'd try and do it, but that I was not sure if you could get the black puddings through Customs. That was the last time I spoke with him.'

Whilst Cynthia had always assumed there was a romance between the two, the lady denies any glimmer. 'I was just a chum. I was fascinated by him but I didn't think he was sexy. He wasn't a college heart-throb. I wouldn't say he was shy. But he wasn't an obvious flirt. Brigitte Bardot was his ideal woman. When he met Cyn all of a sudden her hair started to change colour. She became his ideal woman.'

Perceiving a nasty side to Lennon in the cut and thrust of his college humour, the lady recalls that in those days he had a thing about the Jews. 'People tend to think he was deadly anti-Semitic, but he wasn't. It was just that he used to make up funny stories about them because he found them so funny – especially the Hasidim. Liverpool, Leeds and Manchester are three of the oldest Jewish communities in Europe. He would parody songs like: "I like New York in June. How about Jew? . . . Holding rabbis in the movie show". Or "Bring on the dancing rabbis". But it was funny. He didn't mean any harm by it.

'If he called Brian [Epstein] a "Jew git" it was just his way of being annoyed about something. But he didn't really mean it. He irritated Brian deliberately.'

Mike Issacson concurs. 'John would wind people up. Cynthia said he would drive Epstein up the wall – could send him into a frenzy. Lennon would aggravate him. It was just the way he would talk to him. Vicious. He would have a go at Brian's faith. He was very cruel.'

If Lennon could hate he also could love, his grand passion being the brilliantly eccentric painter Stuart Sutcliffe. 'Stuart and John were close chums. The same kind of character. John idolized

Stuart. Stuart was a little god because he was so talented. John was an overpowering extrovert sort of person and Stuart seemed the opposite. And that's why they probably hit it off. He let John behave the way he did. John got away with murder with everybody. He was very dominant.

'I went once to the flat they shared in Gambier Terrace – six of them together. Stuart did all of his paintings there. What I can remember is that it was one big room. Dirty. Paints were everywhere. It was fine. It was an artist's studio. Mattresses on the floor. No place to walk or sit. They didn't care.'

The flat was leased by Rod Murray, following ejection from a flat in Percy Street taken in Sutcliffe's name. It was John who hooked up with Stuart and Rod, living communally with them and two female students, Ducky and Diz, the latter now married to Rod, who occupied the front room.

A visit to the street was illuminating, firstly because it scotched rumours that Lennon lived in a slum, and secondly because it gave me a chance to meet Murray, now an instructor at the college where he, John and Stuart were students, and to discover that the lifestyle, rather than *à deux*, was *à cinq*.

'Our flat was a whole floor of one of those buildings,' clarifies Murray. 'The first room that I had was twenty foot square. There was a room at the back which originally Stuart slept in and we all used as a studio. John moved in there with him. In the first instance Diz and Ducky had the little room and Rod Jones had it after them. We had a long corridor with a bathroom and a kitchen. It was a very luxurious place.'

Luxurious was not how the newspapers described it when they did their student digs exposé, with banner headlines proclaiming: 'Beatnik Horror'. That Murray and the others participated in the writing of the exposé sealed their fate, and whilst the landlord willingly overlooked complaints about the loud music emanating from the flat when the Beatles were practising, he refused to tolerate the lodgings scandal and asked them to leave promptly.

'One of the Sunday papers came to the local pub and said they wanted to do a story about the living conditions of students. We took them back to our flat and they wrote this absolute garbage – that we were lying in filth, that there were eight people in the flat at the time, and so on.

'Stuart's mother came and took his stuff away. And Rod Jones went off to Jersey. I stored Lennon's stuff until he came back from Hamburg. I had all John's stuff: paintings, drawings, sketches, clothes. And when he returned he said, "Keep them for what I owe you."'

Was that generous?

'No way. These were all sorts of drawings and things for which he had *failed* his examinations. I only kept a bit of it, because I thought the cartoons were amusing. I sold one book, five years ago, for £16,000.'

Whilst John's background was solidly surburban, he always seemed to be short of money and is remembered by almost all of his college friends as lacking funds even for a lager or a coffee. 'There were lots of places in Chinatown where you could eat cheaply. John liked eating. But he couldn't always afford it. If it was a choice between eating and drinking, drinking won.

'Another reason for drinking is that it is expensive to heat a flat, and if it was going to cost five shillings on the meter to stay in, for the same five shillings you could be warm and drink.' He pauses. 'Whilst the bathroom and kitchen were heated by gas, the bedrooms had large coal-burning fireplaces. Nobody delivered coal, so you had to go with a cardboard box to the little coalyards left over from the last century, weigh a scoop of coal, put it in your cardboard box and walk home with it. The Victorians were hearty buggers and they didn't go in for central heating.'

Although Murray complains about journalists trying to elicit bogus stories about John's infidelity, he says, 'John was liked by women but he was also liked by guys because he was "good company". He was not charming, but certainly sarcastic and very funny. Everybody laughed at the sort of things he would say. Usually pointed at someone.'

Was he ruthless?

'He could be, thoughtlessly so,' says Murray, who feels that Allan Williams got a raw deal. 'He put up the cash for them to go to Hamburg. Without his push I don't think they would have gone, because I don't think Brian Epstein would have been interested in those days and they wouldn't have done it themselves.'

Summing up, he says, 'John was a nice guy basically, but he could get angry and was capable of poking someone in the eye.'

Another Liverpool art college student and early Lennon supporter was Bill Harry, founder of *Mersey Beat*, Liverpool's own music publication, which was a premier showcase for John's writings and stories. Harry, the first person to call John a 'genius', elicited respect from John's aunt Mimi with his endorsement of her nephew's talents.

Ascribing the naive and xenophobic qualities in John's work to his mystical Irish origins, Harry describes the city as a gateway into England. 'Everyone came over from Ireland through Liverpool direct, and they came off the boats and stayed. My father was a merchant seaman. So was John's. And his grandfather too. My grandfather was Irish – a pugilist. Lennon's is Irish. McCartney's too, but Unionist and Protestant. And Ringo and George.'

Neighbourhoods grew up around these characters, a prominent one being the Liverpool 8 district where the boys went to school. Recalls Harry, 'The area around John's and Stuart's flat was replete with characters. The guy on the ground floor was a mystic writing stories about life after death. (He said that he had these great secrets.) Another flat around the corner housed a couple of Irish workmen and on another floor a couple of prostitutes lived. You got the folk singers – people playing guitars in pubs and things like that. People writing books – others writing poetry.'

Continues Harry, 'We'd have these overnight parties. We'd go to their flat, talking all the way through the night. John used to devise these games where we'd sit in a circle, and somebody would say something and the person sitting next to him would have to follow it up with a sentence. Another time John would come out with something outrageous. This girl Margaret (Ducky) fell asleep on the bed. John said, "Let's frighten her for when she wakes up in the morning." We got these potatoes which we carved like matchsticks, and we hung them dangling down off the bed for when she awoke.'

Originating *Mersey Beat* as Liverpool's answer to *American Beat*, Harry proclaims the individuality of his circle in wanting to create something unique to the north of England, indeed to Liverpool. 'The idea was to make Liverpool famous, Stuart with his painting and I with my writing. I created the phrase 'Mersey Beat' which is now famous throughout the world and included in the *Encyclopedia Britannica*. John did it with his music.

'We used to go into a pub in Rice Street called Ye Cracke and I used to sit there with John. That's when I asked him about his poetry. At that time there was interest in the Beat Generation and the Beat Movement.'

The myth of Sutcliffe, who died of a brain tumour in April 1962 in Hamburg, looms large. His unrealized potential is mourned by tutors and friends. 'Stuart influenced John a lot. He broadened his outlook. He stretched his mind. Stuart used to sit and talk about the future, mysticism, the things behind life and the rest of it.'

Was he as brilliant a painter as people say?

Harry confirms, 'I had heard a new guy was starting. He was supposed to be a brilliant painter, and I wanted to find out what he was like. I saw one of his works. He put it on exhibition on the ground floor in the art school. It was a painting of a church dome in the style of Van Gogh.

'I got to know Stuart. We became close. He was into the philosophical thing. He used to carry a copy of Kierkegaard in his pocket. We used to talk a lot about making Liverpool famous. We wanted to do a book including all the interesting stories about the millionaire who spends his fortune building underground passages and the sacred tigers of Bengal Street. And he'd illustrate it. I said I wanted one of his paintings. He said he liked the blue jacket I was wearing and agreed to do a painting in exchange for the jacket. He did this oil painting of me and asked how I'd like it? I said, "In the style of Van Gogh." I've got it hanging on the wall at home.'

Sutcliffe's expulsion from art school – owing much to the amplifier which the boys purloined and flogged in Germany – derives from his infatuation with Lennon and willingness to do anything for him. That the group cut its teeth by playing at college dances and socials is a cause of pride to Harry, who recalls the Beatles in their formative stages.

'Stuart and I were members of the student union committee, George and Paul were next door in the Liverpool institute. John and Stuart were in the art college. We used to rehearse in the room upstairs because Paul and George would come in at lunch breaks. It was the time of skiffle and I can remember playing kazoo in one corner and rehearsing in the other. We used to book them at art college dances held in the basement, like the Cavern before its time – a Victorian Gothic undercroft, but drier. We regarded them as "our band". When I was on the committee I proposed that we buy a PA system to lend to them when they played. And that's the stuff that Johnny flogged in Germany.'

And John's responsibility for Stuart's death?

'Years later you have a writer saying that it was a kick at Litherland Town Hall, and another saying John kicked him in the head. But Stuart's mother told me that he had an accident in Hamburg – that he was living in the attic in Astrid Kirchherr's house, and had to come down these narrow stairs. He fell down the stairs, bumped his head and had been having headaches ever since.'

Witness to the changes in John after Hamburg, Harry observes: 'You put yourself in the places of young Liverpool kids coming out of their teens who had no income and no money. Their idea of a holiday, if they are lucky, is going up to the Lake District. They have never been abroad. They have never had their minds stretched by meeting really interesting people. Young people of this impressionable age go to a foreign country where everything is open and there are no restrictions. Whereas in Liverpool the clubs close at a certain time – the Watch Committee is stopping this, and everything is closing – in Hamburg everything is open. There are women, booze, pills. You don't want to go to bed. You want to stay up twenty-four hours. You are not bothering to go to bed. The water is warm. Dive in. They completely saturated themselves in it.'

Liverpool John – a sex symbol?

Virginia Harry replies: 'John Lennon was a man's man. He was very quick-witted. Some were afraid of him. He could be cruel. If you gave him back what he gave you he wouldn't do it. John was cruel to Brian, but Brian allowed it.'

She pauses, 'John Lennon was a funny guy. He had friends that you wouldn't expect him to have. Cynthia didn't know how to get the hangers-on off John's back. Yoko did, which is perhaps why the marriage lasted. John was very much a leader of boys.'

'When Stuart died, John didn't make any gesture of support. He didn't even send flowers,' she recalls. 'Mrs Sutcliffe was upset about it. When the Walker Art Gallery had an exhibition of Stuart's work, John Lennon didn't attend it. John didn't do a thing to help Stuart, and yet he always went on about how important Stuart was to him.'

Virginia says that John went out with other women in the earliest stages of his marriage, and that even after Cynthia had the baby he continued seeing a former girlfriend. 'He just thought it was cool to have a wife and a mistress. She had jet-black hair – pretty. Fringe bangs. Pale and pretty.' Bill Harry confirms, 'When they were married and she was having the baby, he'd be down at the Blue Angel picking up girls. Virginia and I went out with John and the girl.'

Rather than strengthening her confidence, Lennon undermined any feelings of adequacy which Cynthia might have nurtured. 'She was quiet and stayed in the background,' recalls Virginia. 'She used to sit there. Now she is much more vital and confident.'

Billy Harry disagrees, 'I knew Cynthia when she was at the junior art school. She was only thirteen – small, with dark mousy hair, and very timid and shy. To get John she transformed herself into Brigitte Bardot. She was always with him. When we went down to the Jacaranda [Allan Williams' coffee bar] we saw Cynthia and some girls sitting in the corner on chairs holding broomsticks with mikes attacked to them.

'She had to be in the balcony, because if she was around John and the other girls found out they'd claw her eyes out.'

So why did John marry?

'In those days anybody who got a girl pregnant got married. That was the thing. It was in your psyche. John didn't use a condom. And the other girls wore a diaphragm or something.'

Another witness to John's incarnation as an art student is Jon Hague, the painter whose London debut John financed, having also bought him a house and various other gifts. Their relationship, similar to John's with Peter Shotton, but less highly publicized, seems free of the ambiguity characterizing other friendships of John's.

Impressed by John's confidence and wit, even as a neophyte art college student, Hague was taken under his wing, shaped and moulded. 'He was a Teddy boy in those days. He taught me how to have my hair styled in that sort of pompadour with sideburns. I had arrived in my little blazer from the countryside. I was very much the public schoolboy and he was the big city boy. I lived a very sheltered existence at a public school in Lindisfarne and suddenly I was let into the big, wide Liverpool space. I learned to drink with John and all sorts of things with him. He guided me down all these evil paths. Girls were a major topic of conversation. Before Cynthia he was dating a girl called Annette. But when he met Cynthia they spent a lot of time together. We were only students and didn't have any money. We would go to the local little pub, a sleazy little place. There was an abundance of girls at the art college itself. It was a big new experience for me and probably for John as well.'

Confirming John's image as an acerbic clown, Hague recalls that he could be wounding. 'His imitation of cripples is mild. When he was drunk he got aggressive physically and verbally. He could get at someone about their race and verbally badger them in a pub. We got very drunk and he could be hasty. We could drink to the stage of being unconscious. We'd go out on to the pavement and when the cold air hit us we would fall over. We'd sit with these massive mugs of beer and think what revolting stuff it was. But it would be the only way to get drunk.

'We used to go to shows, and John would shout back to the stage performers. He was a heckler. We'd go to Victorian music halls, long since gone, and little theatres – crummy places, where the acts were professionals but not stars.

'Lennon was the sort of person who would entertain in every respect. Even in our classes at college we'd be quietly drawing and he would start to make funny noises and would build it up until he had the whole room in fits of laughter. He would do little things like that. It was his obsession to entertain. He had this gift.

'When John and the group played Llandudno [Hague's home town in Wales] I remember him clowning around behind the stage before the show, making funny noises. He would be the "star attraction" behind the scenes. McCartney didn't have his gift. The others were nowhere near Lennon.

'He was always a fascinating person. When he was at college people were influenced by him. I was a quiet, country boy completely fascinated by John. He showed me a new world – opened my eyes, totally. He was an important person to me at that time. He could win people over.'

Image-consciousness is a characteristic one ascribes to the later Lennon, and which seems incompatible with the rebellious, callow youth. Yet according to Hague this trait was in evidence years before. Rather than eschewing convention, he was impressed by clothes and looks and money and status. 'He was very self-conscious about wearing glasses and would go around almost blind rather than wear them.'

Was he vain?

'Very vain,' confirms John. 'He was forever teaching me how to comb my hair. He was conscious about posing. He was conscious of looks. He used to talk about it a lot. I remember him saying that looks were important and that even his best friends were good-looking. He was conscious of how he looked – of clothes and wearing the right things. I can remember him teaching me everything, like what shoes to wear – winklepickers [pointed shoes which laced up] – and relegating my dreary school blazer to the wardrobe.'

Recalling that John was facile ('He did his cartoon drawings but they didn't take much time') and lazy ('He declined to work part-time and was always broke'), he recounts that he was sly and mischievous to pay his way. 'I remember once that John was in trouble with the college for pinching coal for their flat. He was really worried when he had to go and see the department head. Everybody thought, "Oh, my God. What will they do to him?" When he came out of the interview he had the guy in fits of laughter. He managed to talk himself out of a reprimand. But that was his talent.'

The £100 John was supposed to have received from his aunt on his twenty-first birthday seems apocryphal, for according to Hague John never had any money, literally coming to college every day with the equivalent of 12½p in his pocket. 'He was forever penniless. He could hardly afford to buy a bag of chips. I was the one who was lending him 2s 6d. He was completely broke. He could never afford to buy drinks and stuff like that.'

Being beset by problems at home made it difficult for Lennon to concentrate at college. Hague characterizes him as 'distracted. I was really worried for John. I used to say, "What on earth are you going to do? You'll end up being a fish and chip shop man." Because he didn't do his work. I remember a tutor getting him to one side and asking: "What are you going to do?" And him telling me, "I'm going to be a pop singer." It sounds ironic now, but at the time it was the tutor's worry, my worry and everybody else's worry.'

A queer remark from Hague, who after being launched by Lennon's funds decidedly resigned from painting and opened up an antique shop with financial support from John. It appears that much of Lennon's instability came from the kindness of friends.

'He did mention things like "My auntie says" or "She wouldn't like that". He was very conscious of approval,' says Hague. 'We were at the age when we were trying to analyse what life was about. I think John was expressing that he had been subjected to discipline. I think he mentioned disciplines which he had been subjected to. His aunt would complain about his hairstyle and his dress. She showed her general disapproval about what he was doing. She would have liked him to be an accountant or a bank clerk. She would say things like that. She minded the fact that he was not treading the path that she would have liked. He would be worried about it. She supported him totally and he got this 2s 6d per day.'

Hague recalls one incident that stands out in his mind as

characteristic of the isolation which John projected. 'I remember going with him to a coffee bar at 9 a.m. and picking him up at 4 p.m. at the same coffee bar when I left college. He sat at the same table all day. He had the ability to do nothing. He was thinking. He'd sit and smoke cigarettes.

'He was lonely. He suffered an awful lot from loneliness. We used to joke about it. He hated that time when I'd leave him in the coffee bar. We used to come and be with him. And he would always want to be with people. He used to be almost terrified to be left on his own. We made a comment about it. I remember we were walking along the pavement and there was a bus. We jumped on the bus and left him standing on the pavement on his own. It was like we committed a major sin against him, played this trick on him.'

And Sutcliffe?

Hague considers that the celebrated friendship only developed when they went to Hamburg. 'Stuart was a year or two ahead of us – slightly a mature student. He was a very good artist. He was talented.

'But John wanted somebody to buy drums or a guitar. It sounds ironic now, but at that stage *anybody* who bought drums could be in the group. Stuart had got this £75, a fortune in those days, from the John Moore art award. He spent the money on this equipment.'

Recalls Hague, 'They played at the college intervals and they played old Buddy Holly tunes pretty badly. He practised a lot in my flat. He used to come with one or two of them when I had a room. He was with Paul and they were the Quarry Men. I couldn't believe that they transformed into making such wonderful stuff. I was in Holland when they made "Love Me Do". I was so thrilled. It was like a month after and they suddenly produced everything.'

Confirming Arthur Ballard's concern and affection for John, Hague recounts: 'He encouraged John to do his caricatures. It absolutely amazed everybody. We'd all be doing typical art student stuff – pictures of people at railway stations – and John would do a picture of somebody picking their nose. We didn't believe that you could do that sort of thing for college work.

'Arthur Ballard was our "god". He was a painter – not a successful one, but an important Liverpool painter at the time. We'd go every week and pin up what we had done on the wall. This was the big moment of the week. He would go to every.

person one by one slaughtering you or praising you. That was all college was about. What Arthur Ballard says.'

The crucial class in lettering, looming large in the legend as the cause of John's failing his exams, is another example of John's faith in friends who let him down. As it turns out, whilst Cynthia and Jon did *some* of the work for him, they were unwilling to do it all, and Lennon was completely incapable of fulfilling the lettering requirements himself. 'Ballard was responsible for getting John another year although he had failed his Intermediate. He took it again and failed it again. Part of the examination was lettering. You had to do Roman lettering on a big plaque at the school. Very detailed. It took about two weeks of solid work. I remember doing some of the work for him. And I remember Cynthia doing some of the work. But he made a mess of it.

'He could have got away with his cartoons for the art work, but he couldn't do the lettering. Arthur Ballard was purely the painting side. The lettering had to go off to the examiners. He should never have done lettering. He said that he had wanted to do something else, but that the class was too full.'

'John would have loved Ballard,' says Hague. 'He was unconventional and was an expressive, intelligent man. We were typical angry young people of that age, who hated pompous-type vicars and people like that. He seemed very anti-established people.

'I think this was the crunch of Lennon's separation from people at this time, of a lot of his anger. He must have been extremely disciplined as a child. I think I had been disciplined at boarding school. I had the anger of being disciplined all those years and suddenly you were let into this free existence. We thought we had all the time in the world. He must have had an upbringing not dissimilar from my own.'

The circumstances of Cynthia's having failed to get her teaching diploma rankle, since Hague respects her abilities and diligence. 'Cynthia failed her ATD but passed everything else. She passed her Intermediate. We then did another two years. She passed that. We did a one-year teaching thing. She failed that. She didn't get the university teaching certificate. She passed her four years but not the fifth.

'I couldn't imagine how she could fail, because she was a dedicated, serious student, always punctual, always there. And I should think her academic ability was good.

'She told me that it was a time when she didn't do the work. It was a time when John was in Hamburg, and she was pregnant.

There was all this emotion. She said that the night before the exam was the night that John came back from Hamburg and she didn't get any sleep. All these kinds of things were going on. She didn't have a quiet life. I should imagine that is why she failed.'

A sense of naiveté characterized Lennon throughout the years Hague knew him. Fearfulness and wariness of strangers were traits which intensified with success. 'John related best to those people who knew him at school,' says Jon. 'He told me he couldn't trust anybody. He was very isolated with his fame. They'd have these steel doors and nobody could go past them. When people did go past them they were all in awe of him and did not behave themselves naturally.

'John Lennon was so famous that whenever he stayed in hotels there would be security people around and fans standing around the entrance of where he was staying. When he was in Llandudno we wouldn't go to the local beach – we had to go to a quiet beach. But even then there were people coming. We couldn't go for a little row in a rowing boat because everybody recognized him. He was so famous.'

It is with wry amusement that I elicit from Hague the admission that he never saw John spend any amount of time involved in writing songs alone or with McCartney. 'I was surprised that he had so much free time. I never saw him compose. He didn't go to the theatre until six o'clock in the evening and I'd turn up for him at 11 a.m. I took him around for tea with my mother. We went off to the countryside.'

And his feelings about the divorce?

'Even when he came to Llandudno, he was with some broad. He had a girl.'

And the £100,000 settlement?

'When you consider that he bought my house for £4000, £100,000 was a lot of money in those days. I've only recently learned from Cynthia the amount of the settlement and that she said she has lost all her money. She got married twice, and she is now struggling. She's tried many things and deserves success with this new restaurant nightclub that she has opened called Lennon's. [Subsequently Mrs Lennon has removed herself from the enterprise.] Odd that the other Beatles haven't been around to support her. The only person who had been there was Ringo. I met Ringo's daughter there. Apparently she goes there all the time and must have dragged her Dad along.'

Lennon, it appears, is but a faint memory – the fish and chip shop boy who became a superstar, not by perseverance or even genius, but by a cocky, cunning, confident attitude which stuns, awes, surprises but elicits in the end very little respect.

The formulation of this persona emerged in the touring, where, according to experts, Lennon developed a propensity for 'growing up absurd'.

7

The Tours – Growing Up Absurd

Whilst unwilling to concede that Lennon's lyrical talents categorize him as the century's greatest composer, I categorically maintain that his command of the basics of advertising and marketing – of conceptual analysis – enabled him to create the basis of a pop group which set standards not only in Britain but worldwide. And while we can split hairs about whether he purposefully revised twelve-bar blues with endless streams of run-on non sequiturs, or if he consciously revolutionized lyric writing with Joycean originality, we will not argue that he thoroughly routed the balladeer from his place of enshrined permanence, displacing Cliff Richard, Frankie Vaughan, much less Sinatra, Bennett and Como, with a compost of Goon Show musicality.

Let no one deny that it was Lennon's idea to transform the Quarry Men, a decidedly folk group, into a pop group promoting an indigenous Liverpool sound named after the River Mersey and called 'the Mersey Beat'. A producer *extraordinaire*, Lennon is given too little credit for defining the group's concept and sticking to it despite little encouragement along the way from Brian Epstein, George Martin (EMI), Alan Livingstone (Capitol) and others.

In an era when British popular singers developed and promoted by Larry Parnes tended to have a uniformly beefcake sort of an image – the most conspicuous of whom was Liverpool's Billy Fury (born Ronald Wycherly) – Lennon's schoolboy cheekiness was something to be reckoned with. Simply, he took himself seriously, extending in his professional image those preoccupations that dominated his private life. Intelligent, political, rebellious and original are qualities which provide the basis of the Beatles pop group, all of which define John Lennon. There is barely any occasion, be it *The Royal Variety Show*, *The Ed Sullivan Show* or the EMI record awards, that Lennon hasn't come out with some headline-grabbing witticism. Only when those witticisms forswore a lack of restraint did Lennon begin to lose his following of fans. But that was *after* his break-up with the Beatles and the evolution of a new personality with Yoko Ono.

During those years when he was building the concept of the Beatles act, there is no doubt to my mind that Lennon knew exactly what he was doing and that every hiring and firing, every audition and newspaper interview, every performance and career manoeuvre was calculated as a means of extending the persona he had devised.

Of course, history has proven Lennon right against incredible odds of prejudice and tradition, not only in Britain but elsewhere. And whereas in the beginning his working-class, schoolboy persona was considered rude and unintelligible, later on, by comparison to the punk rockers whom he influenced, he was left pitifully behind: a tragic figure.

That Lennon was able to perceive as a fad and to distinguish what in showbusiness is 'flash' or 'beefcake', and therefore perishable, is amazing when you consider the limitations of his background. Most acts, when they go back to doing other things after doing 'panto', always keep about them something of the baggy pants clown. Lennon was superior to all that. He would not condescend to allow the Beatles to do pantomime, or anything verging on the burlesque.

There is little doubt, on reflection, that Lennon had Brian Epstein dismiss Pete Best, not because he wasn't a good drummer or for any of the other suggested reasons, but for the simple reason that, although intelligent, he lacked the caustic, intellectual edge which Lennon felt was essential to *all* group members. The nasty, acerbic humour of which all the Beatles were capable was something which John considered essential to the act. Let us not forget that it was Ringo Starr (Pete's replacement) who, known for his malapropisms, came out with the inspired title for the Beatles' first (and classic) film, *A Hard Day's Night*.

John's coolness toward the Liverpool reporter who failed to interview the Beatles at the Cavern was symptomatic of what was to occur thereafter. Ignoring Brian's admonition, Lennon continued to mould and shape the group's interview style on a level of politicism and intelligence. Chat about what he wore to bed or ate for breakfast was boring: Lennon was concerned with addressing himself to larger issues and events. His comments to the *Evening Standard* reporter about being 'bigger than Jesus' were typical of the level of John's commentary to the press.

He bridled against restraint, surmounting Epstein's cautions whenever and wherever he could. The notorious 'butcher's sleeve' was fobbed off on America's Capital Records without Brian's endorsement and recalled only when the US suppliers refused to stock the LP.

That Capitol refused to touch the group which had already hit the Number One spot in Britain, having watched while two of their singles languished in the States, is a statement about the then limited potential of British groups in the American market. That the Beatles' 'I Want to Hold Your Hand' was the first single by an English group to rise to the Number One place in the US charts is some sort of tribute to the Beatles' genius in devising an original style and presentation which were appealing not only to the north of England and the entire United Kingdom, but to America and the rest of the world. The early songs, simple and sweet, indicating nothing of what was to explode later for the group, succeeded initially not because of any profundity but on account of a simplicity and spontaneity which Lennon argued should be retained against the slickness of recording industry standards.

Their utter lack of sophistication, giving an impression of something unfinished and a bit jagged, was an irresistible competitor to the stylized elocution of Sinatra or Tony Bennett. That the ballad was thirteen or sixteen lines, without an obligatory chorus, or that inaudible words and phrases were retained, along with acoustical imperfections, all contributed to a mode of performance which was to receive world-wide acclaim, signifying the launch of a cultural phenomenon universally known as 'Beatlemania'.

The look, the demeanour and the rap of the world's first counter-culture pop group is to my mind a well-conceived political credo on Lennon's part, fed up with the glitz of Hollywood musicals and British music hall talent. Something of this was revealed when, in the course of our interview, he compared superstardom with electioneering, arguing that you always had to be that much further ahead.

Reading through the chronicles of those early years is fascinating, since it projects the uphill struggle which Lennon had in trying to make his way into the British music scene without 'selling out' to a Larry Parnes-type promoter.

The Channel 4 documentary about Parnes, Britain's top promoter at the time that the Beatles were coming up, is ruthless in its presentation of a nice Jewish boy gone bad. Both seducer of and seduced by the lads whom he discovered, Parnes degenerates in the course of the documentary into nothing more than a glorified hairdresser. He died in 1989, of anorexia, pursuing a 'strange' lifestyle prompted by both economy and diet.

It is not surprising that he, and many other slick rock promoters, failed to recognize the Beatles' originality and potential, preferring to manage those acts which were non-political, non-controversial and non-iconoclastic. John auditioned for Parnes in May 1960, calling his group the Silver Beetles in an apparently marginal effort to be less obscure and elitist. Something, however, rubbed Parnes up the wrong way, for instead of hiring the Beatles to back up Billy Fury (a Liverpool singer, having begun with the Beatles in 1959, he was already a Parnes star in 1960), he booked them instead to back up Johnny Gentle on a tour of Scotland. It is not surprising, considering their ruthless bravado, that the Beatles failed to make any impact on the tour; they were referred to by the press – if at all – as a backing group called the Beats, Four Beats or Four Beatles, since the catchy 'Beatles' tag was too artsy a label for most newspaper people to manage.

An exclusive interview with Fury's common-law wife, Lee Everett, elucidates why it was that Billy rejected the Beatles, regarding them as 'trouble'.

It is interesting to observe that whilst Billy failed the same 1959 audition, as did the Beatles (calling themselves Johnny and the Moondogs), for 'star-maker' Carroll Levis at Manchester's Hippodrome, within months the native Liverpudlian was a Larry Parnes headliner auditioning for a back-up group.

Observes Lee, 'When Billy's back-up group, the Tornados, had a Number One hit (Billy never went higher in the charts than Number Three) he auditioned for another band. He auditioned the Beatles but he thought that they were trouble. They had a whole attitude about them. He said he thought they would be enormous trouble on tour. They were lively lads. Billy was looking for someone more conforming and quiet.'

Herself a Larry Parnes' talent known as Lady Lee ('Parnes wanted to call me "Lucky" Lee, but I refused') Lee Everett stands by the man who in the British music industry was for many years a showbusiness original – whose name loomed over the stars larger than life.

What is now camp and a Gary Glitter put-on was for Parnes the essence of showbusiness gospel. 'Larry liked flash and glitz,' says Lee. 'Everyone had to be honky-tonk, which is what he felt showbusiness was about. And in those days it was.' She continues, 'He had a thing about names. He changed people's names – Johnny Gentle, Billy Fury, Georgie Fame, Tommy Steele and Marty Wilde. He liked lurex suits and shiny mohair. And platinum hair.'

Whilst Parnes signed all his acts to iron-clad contracts, allowing him to dominate their careers ruthlessly, there were occasions when Fury bridled against the determined course. Whilst the Beatles made a big deal about writing the A-sides of their own records (many of whose credits have been disputed), Fury quietly and modestly penned any number of the B-sides to his songs.

Conceding to go to an acting coach when he began to make films, Fury also went along with Parnes' decision that he should do pantomime. 'He did get talked into doing a pantomime,' recalls Lee, adding, 'but he didn't even start it when he walked out of it in rehearsals. He hated it. He did two nights and went ill.'

That they remained common-law rather than officially married had to do with image, although this was dictated not by Parnes but the fans themselves. 'Billy and I once tried to get married in Jamaica. We discussed it with Larry Parnes and decided against it. One only had to look at what marriage did to Marty Wilde's career. It killed him dead.' (Kim Wilde, currently a hit singer, is the offspring of that union.) 'Billy had to take over for him. Marty was top of the bill. But as soon as that happened, his fans did not want to know.'

Whilst Billy had the ironic distinction of outliving Lennon by three years, his career was shadowed by a heart condition accelerated by being displaced by the Beatles. 'I remember Larry Parnes reassuring Billy that stars come and go. But it [the Beatles] sent Billy into extreme worries. It was like killing off the Old. The Beatles indicated a whole new trend. And Billy sank ever so low in the charts. It was the beginning of his becoming quite ill.'

While Parnes couldn't be bothered, sticking them as back-up men for Johnny Gentle's Scottish tour since he was unable to find any other available band, there was no doubt from the start that John's group with the funny name was something to be reckoned with.

True, times were changing and the Beatles rode the crest of the wave in hair, fashion, and photography with their Sassoon blow-cuts, Mary Quant collarless jackets and David Bailey-style photographs by Dezo Hoffman and others. Recalls Lee, 'Before that everyone had the Elvis coiffe.'

But the Beatles turned all that around. Before Beatles – or BB – you weren't allowed to have an opinion. You weren't allowed to have a northern accent. You weren't supposed to have long hair, smoke, drink or talk dirty. What is more, John *was* married, and whilst he sang 'You've Got to Hide Your Love Away', it was common knowledge that he was both a husband and a father. It was rebellion, and the Beatles led the pack. Here was a group which kept their own names, wrote their own music and talked the same way they did at the village pub about politics, religion and sex.

Having observed John at Brian Epstein's Rushlake Green parties, Lee says that she liked John *less* when he was married to Cynthia, a close friend. 'He was nasty and sarcastic when he was married to Cyn. He'd say things which were hurtful. He was not nice to be near.' When Kenny Everett came to interview John on his first assignment for pirate radio, he refused to communicate, dismissing Kenny with a brief 'Yes' or 'No'.

John's behaviour towards his wife on social occasions was less than ideal, since, according to Lee, Lennon was lusting after her in plain sight of his wife. 'Every time I turned around there was he, looking at me *strangely*. I must say it was very *strange*. It was one of those looks which make you go "Oooh". I went and sat myself down with Cynthia and stayed the rest of the night with her.'

Observing Cynthia after the divorce at parties given at her own Surrey residence, Lee reckons that the marriage broke up because Cynthia was not really John's type. 'She is a very strait-laced girl – simple, quiet and wifely. I saw a lot of her after they split up. She used to come around. I felt sorry for her. She was so distraught. She didn't seem to get over him. Even when she married somebody else, she still retained a fondness for him. When she'd go to parties Cynthia would be found in front of the record player listening to John's records. You could see she was totally unhappy. She was so loyal and devoted to him.'

Observing that John mellowed after his marriage to Yoko, Lee says that she saw more of him since he became more cordial in his attitude toward 'Ev' (Kenny Everett), who on numerous occasions interviewed John in Ascot at his Tittenhurst Park mansion.

'I went to their house a lot with "Ev". I thought they were great. When we first went there Yoko had had one of her miscarriages.

She actually got out of her sick bed and cooked us nut cutlets. She didn't have to do it. Another time she and John took this carriage out and took us all around the grounds.'

Why wife rather than mistress?

Lee considers, 'John wanted to do everything with her. He didn't want to do *anything* with Cynthia. There is that famous photograph of them all going off to the Maharishi in Wales, with Cynthia being left behind. That says a lot about the state of their marriage.'

It wasn't until the release in Britain by Tony Sheridan of a recording they had done in Germany for Polydor (the company which, ironically, released in 1984 John's posthumous last album, *Milk and Honey*), called 'My Bonnie', featuring Lennon and the Beatles as a backing group called the Beat Brothers, that they caused a stir in Britain. Playing at the Cavern when the record hit in Britain brought them to the attention of Brian Epstein, then a local record shop owner, who asked to manage them.

Up until the Helen Shapiro tour in 1963, when 'Please, Please Me' reached the Number One position in the British charts, the Beatles were referred to as the Beat Boys, the Four Beats and so on. Suddenly the idea of Beadles or Beatles congealed, the name no longer sounding too arcane for popular consumption.

An interesting sidelight to the Scottish tour with Johnny Gentle is a song which has surfaced, credited to a collaboration between Lennon and Gentle (now Darren Young), called 'I've Just Fallen for Someone'. What is revealed on this otherwise silly sixties' ballad is John's command of the cliché, brilliantly executed in all of the Beatles songs and played against the spine of the composition. Lines such as 'The best things in life are free' and 'Like Humpty-Dumpty I've fallen and all the king's men can't put me together again' are the sorts of pedestrian observations associated with Lennon, although later on his level of sophistication increases, his style gaining in both strength and stature.

Playing its part in launching the Beatles in Britain was the BBC. During 1962, 1963 and 1964 it added its endorsement to a group which was fast establishing new manners and mores, exposing the Beatles to 30 million people worldwide via the World Service.

While standards of RP (Received Pronunciation) and acceptability in grooming were beginning to give way at the Beeb, there was the odd occasion when old prejudices were voiced, such as the group's encounter with BBC presenter John Dunn who kidded them about their looks. Generally popular were the caricature faces, mop-top haircuts, collarless suits, Liverpool accents and offhand remarks combined with unadulterated lyrics of a suggestive kind.

The evolution of the group's personality during their BBC gigs is perceptible in the 'Lost Beatles Tapes', aired from time to time by the BBC. Mild by comparison to the rap adapted by the Beatles later on, the tapes allow us an early glimpse at a neophyte Lennon testing the waters, fencing with Old Guard presenters and evolving a flip, iconoclastic style which rankles rather than insults.

The relative awe and pleasant surprise at having made it to the BBC is unmistakable: John replies to presenters' questions with a candour that is irresistible. When asked about newspaper items which say he is divorced, Lennon quips, 'I see my wife every day. She knows we are not divorced.' Queried about the price of fame, Lennon retorts: 'I don't miss riding on a bus', adding 'And we got to *certain* restaurants where the people are so snobby they pretend they don't know us, so we have a good time.'

Ruthlessly precise, and unwilling to allow errors to go uncorrected, Lennon was often involved in combat with BBC announcers. Correcting a reference to a little harp as a harmonica, he snapped, 'I play harmonica on "Love Me Do".' Pausing, he gibbed, 'I love these Goon Shows.'

Another time he kids presenter Lee Peters, 'Why don't you do it [announce the next song] in your famous James Mason impersonation voice? . . . Not very good. Can you do Mickey Mouse?'

Asked about the money they were making, John said, 'People say we make £7000 a week, but record royalties take a lot of it. The accountant sees the money. We played three or four years earning hardly anything. We like it sufficiently to play not only for the money. But the money helps. I don't have the patience to practise. But I like to sing and act around and write music. George is interested in instruments – others of us, the sound of the group. I suppose we are crummy musicians.'

During their 1964 first American tour, John was asked by the BBC for his impressions of the States. 'We are on all the news. There are so many programmes on the TV. It is wild. The fans are out of their minds.' Reporting about their first press conference, John said the two primary questions which he had been asked were: 'What do you do with your money?' and 'Are you all bald?'

If the cut and thrust of touring helped to create a style of repartee that was to become characteristically Beatles, then their experiences during the five times they played the German port of Hamburg between 16 August 1960 and 17 December 1962 turned a band of Liverpool scruffs into a band which had learnt how to 'Makshow'. Prior to taking the plunge of accepting an overseas venue, the Beatles had played local gigs at town halls, coffee bars and so on, often confining their rude remarks to themselves. It was only during and after the Hamburg experience, when they developed the stage presence to include the spectators in their act, that they began to play bigger venues – clubs, concert halls and so on.

There is little doubt to my mind that their experiences in Hamburg have been dismissively reported – the Germans having taken a lame British act, polished and reshaped it so that, upon its British return, it was ready to be signed up by an enterprising record shop owner with a view to world renown. In Hamburg the Beatles developed a personality which Lennon later said was based upon 'repressed sex'. Perhaps true. For while larger audiences responded to refrains of 'I Want to Hold Your Hand', what they were subliminally reacting to was much raunchier indeed, something along the lines of 'I Want to **** Your ****'. This, then, was the genius of the Beatles – using innuendo to identify romantic notions with sexual libido.

That the idea worked so well had a lot to do with the lifestyles pursued in Hamburg by the Beatles, Lennon in particular. For if John had pursued a choirboy lifestyle and *then* sung 'I Want to Hold Your Hand' it is doubtful whether the response would have been so volcanic. The truth is that he lived dangerously and sang innocently – the combination was electrifying.

Albert Goldman remarked off-handedly about the juxtaposition of John's personal and musical lives, and while their Hamburg period has been mentioned in various sources it has not been treated with any measure of importance. The fact is that the boys, especially John, were seasoned, not to say embittered, by their experiences in the German port, contributing later on, after they had made it, to a sustained hatred of all bosses, referred to by John disparagingly as 'suit-and-tie' men.

While John told Aunt Mimi that he was earning masses of money he was in reality living on the borderline of poverty, barely scraping enough together to pay for his meals and more often than not borrowing from their 'minder'. Accommodation was sub-standard – dressing rooms with bunk beds within the confines of a cinema, without proper heating or lavatory facilities.

It is telling that, while John and Paul were to become the group's future sex symbols, in the beginning it was Stuart Sutcliffe and Pete Best who hooked up with girlfriends with whom they moved in. (The original Beatles numbered five.) There is the suggestion that John's German period saw his break-up with former lover Stu Sutcliffe, whom he had kicked in the head (culminating in his death) in the heat of a lovers' brawl. However, since I have been unable to confirm the rumour, having questioned Stu's girlfriend Astrid about it, I cannot vouch for its validity. It is interesting to note that when Stu performed 'Love Me Tender' he sang the song with his back to the audience and facing John Lennon.

It is interesting that many of the local Liverpool groups who played Hamburg prior to the arrival of the Beatles objected to their participation, since they had always had a reputation for being disruptive.

One of the most curious aspects of the German experience is the presence of a self-appointed minder, Horst Fascher, who used to boss the boys about unmercifully. He could not be got rid of, and the boys were unable to persuade him to leave them alone.

Fascher, an ex-boxer, was at the time supported by the earnings of a young girl, thus liberating him for his self-proclaimed passion of looking after the British rock groups who came to Hamburg. Part of the British zone in the division of Germany after the Second World War, Hamburg was occupied by soldiers from whom Fascher learned his English. His love of British, as opposed to American, pop came via the records of Tommy Steele, Cliff Richard and the Shadows, and others, which were imported into the zone.

I caught up with Horst at the 1989 Beatles convention in Liverpool, where we discussed his minder role.

'Today it is only money that is important. In those days it was friendship. Let us do it together, man. No matter how, let us do it.

'If somebody was broke, I would lend them a mark or two or five and you give it back to me next time. We were in chicken soup and bean soup together. When we had money it was chicken or steak.'

In addition, Horst was in charge to make sure that the groups got there on time, were sober on stage, did their jobs and cleaned their rooms. 'And every time I came I had something to moan on. Either John was pissed. He had a girl in his room. He did this or he did that. I said, "John, you can't do that here, man." And he'd say, "Oh, yeah, yeah, yeah. You Nazi thing." And I'd say, "Don't give me all that shit." '

Recalls Horst, 'Lennon was always a little more different than the others. He was quiet, but when he drank he would get a bit more talkative. He was always a little bit nasty, sarcastic. He called me "Nazi bastard" and I called him "Limey bastard".

'John was funny. He liked to make jokes. He had his own interpretation. He interpreted how he saw things as he wanted to. When he did little things on stage, everyone was laughing about it. No one said that is against the Germans. He did it like Charlie Chaplin.'

The club district was also the hang-out for much of Hamburg's low life, none of which seemed to alarm or offend any of the Beatles, several of whom were still minors. 'There was a transvestite who used to give John blow jobs. When he found out she was a man, he was amused.' The clubs where the Beatles appeared have now either gone or been reincarnated as discos. Likewise, all the owners for whom they played are dead but for Bruno Koschmider.

It was Koschmider, whom the Beatles deserted for a better-paying employer, who had them deported for allegedly trying to burn down their dorm. Horst is less dramatic, recounting that they only made a little fire in the room to dry their clothes and because it was cold.

'Koschmider hated me like the devil, because I was the one who took the Beatles away from the Kaiserkeller because of the poor conditions they had.

'I was the one who went to Peter Eckhorn [Top Ten owner] and said, "Look, you cannot pay the Beatles less than 50 marks a night when they have been making 35."

'By the end,' boasts Fascher, 'they were earning £544 a week each. First they came by boat and car and are tired when arriving. At the end we fly them in and give them a double room each. But they don't want to sleep alone. They say "I want to sleep with John or Paul." George and Paul were together. And John with Ringo.'

In addition to better salaries and accommodation, they had

charge accounts at the restaurants and didn't have to pay for drinks at the club. Working conditions improved too – two shows a night, twice an hour, with other acts in between, compared to seven-hour stretches in the early days. 'A club could be open from 4.30 p.m. until 5 a.m.,' says Horst. 'Some groups doubled. Some trebled. The big name groups went on for only an hour. How big you were established for how long you would play.'

Observing the change in image over the years, Fascher credits photographer Astrid Kirchherr (Stu's girlfriend) with engineering much of what was to evolve as the Beatles' 'Look'.

'When I met them they were wearing leather gear, which they were proud of – leather pants and all that. Brian changed them into suits and ties.' Astrid cut their hair (mop-top) and took photos of them in Dezo Hoffmann style, wearing Cardin-style collarless suits. 'She really projected their image,' says Horst.

Pete Best's views about Brian's influence confirm Fascher's. 'On stage we used to drink, smoke and eat. We dressed in leathers, had long hair and wore cowboy boots. When Brian joined, he introduced programmes (versus random song selection), suits, and forbade smoking and drinking. He was making us different from other Liverpool bands. He mentioned he didn't want girlfriends travelling with the band. He never dictated. He merely suggested that "It might create a better image."'

If 'image' was important to Brian it was essential to John, and while acceding to Epstein's requests in a token way, he continued unabated in projecting his own image of the Beatles as Britain's euphonious answer to America's Bowery Boys.

Crucial to creating the impression that they were more than this year's 'flavour of the month' was the reality that they wrote the songs they sang. While Brian was equivocal, endorsing Paul's renderings of 'The Sheikh of Araby' and 'Red Sails in the Sunset', John was adamant, insisting that all compositions be credited to Lennon and McCartney. Many of the songs penned by the duo have not been released, while others, as we know, are classics.

But it was Lennon's tenacity at the time when their fate hung in the balance which triumphed over the equivocation of Brian and EMI, both of whom wanted the Beatles to record *other* people's songs. Endorsed, but rejected by John, was Mitch Murray's 'How Do You Do It', a hit for Gerry and the Pacemakkers.

Jack Fallon, violinist on several Beatles recordings, booked the boys before their 'Please, Please Me' triumph and recalls the controversy over writing their own material. 'When George

Martin brought them into the studio and did a test, Ron Richards (the other A&R – artist and repertoire – man) did quite a bit of conferencing about what to do with them and what tunes they were going to record. EMI wanted them to record *other* people's work. It's the old story. When you walk into a recording studio and you're a nobody, they are not interested in recording your tune but want to give it to someone who can sell it.'

An interview with Fallon produced contracts which the Beatles signed when they were earning peanuts and honoured for venues later on. Booked for two-and-a-half-hour gigs at hotels and subscription rooms for £30 a night, the Beatles did hit-and-run one-nighters in Scotland, Stroud, Swindon and Salisbury before pricing themselves out of Fallon's market.

The Salisbury gig was a landmark. Booked into a concert venue at the Civic Centre, the boys filled the 1700-seat auditorium. Cheers Fallon, 'The Beatles came into Salisbury and at the time they were Number Two on the hit parade. They arrived in the afternoon and they didn't leave the building. They couldn't leave the building. They didn't take any chances going out on the streets. I brought them in something to eat and drink. When the crowd dispersed they'd go home. But that would be *before* the real mass hysteria started.'

They were guaranteed £200 for the evening, and it was the last time the boys worked for Fallon, who candidly admits that after that 'they became unobtainable financially. After they made it on the hit parade, I could not any longer afford them.'

Whilst it wouldn't be until May 1963 that the Beatles topped the bill in a tour with Chris Montez and Tommy Roe, in February of the same year they did their first-ever proper UK tour, covering Bradford, Doncaster, Bedford, Wakefield and Carlisle, on a bill headed by Helen Shapiro. They began as a back-up group and they emerged as stars when EMI's release of their single 'Please, Please Me' rose to the Number One place in the UK charts.

Lennon's antics at a Carlisle golf club dance at the Crown and Mitre Hotel caused such a stir that the boys, in party with Helen Shapiro, were asked to leave. The events at the dance compromised Shapiro, making front-page news in the *Daily Express* on 8 February 1963. Whilst no one can give me an exact account of what Lennon did, it appears that he was joking around in his usual jerky way, sending up the Old Guard types who had invited them and doing off-the-wall Ben Elton-type impressions of their idiosyncrasies.

The newspaper account read:

Singing star Helen Shapiro was ordered out of a golf club's annual ball early yesterday as she was dancing the twist.

'It was very unpleasant,' sixteen-year-old Helen said last night before singing at Peterborough.

But 220 miles north, members of Carlisle Golf Club refused to say who told her to leave.

One club member said, however, 'Some of her friends were wearing leather jackets at what was after all a private ball.'

Ordered out with Helen were Kenny 'Up on the Roof' Lynch and the vocal-instrumental group, the Four Beatles.

They had just returned from a concert at Carlisle's four-star Crown and Mitre Hotel.

As they were sitting in the hotel lounge at midnight, dancing golfers in evening dress were streaming into the hotel ball-room.

'Then,' said Helen, 'one of the golf club committee asked us to go in.

'I was asked to do the twist. But while we were twisting someone else asked us to leave. We got out at once.

'We had no evening dress because we were touring, but we were all quite smart and I don't think we were in the least bit out of place.'

The hotel's assistant manager, Mr David Auty escorted them out through a side door 'to avoid any embarrassment'.

Mr Auty added, 'They were very annoyed and upset.'

'I apologised to Miss Shapiro for the incident later.'

Twenty-seven years later, in discussing the incident in interview, Helen generously dismisses it as minor – a nine-day wonder. 'We were thrown out. It looked bad. We returned to the lounge. It was over and forgotten. My manager asked me what happened and that was it.'

The curious thing is how the press got wind of it. 'I heard it was the Beatles' machine.' So had they set her up? 'I didn't blame them. They weren't responsible. We thought it was funny. We were relaxing in the lounge – guys over a pint. I had a cup of tea. We knew there was a dance inside. A guy came out on three occasions asking us to join them. We said no. We were tired. In the end we went in. The guys wore jeans and leather jackets. We went to the buffet and danced. I was dancing with Ringo.

'The next day the *Daily Express* ran it as a headline. I was surprised how quickly it got into print. I thought the thing was stupid.

'Why? We didn't look right. The Beatles and Kenny [Lynch] in jackets and jeans. I was casual, having changed from the show. The Beatles were considered "hairy". We were enjoying it – a bit of a giggle.

'We didn't fit in – Kenny and I from London's East End and the Beatles from the far end of Liverpool.

'A bright, red-faced bloke who looked like a major asked us to leave. We all went out and back to the lounge, thinking what a bunch of wallies.'

Conversation with Shapiro places the group neatly in time, conjuring up an image of the boys in an era when they were just another supporting group and she was the star girl act. How did they meet?

'Arthur Howes [her promoter] said, "For your next tour we've got this group that has this record, 'Love Me Do'." I said, "That's great. I love that record."

'The first meeting was in the afternoon of the first gig for the sound check and all that. They were on stage messing around with amps and pianos and what not. I came in with Arthur, who introduced me. He said, "This is Helen." "This is John, Paul, George and Ringo." And it was Paul who was the spokesman. He came forward and introduced himself personally. The first thing he said was, "It's a shame about the song we wrote for you." I didn't know about it. I said, "What song is that?" They said, "A song called 'Misery'." Apparently they had written that song with me in mind, but they had submitted it to my record producer Norrie Paramor [Columbia-EMI] and he had apparently turned it down in my absence. He didn't think it was suitable. It appeared on their first album, *Please, Please Me*, and Kenny Lynch, also on our tour, released it as a single.'

She continues, 'Paul probably hadn't heard that I didn't know about it. I told him and he was very disappointed. They said, "Oh, Ah, what a shame." And that's when Kenny went away and recorded it.'

I asked Kenny, who had success with the song, why 'Misery' for Helen – a decidedly fetching teenager at the height of her powers.

'They wrote it for Helen, and it wasn't her song. I said, "I like it. I'll do it. I'm doing a session next week and I'll put it on." John went absolutely mad when he heard it, 'cause we had a session musician called Bert Weedon do the guitar solo.' Guitarist Weedon wrote the book from which many novices, including John and Paul, learned to play the guitar. 'Amongst the rock stars he is a bit of a joke – he is a session musician. He played this solo on "Misery" and when I played it for John, he went ape-shit. He said, "You should have got me in" and all that.'

Although Paul was chatty, it was John who appealed, and Helen developed a schoolgirl crush on Lennon. Whilst he never admitted he was married, he was only encouraging in an off-hand, paternalistic sort of way and there is little to suggest that he was seriously interested.

'Helen was a baby in those days,' says Kenny. 'She was a sixteen-year-old kid. She used to sit down in the front of the coach so she couldn't hear us swearing.'

Did Lennon try to chat her up?

'She was too young. He was having a giggle. She was the only girl in the bloody coach. She had a chaperone – a young girl a bit older than I was. They were probably having a bit of a laugh. When you get a bit older we'll see to you. I still kid her that I haven't given her one yet.'

I asked Helen if John had told her he was married.

'It didn't occur,' she replies. 'He didn't know I had a crush on him. I was a kid. I think we knew he was married, but it was hush-hush. I thought what a sexy voice John had, and I developed a thing on him after that. He was protective to me. He respected what I had done in the business. He was a total gentleman towards me, always. He would be the chaperon in a way if there was anybody else around. He called me "Hellie this" and "Hellie that". And later on, when they got big, he would always say, "Come in and sit down."'

When, in April 1964, Lennon was already a superstar and Foyle's honoured his literary achievement with a Dorchester luncheon, Shapiro was asked to attend together with associated hangers-on and Lord and Lady Whatstheirname. 'At the end we all got our free copies and everyone queued up to get their autograph. I was in the queue and suddenly I saw Nellie [Neil Aspinall], who was their roadie. He waved me over and said that he would tell John I was there. He told John and John yelled "Hellie, Hellie" and all that sort of thing. I got to jump the queue and get his autograph.'

Charming and ingratiating in an off-the-wall, wacky sort of way, John acted the fool on the coach – pulling faces at people on the street and clowninng with HHelen.. 'Duriing this tour I was reeading *Melody Maker* or one of the trade papers. There was a headline across a single page which said, "Is Helen Shapiro a Has-Been at Sixteen?" Naturally I was upset, and he was behind, looking over. And it was the hand on the shoulder and a kind remark: "Never mind. It's a lot of whatever it was. It's nonsense and rubbish. Everything's fine and all that".'

For the Beatles this was the tour which commenced in a coach and culminated in a limo. Recounts Helen, ' "Please, Please Me" went up the charts during the tour. Consequently they were promoted and, from being second on, closed the first half of the show.

'By the time we got to Sheffield there were lots of fans outside the hotel. We were up in the lounge, and they were calling out for "Helen" and calling out for "the Beatles". And I have this lovely memory of leaning out the window, flinging out photographs.

'I was with them the first time they ever saw themselves on television. It was a local thing for Granada. We were in the area around Manchester in a TV lounge. We said, "We recorded this TV programme. Let's watch it." There we were. And I can remember John saying, "God, do I really look like that?" He had a fairly ungainly way of moving. And I said, "It's great." The way they moved. Because the only group which we had before them was the Shadows. *They* were the first group.'

Upset at bogus reports about her own conduct towards the boys, Shapiro insists she never played the star. 'A writer said that I never travelled on the coach but in a chauffeured limousine. *I* travelled on the coach. I loved it!

'The point is that during the last two or three days of the tour the Beatles were driven around by their roadie, Neil. "Please, Please Me" had got to Number One. And probably they had to do a TV interview or a press interview. It was for practicality, not status.'

Lynch, known affectionately by Lennon as 'Lynchie', did sixty-two dates with the Beatles and got to know John intimately, on one occasion sharing a room (and bed) with him overnight.

Ruminating about the originality of their style, Kenny says, 'The Beatles were like the musical Monty Pythons – Eric Idle and John. They had a kind of silly humour. But basically, it was an upper-class thing.'

'Over the top' describes the kind of stuff John was writing in the early days – sending up the stultified conventions of a repressive Britain. Kenny continues: 'I remember one time when they'd written something and sang it for me. It went "Whooooo!" I said, "You can't sing that. You'll sound like a bunch of poofs." That's a Little Richard affectation. But they did it anyway.'

So how did he come to share a room with John?

'We were riding along one day in the coach, and they gave us a pamphlet. By that time they were big stars and they'd stay at the best places. They'd pass around a list of hotels in the different towns, and they'd usually stay at the grand station hotels. But I was always having to go out and find digs. I was working every night twice a night and I was getting 90 quid a week. They must have been earning £200-300, I suppose.

'So we were on the coach and they handed out this pamphlet and I saw there was a place where you could get bed and breakfast for 7s 6d. John said, "That sounds great!" So we went to this place and it was a room the size of this table. And when we opened the door, we hit the bed. And we had to share the bed. I couldn't sleep there – it was damp. I remember John grumbling, "Ah, shit. I could have stayed with the lads."'

What was he like?

'He liked to talk serious conversations about music, poetry and books. He used to get silly sometimes to the extent that he became like a kid. He'd throw cakes at somebody. In the cinema he'd throw things at me and burst out laughing. Other times he was down and serious.

'We used to talk a lot about the Vietnam War. I was anti-that. So was he. He wanted to know what the Americans were doing there. He wanted to know why America had the right to tell a country that was so far away what kind of policy it should have and all that. I think basically he was Left. I am too. The more this woman [Thatcher] stays in, the Lefter I get.

'John was unique. Most of the people in the rock music industry don't know what is going on politically. You had to work with guys all the time to find out the few who were interested in something else beside what Wilson Pickett's next record would be.

'He was also aware. I remember walking along with them when they had to meet a photographer to shoot one of their first album covers. And being black, people notice me on the street. I had a couple of hits at the time. So they said, "We're not walking with you any more." Because as soon as people saw me and noticed the Beatles, mobs would descend upon them. They said, "We're

19. Apple Boutique. Sold clothes at cost, but record royalties were standard.

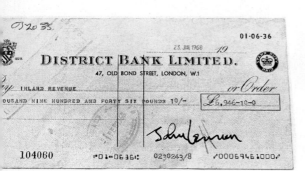

20. Lennon's 1968 tax payment. He was given every advantage in every situation and yet he always complained about discrimination.

21. Apple business adviser 'Yank' Allen Klein. Litigated on Beatles behalf but had to sue for commissions. Glimpsed in front of posh Savile Row Apple HQ.

22. Above: Film-maker Ono before she met John, making 'Bottoms'. She has always said that she ~ shy to look, and absented herself during the filming.

23. Below left: John and Yoko busted for drugs. Lennon was previously warned on several occasic persisted. He longed to be pardonned for the offence so that he could return to Britain.

24. Below right: Lennon with art school friend Jon Hague at the Royal Institute Gallery Piccad exhibition which he sponsored. 'He also gave me lots of presents, bought me a house,' says Ha

John and Yoko at Gibraltar wedding. Tommy [Nut]ter did the clothes. Brother David took the [ph]otos, but was left stranded when Lennon departed without advancing expenses.

. Tittenhurst Park, Ascot – a disgraceful [exam]ple of John's lust for material wealth whilst decrying its corrupting effects.

27. Bed Peace in
Amsterdam – peace
and love and stuff
until John heard
about Dick James'
proposed sale of
Northern Songs, and
bolted back to
London to mount a
campaign to buy the
company himself.

28. 'Obscene' Bag One
Honeymoon lithograph
drawn under mescaline
influence over which
Lennon was taken to court
and won the case.

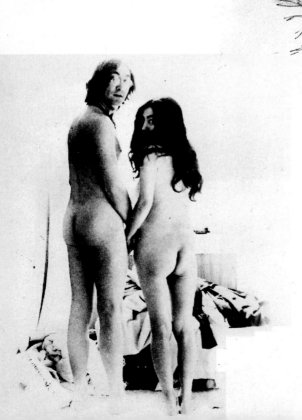

29. 'Two Virgins' – rear
view of album cover. John
wanted to shock, warts and
all.

30. Above: Scottish Holiday. John and Yoko with Kyoko and Julian on a rare Scottish holiday in carefree days, undermined by a road accident in which John and Yoko suffered massive facial injuries.

31. Below: Hassled by United States Immigration for years and years, Lennon got his Green Card in 1975 merely days before the birth of son, Sean.

32. May Pang. Camp
follower-cum-secretary an
latterly John's lover.

33. Lennon's appearanc
with Elton John at
November 1974 Madiso
Square Garden concert w
his last, and evolved *on*
because the duo single
'Whatever Gets You Thr
the Night', reached the
number one position, Joh
first US post Beatles hi
single.

34. Above: Lennon signing autograph for 'fan' Mark David Chapman before the assassination. Chapman waited around to get Yoko's signature and later shot Lennon.

35. Below: The Dakota apartment building. Scene of bizarre film *Rosemary's Baby*. After the assassination, American film columnist Rex Reed moaned 'We felt we were prisoners in our own homes.'

36. Yoko Ono, Sean and Julian at groundbreaking for Strawberry Fields in Central Park at 72nd Street and Central Park West, across from the Dakota apartment building where John lived and died. An oddly reverential show of American respect for a pop star.

37. Sean Lennon with Sam Havadtoy, Yoko's current boyfriend. Her public role nowadays involves devoting energies to the Spirit Foundation and mounting tributes to John's work worldwide in a demonstration of affection for his output as a Beatle.

not going around with you any more because you keep getting us tumbled!" I dropped them off in the alleyway of a photographer in Gerrard Street.'

Observing the tumult of their hasty ascent to stardom, Lynchie recalls, 'The period that they went from troopers to superstars was in about four days. I remember they had "Please, Please Me" out and it went to Number Eighteen. They had written it on the coach and I'd heard it. We were in Coventry on the Sunday and I was in the car. The boys would have a car following the coach sometimes. John or George would be driving. We were in the car listening to *Parade of the Pops* to see if their record had come in at Number One. And it had.'

Good-natured and outgoing, Kenny offered no objection when Brian Epstein, in view of his protégés' accelerated success, changed things around, star-billing the Beatles with Little Richard on a show they were presenting at Liverpool's Empire Theatre, the second largest theatre in England.

'A couple of lads come into my dressing room brandishing the programme of the evening's events, complaining, "Look at the size of the billing these lads have got. It's only because they've got their fan club here with seven hundred people." I said, "Have you got seven hundred people?" They said, "No." I said, "Let them be top of the bill." It's as simple as that.

'Arthur Howes came in and said, "Look, we have to change it." I was on the tour singing five or six songs. Nobody else was interested in doing it. Arthur said, "The boys are getting a lot bigger. I want some more time on stage for the Beatles. So we have to take some songs out." I said, "You can take mine." Everybody else didn't want to know about that sort of thing.'

A huge star before the Beatles, Lynch soon became their warm-up act following the inception of Beatlemania. Continues Kenny, 'I lost four songs on that tour – I ended up doing *two*. On other tours they used to put me on before the boys. They used to do the whole of the second half. The crowd would scream and shout, "We want the Beatles." And I would stand there and not say a word. Then I'd say, "Now if you don't stop, I'm going to sing two or three songs. . . . I'm going to finish and I'll bring up the lights." Then I'd say, "Ladies and gentlemen – the Beatles."'

Just how big they had got and how tight security was is revealed in an anecdote Kenny tells about the time they were doing a gig and used helicopters. 'What they did was to cancel my room, which was at the top of the building, and the four of them stayed in my dressing room. And the guard was saying, "They're not here. They're not here. They're going to come straight in off the roof – jump from the helicopter." But actually they had been there an hour and were sitting in the dressing room having tea and telling jokes. Someone came to my dressing room and asked if I had seen them and I said, "I never see them. They're too big."'

Talking about having clubbed around with John at the Ad Lib and Tramps, Kenny illuminates the moot question of John's marital status. 'He kept his wife a bit of a secret. I think she was still living in Liverpool. I didn't realize he was married. John was the kind of guy who, if he wanted to fool around, would fool around. He was not the type to go home and say to her, "I was fooling around." Nobody knew or cared that he was married.'

How did Kenny discover it?

'I probably said to him, "Come along to London. We'll go out partying." And he might have said, "I'm going home to see the wife." I said, "Oh, you're married." But I never *once* saw her at any of the gigs we played.'

Sighting John first with the girl he was seeing in Liverpool and then with Yoko Ono, Kenny surmises that it *was* the girls who drove the Beatles apart. 'Yoko's arrival on the scene was the beginning of the end. I don't think she did anything. I think her presence did it. She messed up the boys. Sitting around all the time. If they were writing, she was sitting in the corner. If they were recording, she was sitting in the middle of the studio doing her yoga exercises.

'I met her once at the Electric Garden. I was down there one night and they had this group we were going to hear. Suddenly somebody got up on the stage and announced they were going to show this movie called *Bottoms*. And this movie came on with people's arses all over it. John and Yoko noticed me and said, "Hi." I had a few words with John about this movie and she didn't like what I was saying about it. I don't like this artsy stuff. I like *Citizen Kane* and that sort of thing. So I volunteered my opinion to John about this film. And the band was very loud. She must have been screaming at me and I must have been screaming back. I just walked away in the end, because I thought I don't want to have a row with my friend's missus.'

Though they were summed up as 'prisoners of their own

success' in a living testament to Beatlemania, *A Hard Day's Night*, their actual experience of touring differs somewhat from the myth. It is a wonder that they survived in view of the bad receptions they encountered in Japan (where students pelted them with tomatoes), the Philippines (where the Marcoses had them forcibly ejected from the country) and America (where Bible belters burned their records).

Since going against the grain failed to deter John Lennon, it may be supposed that this antagonism merely confirmed in him the will to be no more nor less than himself. Surprisingly the posture succeeded, since John's excess of cheeky rebellion increased press coverage and record sales.

Stories about what went on are legendary, and whether or not we should take it all with a grain of salt, there are recurring rumours about his snubbing British officials at the embassy in Washington, when they requested (but were refused) his co-operation in a charity benefit. The Marcos flap, blown out of all proportion, derives from the same premise, and there was also a charity affair at which Alan Livingstone (then Capitol Records president) asked them to perform but they condescended only to appear.

John's *angst*, well articulated to the press, about not being able to take a piss without some lady wife or local mayor wanting him to kiss their daughter, was what he hated about touring, for he was careless of social courtesy and protocol. Normal, but socially unacceptable, John elected to fulfil his own needs and to forget the rest.

In-house NEMs photographer Robert Whitaker travelled the world with the Beatles, covering the tours of America, Germany, Britain, Japan and the Philippines. In assessing the success of the tours, he says, 'Everything was laid on everywhere in the world – girls and booze.'

So what went wrong in the Philippines?

'When we arrived in Manila we all went to a hotel. Later on in the day we were told that earlier Marcos and his wife had invited us to the palace. We didn't know anything about it. We didn't go. It was as simple as that. There was no communication to say that we had been asked that I know of.

'The concert wasn't over well attended. I am sure that I have photographs of us all getting jostled. I think that one of the Beatles had bought a chess set and it was knocked out of his hand. It was a beautiful set. Yes, we were driven to the airport, very much at gunpoint, and we were only too glad to get on a KLM aircraft and get out of the country.

'I don't think the management was well organized, but I don't think that was Brian's fault at all. I don't know too much about the contractual arrangements.'

Don Short, writing about the Beatles for the *Daily Mirror* (then the biggest newspaper in Europe), having done the first article about them in the national press, was a dogged camp follower of their tours both at home and abroad.

Short, who went along on the Manila tour, recounts his observations of what went wrong. 'Brian Epstein once asked me in the early days whom I thought was the most difficult Beatle to get along with, and I said John Lennon, thinking that would be his answer. He said, "No, it's Paul McCartney." Of course I realized later that he was right. John would sometimes listen to another argument – to reason. Paul was harder to persuade. When he made up his mind he rarely changed it. I can understand it from Brian's viewpoint – "No, Brian. I'm not doing that." And he wouldn't do it. Whereas John might be persuaded into doing something that Brian wanted them to do.

'That often caused Brian embarrassment. "Come and meet the Prime Minister", or "Tonight we have the Russian ambassador." They'd say, "Fuck off, Brian." Brian then had egg on his face because he might have promised someone at a dinner party they'd come, and they didn't come. There were areas there where they did cause embarrassment. They didn't want to play lapdog to anybody, and they didn't want Brian saying to them that they'd have to do this and that.'

Citing another example of John's irresponsibility, Short talks about a Modligiani painting which Epstein had imported from Paris for the day. He had arranged with Lennon to meet the owners at Claridge's with a view to its purchase. The afternoon wore on, but Lennon failed to show up. 'I am sure that John had been well warned to be there and when Brian asked him about it, he waved it off with, "Oh, forgot about it, Brian. Sorry", taking it that it could be rearranged the next day or at any time. That is how they were.'

Yet it was Brian who paid for Lennon's obstinacy in Manila. 'Brian was beaten up pretty badly,' says Short. 'He was a hell of a nice guy. I think they would speak well of him now in hindsight, and did up to a certain point in earlier years. They trusted him. They admired him. And it was only when other ideas came into their mind – about tycoons and yachts and a different living style and the pictures that had been painted in their minds by Allen Klein and what he had done for the Rolling Stones – that they suddenly felt Brian had served his useful purpose. They went off him quickly.

'Brian was very generous and gave them great gifts of cars – a Rolls Royce for one of them. He was the kind of guy who would give anything away. Brian was a soft touch. He was very nice. He would help anybody.'

The exciting thing about Epstein was his genius for merchandising. Before that no artist had ever made a name internationally or conquered America in music. 'Before that we had Cliff Richard who never made it big in the States, but is a tremendous artist here. Then came the Bee Gees. But the Beatles were the first,' says Short.

Describing the tours as the source of the Beatles' combined personality, Robert Whitaker says that, whilst the German trip was 'well organized', the Tokyo trip was the best tour ever – despite the tomato-hurling students. 'It was really the calmest period. They all thought together. They were very peaceful.

'I recall that the Beatles phoned their wives and that we did a painting there. The picture which evolved is superb. I have about four hundred transparencies of them actually making it. They painted their individual pictures in towards the centre – abstracts in bright shades. They each sat at the corner of a piece of paper and painted. It was the most unique period of time.

'While they were painting it, the acetate of *Revolver* had come out which I shot the back cover on (a picture of them at EMI Studios). While that was being painted, we were listening to *Revolver*. They were selecting the tracks. It played continuously.

'*Revolver* was their first esoteric album, with George's sitar for the first time. Intellectual. Sophisticated. Everybody loved it.'

Observing the creative process at work, Whitaker talks about the act of John and Paul collaborating. 'They listened to a lot of different people's records hearing different instruments and beats. Their discussions were very musically minded. I remember "Paperback Writer" being written on the back of a paper bag.'

A tragic postcript to the touring: 'When they stopped touring I stopped working for them. And Brian had his breakdown.'

Why?

'I remember how unhappy Brian was that it all took place and that he had been ousted by the Maharishi.* The Maharishi pretty much led the Beatles. Flower power and everything else. Brian wasn't overly impressed by it all. And I vaguely remember that Brian was hurt by the whole thing because he lost control of the Beatles. And they stopped touring. They were more interested in "getting their minds right".'

Did the Maharishi replace Brian as their guru?

Short says yes. 'There was some measure of compensation because all of them had found meditation. Meditation did help them. There is no doubt about it.'

About the falling out, Short surmises, 'They didn't pay the Maharishi. They felt at the end of the day that they might have been taken for a ride. One of the foibles of the Beatles was if they found something new they'd go balmy about it and then turn around and find they had been exploited.'

And what about the wives?

Short tells a tale about the girls being hidden in laundry baskets during the tour of Ireland so as not to give away the game to the press. 'The press was looking for them everywhere and they didn't want them to know, 'cause in those days they shouldn't have girlfriends or wives. Brian tried to keep Cynthia in the background, suggesting that they shouldn't be photographed with their respective spouses.

'Brian would love to pull the wool over your eyes. He wouldn't always make the Beatles accessible for interviews. He ensured that *he* put them up for the occasional press conference when they were at the London Palladium or when they were about to do a tour.

'We got into Shannon and the Beatles locked themselves in this tower-type hotel. They had a balcony and I climbed over the balcony and into a room that John and George were occupying, with a bottle of Scotch. And the sight of me climbing into their room clutching a bottle of Scotch won great favour. So we had more Scotch and cokes than we could manage.

'Cynthia and Pattie, who was not married to George at the time but was only his girlfriend, climbed into a laundry basket in the hotel and it was pushed past me and into the kitchen and out the

---

* Ironically, Lennon's infatuation with the Maharishi lasted only until shortly after Brian's death, when he publicly denounced the guru on American television. Curiously, Epstein's estate, assumed to be large, was actually modest, suggesting that it might have been *he* who made large donations to the Maharishi. 'In the end', says Don Short, 'John did not pay the Maharishi.'

back. And that is how they escaped from the hotel without any of us realizing.'

Just how marginal a figure was Cynthia Lennon on the tours? True, she used to go about in New York wearing a black fright wig so as not to be recognized. However, any presumption that this was so as to appear to be a member of staff rather than John's wife is dispelled by the caption underscoring John's appearance on *The Ed Sullivan Show*, which read: 'Sorry, girls, he is married!'

The contents of a diary of their appearance in Miami during their first US tour have kindly been made available by Sergeant Buddy Dresner, the security officer in charge of the boys at the Deauville Hotel. In response to my query as to whether John was an absentee husband, he writes,

> John and Cynthia spent every night in their room, called home to England each night to check on their son.
> I got Cynthia out of the hotel many times wearing a black wig and sunglasses. She had a great time.
> The news media missed her because they were killing themselves over the boys. But she appeared everywhere the boys were taken by me.

As a rueful afterthought, he writes: 'I was not pleased with the transformation of John from clean-cut to strange-looking. The need for drugs, bad music, as well as presenting a difficult appearance, was shocking to say the least.'

Nevertheless a certain censorship appears to have existed, since the then Mrs Lennon could barely speak for herself without a roadie insinuating himself between her and the press.

An account of an attempt to interview Cynthia following the American tour, bylined by Helen Mason, says it all.

> *Question:* 'Do fans frighten you?'
> *Roadie:* 'Not at all. We're used to it.'
> *Question:* 'Enjoy America?'
> *Roadie:* 'Not a word, Cyn.'
> *Question:* 'Miss baby John [Julian]?' (Cynthia nods head.)
> *Question:* 'Mind being in the background?'
> *Roadie:* 'She likes it that way, and so does John.'

At this point the writer tells us that Lennon appears, waves and yells to the roadie, 'Get Cyn out of this!' End of story.

The build-up of antipathy leading to a breakdown in touring evolved during the American tours, as a result of first the mobs, and then the backlash against John's opinions about religion.

The perils of the 1965 American tour are recounted by Short. 'At the Cow Palace in San Francisco a wall of human beings trampled over each other. I really thought the Beatles would be trampled to death.'

Then another crisis. 'We were going up to Portland, Oregon and one of the plane's engines caught fire. John and I sat next to each other. We wrote our last messages on a piece of paper and put them in a photographer's 35mm capsule. What happened to them I don't know. We landed safely, the fire brigades and ambulances alongside, and I can remember John screaming from the back of the plane, "Beatles and children off first." '

Events prefacing the group's finale concert at the end of the 1966 American tour at San Francisco's Candlestick Park in August are recounted by Whitaker, who recalls the furore over John's 'We are bigger than Jesus' comments.

'The USA was going to cancel the tour and Epstein had to go to the States to make sure it was okay. John *cried* when he had to go and apologise. He shouldn't have been penalized for saying something which probably was true. And I shouldn't have been penalized for doing the "butcher's sleeve".'

In between the touring there was the recording – the Beatles evolving a style of working which later became commonplace amongst pop groups but which in the mid-sixties was downright revolutionary. The bad boys of EMI, they booked the studio and side musicians indefinitely, were erratic in keeping appointments, tended not to be prepared but to improvise on the spot, and used the best musicians as sidemen. None the less, the effect was not only enthralling but timeless, since some of the best recordings ever made have come out of the dynamic of four boys and a producer sitting together in the middle of the night in a dark room, the sole illumination being a key light focused upon their music stands.

Mark Lewisohn's documentation of the Beatles' recording sessions communicates the vigour and gestation of the sessions. But I decided to follow up his interviews with my own and talked to several Beatles' side men and one woman. NEM's director Vic Lewis, present at the recording sessions, summons up his impression of what they were like – a six-week siege previously unheard of and innovated by the Beatles.

'The EMI studio was booked from 4p.m. until midnight for six weeks, during which time they'd come in for a couple of hours unable to think of anything and walk out again.

'They took so many liberties in making records that nobody else would have ever got away with. EMI made so much money out of the Beatles that they could do what they wanted.

'They'd send out Mal, the roadie, who would come back with bottles of whisky, bottles of lemonade and fish and chips in a paper bag. We'd all sit around the floor and drink out of paper cups. They'd sit down. Paul would sit at the piano. "What do you think of this?" "I don't know." "Let's meet tomorrow." This went on for week after week after week.'

Lennon, whom Lewis did not like and thought to be arrogant because of his disregard for any music other than rock 'n' roll (Lewis had been a bandleader in the big band era), nevertheless is credited with 'having more to say than McCartney. You'll always hear Paul's songs, like an Irving Berlin. But you won't hear John Lennon's. Yet he had great integrity about what he was saying.'

Classical musician Dave Mason, who played the now famous 'piccolo' trumpet on 'Penny Lane', recalls the utter disarray of the sessions. 'There were hangers-on. People came in. It was distracting. Some of the sessions were a bit of a party. Always plenty of time with us hanging about. They experimented all the time. They weren't professional musicians in that they were not trained. None of them played the piano to any extent at that time.

'When they turned up they hadn't written anything and I said, "What do you want me to play?" And I think Paul said, "Oh, I dunno yet, mate." Paul did most of the talking. They said, "Can you go da–da–de–da–de–da–da?" And I said, "Oh, you mean, da–de–de–da–de–de–da?" "Yes, that sounds all right. But can you do it a bit higher?" So I tried another trumpet – I took about six trumpets along.

'That took three hours. They hadn't written it. We merely improvised according to what they wanted. When they had written down what they wanted, the recording only took twenty minutes. George told me the lead-in and I just played what I did. They hadn't decided what they wanted. That is where Paul was so good. He knew what he wanted, but didn't know how to do it technically.

'My own impression is that they were a bit jealous of Paul McCartney. He had the most dominant role, really. George

Harrison took a secondary role to John and Paul. Ringo was quite happy to sit there playing his drums. Lennon sat around and listened and made a few observations.

Recruited by Mason as part of the trumpet trio for another Beatles song, 'Magical Mystery Tour', Elgar Howarth has keen memories of his experience at a Beatles recording session. Four years Lennon's senior, Howarth was then chairman of the Royal Philharmonic Orchestra.

'We were called for all day, which was very unusual for us because in our world – the classical world – you are called for very strictly adhered to times. There are three-hour sessions. You work quickly and in a controlled way in the classical business.

'When we turned up formally dressed at Abbey Road at one o'clock the commissionaire said, "Who are you looking for?" And we said, "We are looking for the Beatles." He said, "The Beatles won't be here yet. They never seem to get here until later afternoonish." So we hung around for a bit. Eventually someone from the company said, "Well, if I were you I'd go to the pub and have a drink." So we went, and returned at half past two. We sat around and read books or whatever. Eventually the Beatles did arrive at about 5 p.m. They had just come back from the Maharishi. They were casually dressed and had young ladies with them. I presume they were their wives. They didn't look like "groupies" or whatever groupies were or are.

'We said to George Martin, "Where is the music for us to play?" They said, "Oh, we haven't written it yet", which again amazed us because in my world everything is very carefully prepared for you. There isn't that sort of money to throw away all the time.

'So Paul McCartney sat down at the piano and started to play with one or two fingers notes to fit into a tape which we had, which was to be our trumpet parts. George Martin said, "Look, it will take them a little while. If I were you I would go off to the pub. Better than you hanging around here." So off we went to the pub again. It was half past five by now and we were working on overtime. We went off to the pub for three-quarters of an hour, and when we came back our parts were ready for us.

'So we played and played. Eventually it was getting on towards ten o'clock. Paul McCartney said, "Okay, good, you've got it." So we started to pack our instruments away, and then John

Lennon asked, "Where are you going? What are you doing?" We said, "We've done it." And he said, "You've done that bit. But there's some more yet." So one of us asked, "Where is it?" And they said, "We haven't written it yet." We were getting a little fed up. I was the first trumpet in the Royal Philharmonic by that time and we always had jobs to go to the next day. I wasn't looking to go on until the early hours of the morning, as attractive and novel as the situation was.

'One of us said to John, "Tell it to him and he will write it down for you." Lennon asked, "Can you do that?" And I said, "Yes, I suppose I can. I have here the harmony, and you sing me if you know how you want the trumpet parts to go." He sang the trumpet licks to play, and I played them and scribbled them out. It was only a few bars. We recorded, and that didn't take so long.

'Perhaps they could see that we were getting a bit fed up with them. I suppose we got out of there at 11p.m. and they were still there. They shook us all by the hand and off we went into the night.'

Harpist Sheila Bromberg recounts a similar experience, having been hired to play on the Beatles' 'She's Leaving Home'.

'I was booked to be on this session at Abbey Road from 9 p.m. until past midnight, and I got there very early because with a harp you have to spend quite a lot of time tuning it. Suddenly I was aware that this figure was standing near by me. I was busy tuning and then this voice said (in Scouse dialect), "What ya got on zee dots?" I turned round and all I could see was hair. I said, in my poshest voice, "I beg your pardon?" And this man standing beside me said, "What ya got on zee dots?" I couldn't understand what he said. I said, "Excuse me. What are you saying?" "What have you got on the dots?" – meaning dots of music – he says. "Could you play it?" I played it. "I don't want that. I want something. . . ." I played it a little differently. "I don't want that. I want something . . ." And I played it differently again. This went on for half an hour. Eventually I found out it was McCartney.'

She continues, 'By 12.45a.m. we were absolutely knackered. My fingers were dropping off. And all I can remember is George Harrison sitting in the corner practising his sitar, looking out of it in a sort of dream world, and Paul McCartney popping in and out but not making his presence greatly felt because George Martin had taken over by the end of the session.

'The leader of the orchestra, a very fine fiddle player, stood up and said, "Now we all have to go home because we are working in the morning." And this voice from the control box said, "Well, I guess that's that, then." No thank you or goodnight, gentlemen (and woman). And we all toddled off.'

Pleased with the innovative mixing on the record, and of the sound of the harp (mechanically repeated) Bromberg asked George Martin about *how* it was done. 'I asked George and he couldn't (or wouldn't) tell me.' She pauses. 'The music is very simple really, but the production of the thing is incredible. George Martin wrote the arrangements for the musicians and was there all the time.'

A graduate of the Royal College of Music, Bromberg complains about being confronted 'with these young kids who don't know what they are doing or how to achieve it. Suddenly out of this chaos, which is all I can describe it as, comes this album that everybody fell over themselves to try and buy.'

Having also played with Sinatra and Crosby, Bromberg compares them to the Beatles. 'Sinatra came in casually dressed but smart. I suppose I was in the same age bracket as the Beatles, but I wouldn't have dreamt of going to work looking like that. Mind you, afterwards I did. I thought, "Christ, if they can get away with it, so can I." So I did. They began to call me "the hippie harpist".'

Following Paul's initial discourse, none of the group said hello or goodbye to the band. The only contact was via George Martin. 'Most big stars would introduce themselves to the band: "Hi, folks." If they'd seen someone before they'd have a word: "Nice to see you back. How's the family?"' She pauses. 'I'm probably the only person of my generation in the whole of Great Britain who didn't go bananas about the Beatles.'

Three events turned it around for the Beatles, transforming an exclusively British act into one of international stature. They all happened in America within months of each other. In December 1963 Capitol Records, a subsidiary of EMI but wholly autonomous, after passing on the group's first two American releases signed the Beatles. Their single 'I Want to Hold Your Hand' was released on 14 January 1964 with an album of material to follow, and a massive publicity campaign was pledged.

Topping the charts of *Billboard*, America's premier music trade magazine, the single confirmed the group's mandate to honour their commitment to promoter Sid Bernstein and to perform at New York's Carnegie Hall. It would be the first time that this classical venue had featured a popular music group – something which Bernstein, as modest as he is, must admit is among the publicity stunts of the century.

Since they were booked on *The Ed Sullivan Show* on both 9 February (before the Carnegie double-nighter) and again on 16 February (after the big event) and seen by 73 million Americans, the group's reputation in the States was assured. (Sullivan had been in London the previous summer and, having seen the furore caused by the Beatles at London Airport, negotiated with Brian Epstein to book them provided that their single went to the Number One position in the US charts.)

Catching up twenty-seven years later with Alan Livingstone, then international president of Capitol Records and now president of his own animation company, Rim Productions Inc., I enquire why there was a delay in signing up the Beatles.

'Capitol had the right of first refusal on any English product from EMI, and the Beatles were submitted to us along with other product. At that time English product was not selling well in this country.

'I had heard about the Beatles because I read the English music press, and I asked my colleagues whose job it was to screen all the product that came in from EMI, "What about this English group – the Beatles?" Their response was, "Ah, they're a bunch of long-haired kids. They're nothing. Forget it."

'And I would bring it up again at a meeting. "No, they're a bunch of long-haired kids. They're not worth bothering with. Forget it."

'So when Capitol didn't take the Beatles, EMI began to shop them elsewhere – to RCA Victor, Columbia Records, Decca Records and a lot of small companies. Everybody turned them down.

'In desperation EMI gave the Beatles to a very small company called Vee-Jay Records. Vee-Jay was on the verge of bankruptcy. They had no money. They took the Beatles record because they got it free to put out. So they felt – why not? They put it out and (I researched this later) it sold sixty-some copies. It was totally unsuccessful. They called EMI and said, "We don't want them any more." So they gave up their rights to the Beatles.

'EMI went shopping again and got Swan Records, a Philadelphia company, to put out four sides – and nothing happened. It sold in the hundreds. Swan said, "We don't want them any more."'

What turned it around at Capitol was the intervention of one man, Brian Epstein, which is why I get so damn angry when people in Liverpool tend to disparage his contributions to the group's success. It was Epstein who, in his highly polished, public school, urbane English way, personally phoned up Alan Livingstone enquiring *why* the company hadn't signed the Beatles.

'I was sitting in my office one day and I get a call from London from the Beatles' manager, Brian Epstein,' recalls Livingstone. '"Mr Livingstone," he said. "We don't understand it. They're doing well here. Why won't you take them?" "Frankly," I said, "I haven't heard them." "Would you please listen and call me back?" I said, "Okay." So I sent downstairs, got a copy of a Beatles record, listened to it and liked them very much. I rang him back and said, "Okay. We'll take them."'

It was Epstein who at this juncture did an about-face and made demands which Capitol incredulously agreed to. '"Just a minute," he said. "I'm not going to give them to you unless you agree to spend $40,000 on their first release." At that time it was a lot of money to spend to promote a single record. We said, "Okay." And we took the record, "I Want to Hold Your Hand". We hardly got through the first twenty thousand copies when it exploded. We followed it up with an album, and the rest is history. It became an absolute sensation.'

While the rest is indeed history, it remains a fact that it was Alan Livingstone who, on account of a rapport with Brian Epstein, personally got the exposure necessary to launch an act both British and a group in the hitherto unconquered American market, paving the way for any number of other British groups to follow.

'I didn't pay anybody off,' protests Livingstone. 'It goes on now, but in those days it wasn't done. At least *we* weren't doing it. We sent mailings to the disc jockeys to encourage them to play the records. We made a special effort to see that when the DJs got the records, they were also in the shops.'

Was there resistance, and if so how was it overcome?

'By persistence, pushing, pleading and begging. Making it sound like we were really behind them. I made personal calls. So did my vice-president in charge of promotion. "This is special. Please play it. Just try it and get a reaction." They tried and got a reaction. It took a lot of work to get the records on the air. Once they were on the air, that was it. And it changed the international face of music.'

Asked what he considers accounted for the pandemonium, Livingstone surmises, 'The cheeky, English, working-class funky sound. And the Look. What was then long hair is today short hair. And the music. It was a change in sound which *nobody* had before. It was different from Elvis. It was a whole different kind of thing, out of which grew the whole electrified guitar hard sound. And not only that, but the songs that Paul and John wrote were marvellous. I don't think the Rolling Stones would have happened without the Beatles paving the way.

'You look back in history and at the milestones where music has changed. You go back to Guy Lombardo who created a very saccharine sound. After that came the big bands – Benny Goodman, Tommy Dorsey and so forth. And then along came Elvis Presley and he made a mark. And then came the Beatles, which was the biggest mark of all. And it just expanded.'

He pauses, 'The "groups" have taken over, and the groups write their own material. Mick Jagger and Elton John. And the new groups coming up like Bon Jovi, Milli Vanilli, and New Kids on the Block. The sad thing is that the big band singers of the past cannot get record deals today.'

Since it was Capitol upon whom Lennon launched the notorious 'butcher's sleeve', I asked Livingstone about how they coped with the group's politicism.

'The original contract we had gave us the right to do the album covers, but the Beatles wanted to do their own. We said okay. They sent us this "butcher's sleeve" cover and I called and said, "What *is* this?" And they said, "It's our comment on war. All the dismembered bodies." I said, "I don't know. You had better give us another cover." They refused. They wanted it out. So we issued a few hundred and sent it out to all our dealers. It came back – "We won't stock it. We won't sell it." I rang London back and said, "I can't sell this. They won't accept shipment." When the boys got too political, the public turned its back.'

Recalling another experience of having to cope with the obstinacy of Lennon's convictions, Livingstone discusses the *Two Virgins* cover. 'They sent us a cover of John Lennon and Yoko Ono. And the picture on the front was of John and Yoko bare naked, frontal view. On the back of the album was bare, naked, rear view. And I must say that her body was nice but not fantastic. His was worse. He sagged pretty good. Anyway, we got that and said, "We won't put this out." They said, "Give us permission to sell it someplace else", because they were under exclusive contract. And we said okay. A company hire took it and put it out with a brown wrapper. A lot of the dealers wouldn't handle it.'

Whilst the *Two Virgins* debacle brought it out into the open, there was always controversy brewing within Lennon. Having got to know the boys pretty well during his presidency of the company (terminated shortly after the group broke up), Livingstone says that 'Lennon had a chip on his shoulder and what that was about I do not know. I think he was anti-social and anti-Establishment, certainly.

'I don't know where John said it, but he was quoted as having said that "The entertainment industry is an extension of Judaism" or that "Judaism is an extension of the entertainment industry". There was a lot of flap about it.'

Having first-hand recollections of how they behaved socially, Livingstone confirms that John was the most difficult to get along with.

'I was the friendliest with Paul. Paul was the most outgoing. I sat at the piano stool with him while he played me melodies and things like that. I enjoyed his company. I had a hard time with John. He was never communicative. It was hard to enter into a conversation with him. Ringo was friendly and a charming man. And George was also difficult in a different way. He was lost and finally went off to India, where he spent a lot of time.'

When the group came over to the States, Livingstone gave a couple of parties for them to meet Hollywood stars.

'They were all people you would think they would be delighted to meet – heads of studios, movie stars, prominent people who came by invitation only. I remember sitting in my office and Edward G. Robinson called, "Alan, I didn't get an invitation to this. Can't you include me?" I got a wire from Cary Grant. Because they wanted to meet the Beatles more than the Beatles wanted to meet them.

'Paul McCartney was charming and delightful. Ringo was very friendly. George Harrison didn't show up. And John Lennon came, but stood in a corner and would hardly talk to anybody. I had the greatest respect for John as a lyricist, but he was always the outsider. Different. You never knew where he stood. At the time I was never sure if it was an act or whether he was that way. And I think he really was that way. He did not enter into society easily. It was not shyness. I do not think he meant to be rude. That was just his manner.'

Another time Livingstone gave a party for his favourite charity and, whilst the Beatles considered that it was an imposition to ask them to perform, they did agree to make a collective appearance.

'It was the most fantastic event you can imagine,' enthuses Livingstone. 'It was by invitation because the demand was so great that we couldn't handle it all. There were almost riots, because we tried to keep the location a secret. The secret got out. We had the riot squad there. If Paul McCartney would be smoking a cigarette, drop it on the ground and step on it, there would be a mad rush to get it. It was absolute hysteria. A picture of it was on the front page of the *Los Angeles Times*. People are still talking about it. It is probably the most exciting charity event this town has ever seen.'

Probably the most illuminating interview about the Beatles' American breakthrough was with Sid Bernstein, the man who brought the Beatles to Carnegie Hall. The significance of the achievement has never properly been credited. However, in conversation with Bernstein all the dynamic of that fateful event surfaces.

Then an agent for GAC (now ICM) for Dion, Fats Domino, Brenda Lee and others, Bernstein had a hankering to become an impresario – a promoter of musical talent. To take his mind off his quest, he enrolled in Max Lerner's political science class at New York's New School for Social Research.

Part of the course consisted of consulting foreign newspapers. Reading in the London press about Beatlemania made Bernstein curious in the Liverpool group, prompting him to make the first of many transatlantic phone calls to Brian Epstein.

'He was working out of Liverpool at the time. I got him at his home and Queenie, his mother, answers the phone. She asks me about New York. It was a lengthy conversation. She was very curious about New York and about the Book Review section of the *New York Times*. Finally she said, "I must be wasting a lot of your money. I'll go and get my son." And Brian got on the phone. When he came on the phone it was a premonition for me in history. I lost my voice. It took me a while to say hello. I think it was the moment. I felt something important was happening.

'Anyway, we made the deal for a year hence. Brian said, "Where would you present them?" I wasn't prepared. I thought the most unique place would be Carnegie Hall. He said to me, "You are going to present my boys at Carnegie Hall?" I said, "Yes." Little did I know that they didn't accept rock acts. And *that* turned him around. We made the deal on the phone. *We never had a contract.*

'When the booking lady, a little Romanian woman with a heavy accent said, "Mr Bernstein, what kind of a group is this?" I said, "They are four young men who are a phenomenon in Britain." She later told me that when I said four men she thought I meant a string ensemble. I ordered the tickets, which went for $3.50, $4.50 and $5.50. On the street the scalpers were getting $150. We got requests from all over the country. Everyone wanted to come.

'When Ed Sullivan found out that a New York promoter named Sid Bernstein had them for 12 February he called and asked, "Sid, what are they like?" I said, "I haven't seen them." I hadn't heard a note of their music. You couldn't *get* their records here. I am still going by the English newspapers. "Sid, I just bought them in front of you for Sunday, 9 February and in back of you, Sunday 16 February – twice.' The programme of the Carnegie concert, now a collector's item, incorrectly lists the band members as John Lennon, Ringo Starr, John McCartney and George Harrison.

The rest, as they say, is history, Bernstein having again presented the Beatles in 1965 at Shea Stadium where they played for twenty-eight minutes. 'From $6500 for two shows in 1964 I went to $180,000 for one show in 1965 at Shea Stadium. Nobody cared. They were there.'

Whilst Bernstein unsuccessfully tried to reunite the dissenting Beatles with a bid to appear in tandem at Madison Square Garden, he is planning in tandem with Cynthia Lennon a tribute to commemorate the tenth anniversary of John's death in 1990.

Bernstein was asked to speak at the Central Park memorial service honouring John after his death on 14 December 1980. Cremated at the Frank Campbell mortuary on the east side of Manhattan, Lennon's ashes are scattered in Central Park in and around Strawberry Fields, a part of the park on West 72nd Street, purchased by Yoko Ono, which commemorates John's work and life and where he used to like to stroll.

Recalling the events of the ceremony, Bernstein says with regret, 'Two hundred thousand people were there. I was standing on the top of the truck being interviewed by ABC and was asked what I had to say about my friend John. "We are resting here where his ashes are resting and enrich this earth to pay tribute to a man who gave us so much." And I started to cry. I am trying to regain my voice. And I see my daughter in this crowd, aged twelve or thirteen, crying. I was here when John Kennedy was shot, and it wasn't the same.'

From September 1971, when Lennon began to live in New

York, his path crossed intermittently with Sid's. There is a running joke about Bernstein meeting up with John accidentally on the streets of New York around Columbus Avenue, where he lived at the Dakota apartment house. Each time they met John would introduce him to Yoko Ono. 'John, I've met Sid a number of times. How often are you going to introduce me?' The incident is ironic in the telling, since Yoko Ono Lennon is mildly irritated at Bernstein's proposal to present a Lennon memorial jointly with Cynthia. She has, in fact, mounted her own tribute, which was a triumph.

Sid pauses. 'I was presenting Jimmy Cliff for the first time at Carnegie Hall. My three oldest children, my wife and I were going to see Jimmy Cliff. John calls me at home, "Sid, I can't get a ticket to see Jimmy Cliff. I've got to see him. Would you have three tickets?" He was taking May Pang and a marvellous friend of his from London. I asked my kids, who were then only nine, twelve and fourteen, would you give them up for John Lennon? So my wife and I, John and May and this other young man went. And during the intermission John said to me, "Sid, do you remember Shea Stadium? A thousand press people from all over the world?"

'I met them again one day in a Chinese restaurant when Szechuan food was just starting. It was the first Szechuan restaurant in New York. I used to bring our kids there a lot because they liked Szechuan food. John and May were sitting at the next table, and he said to me (espying our gang), "Trying to raise a baseball team?" I said, "I'm close." We talked a little bit, and I introduced him to the kids.

'Then one time he rang me up and asked me for a good Italian restaurant. I recommended Paolucci's on Mulberry Street in Little Italy. I gave him the favourite dishes of this restaurant – chicken cacciatore, veal parmigiano. He couldn't spell it. So he said, "Wait a minute. Harry Nilsson is here. Why don't you tell Harry?"

'Two days later two guys walk up with flowers and fill my office room. I said, "Must be a mistake." They said, "Sid Bernstein, third floor." And the card read "Harry and John". I said, "Okay. Leave them here. If somebody calls for them you'll come back." My secretary said, "Didn't you tell me a couple of days ago that John called you and put Harry Nilsson on the phone?" I said, "Harry and John." So I called Paolucci's and they told me that John came down with eleven or twelve guys – Alice Cooper, Nilsson, Yoko, more rock stars. She said they were the most mannerly, well-behaved group. Nobody bothered them. They left the biggest tip in the history of Paolucci's. So he was sending me a thank you with all these flowers.'

A rather oblique aside to Sid's friendship with John is his relationship with May Pang – John's girlfriend during his fourteen-month estrangement from Yoko – which continued, according to Pang, until the day he was shot.

'May Pang was my baby-sitter,' says Bernstein. 'She would baby-sit our kids when she was a young teenager. She lived at 87th and Third and I lived at 84th and Park, so she was close by. She followed the Rascals to Hawaii. We were there. May showed up. She was at the house, watching the kids. Later on she became Lennon's secretary. Then his sweetheart. Whatever the relationship was.'

Touring days over, Beatlemania plummeting, the Beatles embarked upon a film career which, whilst promising (even classic), ended inconsequentially largely due to the group's belief that they could do it better than the experts and because of their unwillingness to continue to work together.

8

The Films – Day for Night and Hard

When the Beatles decided they no longer wanted to tour but to concentrate their energies on recording and film-making, they hooked up with producers and directors who assisted in their success. After the making of *Help*, they decided to make their own movies, and hire their own creative team. It is astonishing, considering the care and expertise, not to mention affection, which producer Walter Shenson and director Richard Lester lavished on the Beatles as a result of their three-picture film deal with United Artists, that they elected to change their previous arrangements. However, the collective decision to do it themselves evolved out of John's idea that they were somehow being ignominiously used by the masters.

That all this transpired *after* Brian Epstein's death is another example of the talent he displayed for making good deals on their behalf. Albert Brodax, producer and co-writer on *Yellow Submarine*, recalls the numerous submissions of treatments on the project, only to have such top writers as Ernie Pintoff and Joseph Heller rejected by Brian for some odd reason. Recalling his frustration with being fobbed off, Brodax says on one occasion he grew so cross that he threatened to assault Brian Epstein.

And yet, Brian's capacity for equivocating until a project was precisely right is precisely *why* the Beatles charade prevailed for as long as it did without confrontation.

It is no mere accident that the Beatles' persona emerged, stylishly reinforcing the wit and pith of their concert personalities. All this had to do with packaging the finest unit to be had: putting together writers, directors and producers to project an extension of the

Beatles myth created by John and generated by Epstein for mass consumption.

As offhand and offbeat as they seemed, the Beatles were cleverly conceptualized and promoted to the public, and whilst produced miles away, they were as carefully scripted and publicized as anything made at the Hollywood Dream Factory. In my interview with producer Walter Shenson at his Beverly Hills office, he admits that what we got in *A Hard Day's Night* and *Help* were *romanticized* versions of the Beatles. 'There is no law that says we have to show all the warts,' he told me, adding, 'I certainly didn't want to be responsible for disillusioning these little girls who were screaming their heads off at concerts by showing the Beatles *not* in a good light.'

Rebelling against commercial pressures, the group, displaying contempt for the traditions of film and film images, repudiated the ideals which had been fashioned by the experts, electing to make their own films a lot closer to what they perceived to be 'the truth'.

This effort consisted of three ventures – the first being the television film *Magical Mystery Tour*, released by NEMS owing to their failure to get proper distribution. The second was *Let It Be*, the last film of their three-picture United Artists deal, produced by Apple. The last, *Yellow Submarine*, produced by Apple, involved the Beatles mainly in marketing and promotion.

Had Brian been alive at the time the Beatles made *Magical Mystery Tour* he surely would have encouraged them to use a professional scriptwriter, director, cinematographer and producer, rather than allowing the Beatles to do it all themselves. What transpires is not only a piece of technically inadequate film-making, but a bit of celluloid which, once again, allows for a glimpse beneath the veil of the true collective Beatles psyche without benefit of expertise by the 'suit and tie' men. Left to their own devices, the Beatles demonstrate that their film-making was uniformly self-indulgent in the pursuit of experience.

There are a few bits which even the British censor had asked to be removed. Judging from what was left in, the excisions must have been excessive indeed. For those who did not see the film, let me recap on the high points – Ringo cuddling up to a woman whose sole distinction is that she is obese; John, a singing waiter, shovelling a heap of vomit upon a customer; and John and George getting it off at a strip show.

Without the professionals to write their material, the Beatles' output was patchy; and whilst we get to glimpse the unorthodox sides of their natures in diversionary episodes such as *Magical Mystery Tour*, for the most part 'the Beatles' was a well-conceived act articulating high-minded sentiments and ideals aided by Brian Epstein, Walter Shenson, George Martin, Albert Brodax and others wise in the ways of the marketplace.

Bridling against this phoney charade, Lennon elected to go his own way. But when he was allowed to ride unharnessed, he rode himself roughshod into the ground. The course pursued after Brian's death and in tandem with Yoko Ono is more truly reflective of John's nature, but it is a coarse, crass, rude, belligerent image previously confined to his private life.

An interesting observation on the buoyancy of the Beatles' cinematic image came from reading that anti-heroic playwright Joe Orton actually became involved in developing a script for them; and what is more, that the script was a 'blue' look at the boys at a time when they could do no wrong.

Orton says: 'Basically the Beatles were getting fed up with the Dick Lester type of direction. They want dialogue to speak. Also they are tired of actors like Leo McKern stealing scenes. Difficult this as I don't think any of the Beatles can act in any accepted sense. . . .'

Having been hired by Walter Shenson to punch up a script which was being considered as the follow-up vehicle to *Help*, Joe Orton describes how they discussed and evaluated a number of ideas, such as *The Three Musketeers*. '"Oh, no," I said, "that's been done to death." "Brigitte Bardot wanted to play Lady de Winter," he said. "She's been done to death as well," I said.'

Observing Shenson's paranoia about projecting the right image, Orton recounts that he 'was most concerned to impress me that the boys shouldn't be made to do anything in the film that would reflect badly on them'.

None the less, *Up Against It*, conceived for the Beatles and derived out of his perception of their collective personality, is controversial: finding the boys *in flagrante*, in dubious political activity, dressed as women, committing murder, being put in prison and committing adultery.

Incredibly, the film was set to go and would have but for Orton's suicide; producer Shenson failed to get a suitable person to rewrite the script.

The Beatle most significant as a film star is, of course, Ringo

Starr, while it was John Lennon who first embarked upon a solo career in a minor role in *How I Won the War* and Paul McCartney who, to my mind, has the undeveloped potential of a Nigel Havers or a James Stewart.

Undoubtedly, the way the Beatles were greatest was collectively, and the fact that they didn't generate a succession of films of the *A Hard Day's Night* calibre is sad in retrospect since there is so little of their product in film archives. And yet, at the Beatles convention in Liverpool, members of the group's own former coalition debunked their film potential as marginal. The fact is that both films, though low-budget, have generated vast fortunes for United Artists, Walter Shenson and the Beatles, both in reissue and on transfer to video cassettes, discs and so on.

The origin of the United Artists deal, of astonishing simplicity, derives from the company wanting to get hold of the music rights to the soundtrack, and to this end they cooked up the red herring of making a film. Conceived as a throwaway, the film, unnamed at the start, was given a limited £200,000 budget and a six-week shooting schedule (6a.m. to 8p.m.) commencing in March 1964, and premiering in London on 6 July that year.

The London première, with Princess Margaret in attendance, was a bit of a non-starter. The Beatles had been holding out for a Liverpool show reminiscent of *Gone with the Wind*'s Atlanta première or the Southern locale where *Steel Magnolias* was first shown. United Artists' head of sales and marketing for north-west England, Max Nathan, a Menlove Avenue neighbour of John Lennon, recalls the fuss made over where the première was to be held.

'When I saw a preview in London of *A Hard Day's Night* I said to my boss, "What a wonderful opportunity. Let's hold the première in Liverpool – the place of their birth. I think I can arrange a civic reception because the Lord Mayor is a fellow with whom I grew up. I will organize it. You get the okay." So he said, "Marvellous idea, Max. You go and do it."

'Two or three days later he calls me up and says, "Max, I've got a bit of disappointing news. You can have your première. But I'm afraid it won't be the *world* première, because Brian insists upon the world première being in London."

'What had happened was my boss had mooted my idea to Brian. Brian would under no circumstances let anyone take any kudos or glory where the Beatles were concerned. Although he loved my idea he wasn't going to let me get the credit.

He made the right moves, oh yes. But the ideas had to come from him.'

Hired by United Artists as producer was Walter Shenson, who had lived in London since 1955 and was noted for his ability to deliver small films on time and within budget.

Recalls Shenson, 'I had made a small comedy called *The Mouse on the Moon* in 1963 for United Artists, having a few years before that made a very successful comedy with Peter Sellers called *The Mouse That Roared* for Columbia Pictures. Because of making *The Mouse on the Moon* the United Artists producer in London (David Picker) knew me as a competent producer of low-budget British comedies, and they asked me if I would produce a film for them. Normally an independent producer approaches the distributor with a package or a script in order to get the money to make the films. But they asked me if I would make the film. And I said if I liked the script, I would. I said, "What do you have?" And they said they had nothing. All they had was an idea to make a film with the Beatles.

'As you can imagine, being a man a generation older I said, "Why would you want to do that?" Those boys with the long hair and the loud music. Although my own kids were playing the records, and obviously one could not avoid the fact that the Beatles were popular in England at this time.

'And they said, "We can work out a deal with the publishers of the Beatles music and the Beatles management so that United Artists Records, an American company, would get the soundtrack album distribution rights." This was probably the first time that a film was made for the express purpose of getting a soundtrack album.

'I said, "That is a noble enough reason. What do you want me to do?" And in essence they gave me a mandate not to spend more than £200,000, to make sure that the Beatles showed up in the morning and to have enough music in it for the album. In other words – to make whatever I wanted.'

Shenson owns the full copyright to *A Hard Day's Night*, which reverted to him in 1979, fifteen years after the film had been made, and a shared copyright with the Beatles to *Help:* revenue from both has made him a multi-millionaire, ensuring that he never has to work again. Yet he chooses to remain a vital part of the motion picture business, jockeying for deals in the heart of Beverly Hills at his office on El Camino Drive, across the road from the Beverly Wilshire Hotel.

Peering at a photograph of himself deep in conversation with John Lennon snapped on the set of *A Hard Day's Night* summons up Shenson's recollections of that first meeting with the Beatles.

'The first step was for me to meet the Beatles' manager, Brian Epstein. He said, "Do you have an office?" I said, "Yes, I have a small office in Mayfair on Shepherd's Market and Hertford Street." He said, "Why don't I bring the boys over?" I said, "Fine." I had a very young English secretary, and when I told her that the Beatles were coming in she was a nervous wreck. She got biscuits and tea ready and cokes and all that stuff.

'On the appointed day Brian Epstein showed up but not the Beatles. He said, "I don't know where they are. They still all live in Liverpool but we do have a flat in Mayfair. I can't get them on the line. It is engaged. We'll just have to arrange this meeting when I can get them all together. I'm just going to have to go and look for them. We have an appointment out at EMI Studios at Abbey Road, where another group I am managing is recording a Beatles song, and the boys want to be present at that recording."

Perceptibly thrilled by the memory, Shenson recounts, 'So I said, "Why don't I go with you?" Brian replied, "That would be marvellous." So we jumped into a taxi and stopped at the flat in Green Street, Mayfair, and sure enough the Beatles were just coming out of the building, hailing a taxi. They piled into ours, and that made six of us in a London taxi which only seats four.

'We went to Abbey Road. It was an experience for me. John and Ringo were aged twenty-three and Paul and George were aged twenty-one. They asked the driver to stop at every corner because there was a newspaper with some screaming headline. Beatlemania was going on at the time. And these kids were just delightful. It all registered and I said, "This we have to capture on film."

'We arrived at Abbey Road and we found a vacant office and I sat down with the fellas. I guess Brian had briefed them and told them who I was. I guess they were impressed with the fact that I had made a comedy with Peter Sellers. They were fans of Peter's. I think one of them, it might have been Paul, said, "Who will direct this film?" I said, "This young American who lives in London," as I was living in London, "called Richard Lester, who directed all the Goon television shows." They said, "Oh, get him." It was the key word. I just knew what they would go for. They wanted to meet Dick and I said I'd arrange that. John took out his little pocket diary and he said they were going to be doing some broadcasting for the BBC in some theatre, and if we could come down a couple of days from then and have tea in the canteen, I could introduce Dick to them. I did that. And they got on well, because Dick has a marvellous sense of humour.'

Since the Beatles, particularly John, had got the reputation of being shrewd businessmen, I asked Shenson if there was any contention over contractual details.

'I think all the Beatles always had to be a little bit on guard at that time – at the height of their careers – about people moving in on them wanting tee-shirt rights and that sort of thing. And when they saw that I was just wanting to get on with making movies and had another life of children and another world that wasn't built around the Beatles, they relaxed. Their manager took care of all that and it didn't dawn on me to say, "Can I have these merchandising rights?" I am not the best businessman in the world, but I do think that I am a good movie producer. I shared in none of the record profits, only in the movie itself.'

Alun Owen, a Liverpudlian 'kitchen sink' dramatist hailing from the working class, wrote the script, which was to be nominated for an Academy Award. The idea was to write about people who are 'prisoners of their own success'.

Recounts Shenson, 'When Alun Owen started to write the script, he said to Dick Lester and me, "What am I going to write about?" We said, "You are going to do an exaggerated day in the life of the Beatles." I had heard that the Beatles said something like "We don't know where we are. When we are in a concert we are in a room. Or if we are here, we are there." We sent Alun, who hadn't met them, up to Dublin where they were doing a concert, and let him come back and tell us.'

That Lester failed to win an Oscar is truly lamentable, since the film captures for posterity the magic and myth of Beatlemania at its height. 'We were *not* making a documentary,' protests Shenson. 'There *was* a documentary which we later saw which had a similarity by the Maysles Bros. They had a train and we had a train, but only because it is obvious if you have something reflecting the Beatles they go on trains.'

Mildly defensive when confronted by the claim that he sanitized the Beatles' image, Shenson objects, 'We didn't want to sanitize the movie. If that movie were made in Hollywood it wouldn't be as good as it was today. One of the things I was grateful for was that we were making the movie six thousand miles away from Hollywood. The idea was *not* to make a Hollywood film in Britain.'

When pressed, Shenson admits that he set out to make a family film. 'United Artists knew that I was bright enough to make a film for the audience that was there for the Beatles – kids, pre-teenagers and teenagers.

'There is no law that says we have to show *all* the warts. I used my own discretion and taste. The boys smoked a lot – cigarettes. I somehow felt that was not the best image for little kids to see their idols smoking all the time. I didn't censor them in any way, but slyly, every time they were about to make a take, I'd take the cigarettes out of their mouths and say to Dick Lester, "Start shooting."'

Conversely, many of the un-Hollywoodisms which rankled with film executives were retained on account of Shenson's perseverance, contributing to the film's overall cinema verité style. These objections focused upon three areas: the fact that it was shot in black and white; that a hand-held camera was used; and that the dialogue was incomprehensible.

Shot in black and white because the process for shooting colour with a hand-held camera had not yet been perfected, the idea was mooted by Lester who queried Shenson about it. ' "How would you feel about a hand-held camera?" I replied, "I think it is right – absolutely perfect for this thing."'

Nevertheless it scared the pants off UA executives, who rang up hysterically after having seen an early print. 'They wondered if I was aware that an arc-light flashed right into the lens of the camera (when Paul McCartney was singing his solo on the TV sound stage). I said, "It took us all morning to set that up so that it would do that." They thought we didn't notice it.'

Rhapsodizing about the shot, Shenson describes, 'Dick had the camera swing 360 degrees on the solo of Paul McCartney up very close. It is one of the most artistically designed shots in the film. There is a flash and then Paul goes instantaneously into silhouette. There is lovely camera work by the cinematographer and his crew. And Dick knew what he wanted. I encouraged them to do it. But Hollywood didn't want to know.'

Executives who saw the rushes found the dialogue singularly off-putting. 'I said it is difficult on ears who are not used to the northern accent. But that is the way they talk, and we didn't want to show the Beatles in a phoney light. That is the charm of the movie. We captured the Beatles as they are.

'These were English executives,' Shenson emphasizes, 'and they were saying – "We are going to have to revoice Ringo Starr. Nobody understands a word he is saying." I said, "Not a chance. This is what we bought." But they thought that his Liverpool accent wouldn't be understood.'

Nevertheless each of the Beatles had to do his share of 'looping' (or re-recording film dialogue), and whether or not additional weight was levied against Ringo, one bitter exchange when they were filming *Help* is recounted by Shenson.

'I remember one time when an assistant director told Ringo that he would be free the next day. He made some personal plans. The man who was creating the title sequence of *Help* said, "I see you don't need Ringo for what you are doing tomorrow. I want to use him for the title sequence – a couple of shots I have to make." I said, "All right, I'll tell the assistant director." So I told him, "Tell Ringo he has to work tomorrow." He said, "You better tell him, because he is planning to take the day off."

'I found him sitting in the back seat of a limousine talking with Paul very seriously. I said, "Excuse me, Ringo. They need you tomorrow." And he says, "Piss off." I said, "Get it off your chest." I know when something is bothering somebody and it is not me. If I am going to be the butt of that problem I will handle it. Paul was very embarrassed. He said, "He didn't mean that." I said, "It's okay. What's the matter? What's bothering you, Ringo?" And he said, "Oh, I was told I'd have the day off." I said, "Look, you are needed for the schedule tomorrow. The schedule is tight." He said, "Well, I won't come in until 3p.m." I said, "Fine." Let him have a little victory and I will still get the job done. Whereas the assistant director would probably have said, "If you aren't in by 11a.m., forget it."

'Next day when he came in he came over to me and said, "I am very sorry for what I said yesterday. You don't deserve it." I said, "Forget it. It's okay. We all have to blow off once in a while."'

Looping was easiest for John, about whom there was the least resistance: his lilting drawl, southern Liverpool in origin, as opposed to Ringo's northern Dingle accent, being amongst his primary attractions.

'I was taking each of the Beatles and doing the looping at night while Dick was shooting during the day, because we were on a tight schedule. So it was the night I was with John. Just the two of us were alone and we were at Twickenham Studios running these loops, clarifying a line one at a time. All the John loops. All of them were good. He had the rhythm. These guys loved the "technical" parts of filming. John was getting a kick out of it. All new and fresh. John knew what we were after. I'd say, "That's a good reading. Play it back. Next."'

It is amazing how incredibly good the Beatles were at playing comedy, without benefit of coaching or formal training. When you consider the performance in films of Cliff Richard (whose *Summer Holiday* flick is run to distraction) or Billy Fury – Tommy Steele is the only contender for stardom – the Beatles suddenly seem worthy of their success at the box office.

Appreciating the extent of this distinction, Shenson highlights the talent of the boys to be themselves. 'Any trained actor will tell you that the hardest thing to be is yourself. Peter Sellers used to say to me, "Walter, I'll play any role but do not ask me to play Peter Sellers. I want to hide behind make-up. I'll play an old man. I'll play a woman. Give me another accent." And conversely it is the other way around with the Beatles. Can you imagine the Beatles playing anything but themselves? It is pretty hard. Furthermore the audience cannot separate that.'

He pauses, 'Lawyers, agents and others have asked me to make films with their groups, and I have said, "You're asking me to catch lightning in a bottle twice. The Beatles had personalities. The first day's rushes that I looked at, I wasn't paying attention to the dialogue or the direction or the music. Just them. And you can't keep your eyes off them. They had "screen presence". Body language.'

Written off as a low-budget, inconsequential flick aimed at exploiting the youth market, the charming and artless film Dick Lester was creating was ignored by UA until the boys exploded on *The Ed Sullivan Show*, America's Sunday night prime-time television programme, watched by 73 million viewers.

'I got a phone call from New York from the executives at United Artists the morning after *The Ed Sullivan Show*, and all of a sudden it dawned on them that Walter Shenson was making a picture for them and 6 million Americans have now seen the Beatles. They must have said, "My God, we are on to something. Get a hold of the producer and make sure he is doing it right." So they called me and said, "How are you coming with it? Will you finish on time?" I said, "Everything is in order. Don't worry." They almost said, "If you need more money, don't worry about it."'

UA's myopia in recognizing what it had got prevailed until the very end when, after the first weekend of the film's release, they recovered the whole of their investment, plus interest, as well as the cost of the film, distribution charges and marketing costs.

'When I sent UA in New York the first cut, having brought the picture in on time and just under budget, they said, "We have an important question to ask you. Do you think the Beatles are going to last?" I said, "I haven't a clue. Why ask me?" They said, "Well, do we put out a lot of prints of this film and cash in on their popularity, or do we take our time and book it wherever we want?" I said, "I'm not a distributor. I don't know. I think the movie is good." Prints in those days were very inexpensive. Advertising was inexpensive. I said, "You have nothing to lose. Why don't you put out a lot of prints? And you'll be covered in case the Beatles don't last." They put out several hundred, and I think it holds the record for that company for the fastest recoupment of the investment.'

A Hard Day's Night surfaced as the film's title almost when they were ready to wrap – for weeks the movie had been called nothing less or more than *Beatles One*. Recalling the panic to find the right title, Shenson recounts frantic calls from UA's New York publicity department asking, 'What is the name of the movie going to be?' '"I don't know," I'd say. "Call it *Beatles One*. I don't know." They said, "How can we publish without a title?" I said, "I'm making the movie. I've sent you a rough synopsis of what the thing is." "Well," they said, "we can't get anything out of it."'

He pauses, 'John and I used to sit and talk quite often – just the two of us in this canteen or commissary at Twickenham Studios during the lunch break, and then we'd go back to the film. And one day he said to me, "Have you ever heard Ringo misuse the English language? I'll give you an example. We'd do a record session until 4 or 5a.m. and the next day when we'd meet Ringo would say, "That was a hard day's night." I said, "That is so descriptive. That would make a good title." John said, "Why not?" I said, "Hey, guys, listen to this." I ran it by Dick. They all said, "That's it. We don't have to think about it any more."

'I called New York and they said, "What? What does that mean?" I said, "Everybody here likes it." I said, "Ask the secretaries in the office. Ask the office boys. Ask the kids." They called me back and said, "Everybody loves it."'

Shenson's deal with the Beatles consisted of them not only appearing in the film but also, and more importantly, writing a new score for the movie, which would be intercut with the storyline. Some of the songs would be sung on camera, others in the background.

Consequently, with the advent of the title came the responsibility to write yet another new song – a task which appeared to daunt Lennon who, it is presumed, did not *like* to compose.

Recounts Shenson, 'I said to John, "You know they accepted *A Hard Day's Night*. Do you know we don't have a song called 'A Hard Day's Night'? What kind of a producer would I be to put out a film called *A Hard Day's Night* with the Beatles and *not* have a title song?" He said, "What do you want?" I said, "You and Paul *have* to write me a song." He said, "Oh, oh, Wal. No." I said, "We gotta have it." He said, "What do you want?" I said, "A hard day's night until I come home to you." He said, "Where will you put it? We've finished all that." I said, "Over the titles. The scene where the kids are chasing you. You don't have to sing it on camera." "Okay, okay."

'We finish our looping session at 10p.m. and get into his car and drive from Twickenham into London. John said to the driver, "Hurry up and take me home before you take Walter home. I have to do some work." I said, "I'll see you tomorrow, We're still shooting." "Fine." "Goodnight." "Goodnight."

'That was 10p.m. at night. I am on the set at 8.30a.m. talking to the director, and the assistant director comes up and tells me that John wants to see me in his dressing room. So I go in there. John is there with Paul. They've got a little matchbook cover and written on it are all the lyrics to 'A Hard Day's Night'. *That* is writing a song on demand. I called George Martin and said I needed another song recorded. He said, "Uh, uh, uh." And I said, "Yes. It's called 'A Hard Day's Night'. When can they record it?" He said, "Tomorrow night. We've got time." The next day they handed me the tape. It was a Number One hit song.'

An interesting aside to Shenson's account of the origin of the title song is rendered by John Junkin, who played the part of Shake, one of the two roadies in the film. Partying with the boys at the London clubs after the day's shoot, Junkin recounts that Lennon was indeed partying the night he wrote the song. 'We'd be together in the studio from 6a.m. to 8p.m. and then I'd meet them again at the club. John used to go out to clubs until 3a.m.'

So when did he write 'A Hard Day's Night'?

'He had an incredible facility,' declares Junkin. 'Once the idea was there – bang!'

Although Shenson was closest to John, he has the distinction of introducing George to Pattie Boyd (an extra in the film) and occasionally socializing with Paul: one engagement crystallizing the extent of Beatlemania at its peak.

'One night at the end of shooting, everybody was going home and I could see that Paul hadn't connected for the evening. I knew that he was living with Jane Asher and her mother in Wimpole Street. He kept saying, "What are you doing tonight?" Everyone had something to do. I said, "What's the matter, Paul? You loose tonight?" I think he was twenty-one years old. His girlfriend was seventeen years old. I said, "My wife and I are going out to a friend's house for dinner, and I am sure they would love to have the two of you come. Why don't I pick you and Jane up at Jane's house at 7p.m.? You'll be our guests, and I am sure my host won't mind.

'So I quickly called this guy, who is a bachelor friend of mine who wrote *A Funny Thing Happened on the Way to the Forum* – Burt Shevelove. Burt is very social in London. So I called him. He had rented Oliver Messel's house, uncle to Tony Armstrong-Jones [Lord Snowdon, then married to Princess Margaret]. Burt was very grand and the show was on. He always had celebrities over there. So I knew it would be all right.

'I called and asked if I could bring Paul McCartney and his girlfriend. He said, "Can you bring them? My God, it'll be the social hit of all time." Nobody was going to top a Beatle, except maybe all four.

'So I picked them up – these two kids – with my wife, and I took them to this party. There were celebrities all over the place – Joan Sutherland, the famous opera star, and people like that. Of course Paul dominated the whole evening, not because he wanted to but because he was Paul McCartney. Paul and Joan Sutherland enveloped each other for the whole evening. And I was trying to be social with the young lady – keeping her with my wife and me. But she knew what she was doing. Joan Sutherland asked Paul to autograph something for her teenage daughter. It was very sweet.'

Shenson's friendship with John, although more casual, was a lot closer; Lennon often dropped into the producer's office for a chat.

'I think I recognized in John an interest in people like me, a generation older – in his mind a Hollywood film producer from California and a totally different background. He was very curious. We talked a lot. He would come by my office by himself without the other Beatles and we would talk about many things. We would chat and discuss our films. He would come up to my office to ask how it was going and look at all the film cuttings from America which were sent to me by our distributors. Apparently our critics saw some symbolism and allegory and things like that in the movie. It gave John a big giggle, because he said, "Didn't we just make a little comedy?" I said, "Of course we made a little comedy, but if these people want to read something into it, why not? It gives them something to write about." He didn't like pretension, and that was pretentious. He had found a friend in an older man. It was just that simple, and the more we worked together the more he realized that I was a professional.'

Legend proliferates about the group's inveterate clannishness. Was Shenson ever the odd man out? 'I was very much aware that if they wanted to get together and discuss somebody and exclude them from the conversation, they had a shorthand of their own. You could be standing there and you might as well have been a hundred miles away. If you were insensitive to it you would make a fool out of yourself. If you were sensitive you would walk away. You did not want to be pushy. You let them lead as far as a social relationship. You know when people like you and when they don't like you.'

Aggression only surfaced after Shenson's relationship with the Beatles on *A Hard Day's Night* and *Help*. 'I think it was Paul who went on record as saying, "We don't *need* Walter Shenson. We don't *need* Richard Lester. We will go on and do our own things." We said, "Fine." The marvellous thing is that Paul has come around that. Today, as we are sitting here talking, Dick Lester is filming the Wings tour.

'I do remember John saying after we made *Help* that the Beatles were merely puppets and all the other actors in the thing were strong. It wasn't true. In casting the other parts we tried to get the best people available – the very best – Shakespearean actors like Leo McKern. England is just loaded with talented performers. Why not get them in the film? I never made a film where the main actor's ego wasn't such that he said, "Get the best people you can for the supporting roles. I will work harder to stay up with them.""'

And yet, in spite of the grumbling and the bitching, one takes

Lennon's point. Shenson recounted: 'Did you see the film *Imagine* where John is yelling at some lady journalist, "You want it to be yeh-yeh *A Hard Day's Night*?" He wasn't referring to the film in a derogatory way. He was saying, "Look, I am a different person. I have changed. It's ten years. Twenty years. Twenty-five years later. I have different attitudes. Stop hanging on to the past." He has the right to do what he wants. But the question is whether the public responds to it. And I agree with you, that it is far more pleasant to see John running around in *A Hard Day's Night* than what he did to himself later on. And you and I and the audience have our right to like one thing instead of another.'

Although afterwards complaining about the working environment on *Help* – the location (the Bahamas – ugh!) and the actors – filming appeared to commence on a harmonious note. 'They appeared to have a ball. We had fun!' insists Shenson. 'It was nice. They were not as satisfied with the movie as they were with *A Hard Day's Night*. I had the feeling that they were looking for things. We weren't there long – a couple of weeks at the most. And then we went to the Austrian Alps. Fun in the snow. I think they were let down with the film itself.'

He continues, 'Touring had ceased to interest them. They were getting fed up. It was physically hard and dangerous. They were getting mobbed. It was getting to the point where they were looking forward to coming back to London to start the second film. The first one had been such a pleasurable experience. But a successful experience. Now they were coming back to their "other" family – that is me and their film family. The crew. And Twickenham Studios. I think they were looking forward to that. We kept the crowds away or inaccessible. And they are quick studies. They learned on *A Hard Day's Night* why a director asked this or that from them. They were eager to get back to us to do another film. We were good guys to work with.'

The UA deal called for the boys to do three films – the third picture being the proverbial straw that broke the camel's back.

'John was the spokesman, the spiritual leader of the Beatles. There is no question,' recounts Walter. 'They wanted to keep progressing. Unlike Elvis, who made 'Elvis in the Army' [*GI Blues*] and 'Elvis in Hawaii' [*Blue Hawaii*], they wouldn't do that. They made *A Hard Day's Night*. Now the next one cannot be another day in the life of the Beatles. I said, "Fine. We'll make it an adventure. We will make it a movie-movie. And we'll film in colour instead of black and white. So we did *Help*."'

Third time around they wanted to do something different again. 'So I said to John,' recalls Shenson, '"You are a writer. You are a published poet. You come up with an idea." John said, "Walter, I don't know what we can do. Do we have to be the Beatles?" I said, "*You* invented the Beatles. I think you are always going to be the Beatles." He said, "We have been talking for an hour and you haven't called me John and I haven't called you Walter once." I said, "I can call you Stanley and you are still going to be the Beatles, and there is still going to be Beatles music in the movie. I don't know how we can make a film with you not being the Beatles."'

Discarding several ideas before deciding to produce a cinematic account of the *Let It Be* album sessions, the boys discussed any number of other projects including *A Talent for Loving* (to which they bought the rights) and *The Three Musketeers*. 'John thought it was a lousy idea,' says Shenson. 'I agreed with him. Although Dick Lester made it with others. It would have been a good idea. But they thought it was a little on the nose – a little bit obvious.'

Negotiating to extricate himself from any obligation to produce *Let It Be*, Shenson claimed a small percentage, thus leaving the Beatles free to do their own film – to employ their own crew and get their own financing. 'They got a television director – a good one – and they made it. It was not scripted. In the film was Yoko. In the film was Linda. To me, and to Beatles fans, it was a sad film, because one detected the breaking up of the camaraderie. The die-hard Beatles fans were uncomfortable watching the film. The darlings that they once were were the darlings no more. I am certainly not one to blame the women for coming into it and causing it. But the die-hard fans would have loved to see them be single and stay together forever.'

Of all the actors Wilfred Brambell, playing Paul's scrupulously clean old grandfather, an idealized version of the actual father about whom Brian Epstein was ashamed on account of his drink problem, is my favourite in *A Hard Day's Night*. The two roadies, Norm and Shake, come in as strong seconds.

Screenwriter Owen declined to model the characters on the real roadies, Malcolm Evans and Neil Aspinall, explaining that he didn't get to know them all that well, and substituted the personalities of two of his own buddies from the acting world – John Junkin and Norman Rossington – turning what in reality could be very sour exchanges into a wistful camaraderie. Much of what Rossington and Junkin describe as off-camera remarks between the Beatles and their roadies whilst in production, hitherto unreported by the press, contrasts profoundly with what occurs on camera.

Hailing from the Allerton-Woolton southern area of Liverpool, home to John and Paul, Rossington lacks the guttural Scouse dialect indigenous to the north. A classically trained actor and former member of Lord Olivier's Old Vic Company at Chichester, Rossington follows in a tradition of the great Liverpudlian actors incuding Rex Harrison and Basil Rathbone. Having been in theatre and television since 1950, he began making films in 1955, eight years prior to his legendary role in *A Hard Day's Night*.

'I never even read the script,' recounts Rossington, talking to me about the film's ascent to something of a cult favourite a quarter of a century after it was made. 'They just asked me to do it and I said, "Yes, please." "Would you like to do a film with the Beatles?" "Yes, please." It was as simple as that.

'I don't think anyone realized that it would be such a huge success and the classic it was. I remember the first day of shooting we started off at Marylebone Station in London (doubling for Liverpool's Lime Street). We were shooting on the train as we were supposed to be coming from Liverpool down to London. It was totally hush-hush – top secret. Nobody knew about it. We all piled on to this train, got up steam, got outside London and each station from London to Somerset – bang!! with kids screaming and shouting. That was great fun.'

Did he find them intimidating?

A lingering memory of Rossington when he was a 'big TV star' returning to Liverpool to open a bowling alley broke the ice: Paul McCartney recounted having actually met him just before the group had scored their 'Please, Please Me' hit. 'On the first day of shooting Paul McCartney said to me, "You don't remember me, do you, Norm? You came to Liverpool last year to take part in the opening of that new bowling alley. You came back afterwards with your girlfriend and you were bowling. You remember two cheeky lads in the bowling alley?" I said, "Vaguely." "It was John and me. And I've still got your autograph."

Comparing the boys to a gang reminiscent of the *Our Gang* comedies, Rossington cheers both the cohesion of the unit and the local Liverpool humour and wit. 'There was virtually no outside influence,' he observes. 'They concentrated on the work. The Beatles as a group needed that cohesion. That was part of their strength. The controlling talents were Paul and John.

'They are very Liverpudlian and you have to be born in Liverpool to understand them. A lot of the Liverpool character is aggressive and funny.

'When I became an actor you had to speak with a southern English accent. But when the Beatles came along it was fashionable to speak Scouse. They could do what they liked.'

Confirming the general impression that they were four naturally gifted comedians wholly without formal training or coaching, Rossington recalls observing during the course of the filming their artless lack of technique.

'It was their first film and it was a new technique and a way of working. They didn't realize they could alter the script if they wanted to. When they realized that, whoopee! – away they went. They thought that you had to say what was written down. Once they realized that you could ad lib – write your own dialogue – they were away. Richard Lester encouraged their enormous creativity. Most of it was written apart from the actual visual stuff which Dick did. The press conference was ad libbed.'

He continues, 'Lester got on well with the boys. He is a great fun fellow who absolutely adores Liverpool. He was exactly the right director. "Go ahead, lads. Do it." And they did.'

Was the opening scene rehearsed, since various sources disagree?

'Absolutely rehearsed. They were wearing make-up. You can't have the train pulling into the station six times without knowing what is going to happen. The fans were paid extras. By that time they were starting to act a bit.'

Intended as another rock 'n' roll musical along the lines of *Summer Holiday*, the film was quickly declared a major release. Rossington recounts the feedback from Hollywood after they had seen the rushes. 'It was intended as a small-budget film. And very soon the word came back – Walter wanted some extra dough – "You can have what you like."'

Reflecting on the aftermath when Lennon disparaged the Beatles' films, Rossington surmises, 'I don't think it was as enjoyable or creative on *Help*. I don't think it had the unique quality which we did. I think it was a mistake to go abroad. They should have stayed in England and done one in Liverpool.

'The combination on *A Hard Day's Night* was incredible. It was unique to get a producer like Walter Shenson, a director like Richard Lester, four lads like the Beatles and the rest of us.'

Stars versus director?

Despite, or perhaps because of, the film's cohesive brilliance tending to obscure the singular performances of John and the other Beatles, Lennon bit the hand that fed him. 'That was John,' says Rossington. 'He was direct and he spoke his mind. He didn't go out of his way to be diplomatic, and neither should he. One observes the way the boy behaves. He was a strong personality. Together. He knew what he wanted to do. Where he was going. In which direction. How it manifested itself later on one did not know. But he was going somewhere.'

John Junkin got to know them much better, socializing as well as working with the boys. While it was a friendship which continued over the years, particularly with Lennon, the thing almost did not happen: Junkin was nearly passed over for the role of Shake on account of his southern English origins (he was born in the London suburb of Ealing).

He was put up for the part by Alun Owen, who had used him as a role-model for the character of the roadie, but his hiring depended upon the approval of the Beatles. It was therefore with some measure of trepidation, Junkin recalls, that he heard from Owen that 'The boys are very nervous and want to be surrounded by bona fide Liverpudlians.' Recounts Junkin, 'So he said "My advice to you is, from the moment you meet them, 'Speak Scouse'."'

Having initially fooled the boys, it wasn't until Junkin was present at a television recording session a few weeks into filming that the deception was discovered.

'We started filming, and the Beatles were invited on to a live programme called *Ready, Steady, Go*. They said (in Scouse dialect), "Come on along. We'll ask you. Why not?" So I went along to the studios and we were sitting in the Green Room when the producer of the programme came in and, assuming that I was actually the road manager, kept giving me instructions about getting them a Coke. Well, I did it until a lovely lady called Alma Cogan (who died of cancer), whom I knew, came in to the Green Room and said, "Junkin – what are *you* doing in this film? You are about as much a bloody Liverpudlian as I am." I thought, "The whole thing is blown." There was a silence and Lennon said, "Junkin (sounds like funkin'), where exactly *are* you from?" "Actually, John, it's like Liverpool. It's a little suburb outside. It's called Ealing." He looked at me and said, "You bastard." By then they were happy enough with me not to fuss.'

Showing steadfast patience and unerring devotion, Junkin fast became a friend of Lennon's to whom he appealed because, as Lennon himself declared, 'You are one of the few people who argue with me.' 'I was *very* pleased when he said that one night,' recalls Junkin. 'I said, "Why wouldn't I argue with you? When you are talking crap why wouldn't I say you are talking crap?" And he said, "Because it is reaching the stage where I can bang a bent nail into a piece of wood and call it a work of art and people will agree with me." What he said to me was that he wanted people to challenge him. He wanted to write or sing something and for people to say, "John, that's awful."'

Recounts Junkin, 'When I knew him John had opinions and ideas about everything. If you had a discussion with him about politics or religion, John would not take a position and staunchly refuse to budge. John would argue.

Portraying the group as four happy-go–lucky lads who had the time of day for almost anybody – the constable on the beat, a 'bird' on the train, a lady reporter – the film tends to obscure what in reality, and without inference, could be conceived of as exceedingly harsh exchanges. In brief, on occasion the Beatles could be remote and caustic.

Observing Lennon's treatment of the roadies, for instance, Junkin recounts, 'He'd tell one of the roadies to get him a sand-wich, and when they'd come back he'd say, "I didn't want tomato sauce, you stupid bastard. I wanted brown sauce." I could read that line a hundred different ways and it would sound different each time. It was a term of affection, almost. But that was the guy's job.' (Roadie Neil Aspinall currently holds a top job at Apple.)

'I have never heard John being gratuitously nasty to anybody, including the two characters that Norman and I played – Neil and Mal. I heard him get terse. I heard him get bad-tempered. But I never heard him get venomous. But if I took down the lines which John said he would come over as the most unpleasant man in history.

'I remember sitting in the Scala Theatre with Ringo (the TV studio scene). He and I weren't wanted in this particular scene. Somebody had left a pack of cards on a coffee table. He said, "Do you want to play cards?" So we played cards. He said, "I'm sixpence." I said, "Your sixpence and up sixpence." And I won. I won about five consecutive hands. The next time we played Ringo said, "Your sixpence and I'm a million pounds." I said,

"Your million pounds up sixpence." And I beat him. We both laughed. Quote the conversation and Ringo comes out like an arrogant bastard. He wasn't. He was being funny.'

Although he mellowed with time, Lennon was idolized in his prime for his scathing and sardonic wit; Junkin recounts an episode which describes this characteristic. 'We were sitting in the circle of the Scala Theatre and everyone had a late night. John was sitting with his cap down over his eyes, for all intents and purposes asleep. George, Paul and Ringo were sitting around and I was talking to them, and they started reminiscing about early days. Paul I think it was who said, "Do you remember those digs we stayed down in the West Country?" (Apparently they stayed in digs with a very eccentric landlady who had a dog with no legs.) And from under John's hat came the retort, "That's right. She used to take it for a slide every morning." That line was irresistible.

'There was another instance at the same theatre where we were sitting with Lionel Blair and the dancers. It was a beautiful sunny day and we were sitting outside the stage door and there were four or five dancers. We were chatting. And suddenly along the street came a young Negro who looked like burnished copper – slim, twenty years old, beautifully, elegantly dressed up as though he owned the world. And as he walked past the girl dancers, their conversation faded and they watched this wonderful, beautiful man. And before they could speak, John said, "That's all very well. But how would you like your sister to polish one?"

'It wasn't a racist joke. It was just John taking the moment from the girls and converting it and finding a beautiful, very funny line. If John made a comment like that in company and someone took exception I think he would have been mortally upset. John liked to manipulate the moment and the situation and find a funny line.'

Confirming Norman Rossington's observations of the Beatles' strength as a cohesive, secure unit, Junkin describes three instances where they could have been thought rude but where they distanced themselves from the public so as to preserve their safety as well as their sanity.

'We did the train journey from London to Somerset and somebody *always* leaked where they would be when they stopped at a station. And each station was always mobbed with ten or twenty thousand kids. One night towards the end of the week we pulled into Paddington and these kids were there and there were the police. And I said to John, "What do you think would happen if one night you got off the train and policemen weren't there?"

He thought for a minute and he said, "They'd kill us." I said, "Come on. Why would they kill you?" And he replied, "They wouldn't want to kill us, but the thing is at the moment all they want to do is *touch* a Beatle. If the policemen weren't there they'd *touch* a Beatle. And the next ones would want a button or a piece of your jacket. Or your tie. And the next ones would want to *grab* and they'd grab your hair. By the time you got to the back of that crowd you'd be dead." It was very logical. It wasn't manipulative from their viewpoint in any way.'

Another time the Beatles, keen to view Junkin in cabaret with Ronnie Corbett at a club (now closed) called Winston's, suggested that they meet up for a meal at the Beachcomber restaurant in Park Lane's Hilton Hotel before wending their way to the show.

Recounts John, 'Paul wasn't there. He had a stomach upset. Ringo was there with Maureen. George was there with (I think) Pattie Boyd, and John was there with Cynthia. I was there with a girlfriend. We had a meal and suddenly I heard John say, "Oh, God." I said, "What's the matter?" He said, "Look over to your right." And there was a woman with about five kids, giving them pens, pencils and bits of paper. And you knew that the moment she arrived at the table the rest of them would come too.

'The woman came marching towards the table. So I said, "Excuse me. The boys have just ordered a meal and it's about to be served. Would you mind waiting until they have finished?" She looked at me, didn't utter a word to me and turned her eye towards George, Ringo and John and said, "Who do you think you are? . . . These kids want your autograph. It is people like *them* and people like *me* who have put you where you are buying your records." And she harangued them for what I said. And the three of them just sat and slid in their chairs. John, I thought, was going to rise to the bait, but he didn't. And she abused these three because they weren't prepared to give up their meal and give up their privacy and sign.'

Having excused himself, Junkin left early so as to arrange for the Beatles' presence at the cabaret. 'I told the manager: "Arrange for them to get a little bit of protection and you can run the club for a year on the fact that the Beatles have been here." Because they never went to old-fashioned cabaret clubs.'

He continues, 'They came. They watched the show. And the waiters were ignoring the customers and getting their autographs at £25 a throw. It was *horrendous*. I came offstage and there was a message from them saying, 'See you at the Ad Lib.' I went to the Ad Lib, spent the evening with them and the following day I phoned John.

'I was slightly embarrassed by the whole thing. John came to the phone and said, "What do you want?" I said, "I'm just ringing up to say, 'Thank you so much for coming last night.' There was a short pause, and he said something I learned as a child, "Thank you very much for having us." I thought, "How wonderful. No abuse for the treatment they had."'

Having worked as a supporting actor with several international stars, including Peter Sellers, Rex Harrison and Warren Beatty, Junkin surmises that Lennon was the nicest of all. 'In his private life he was gentle, generous and courteous.

'I went out to John's house at Kenwood in Surrey a few times. I can remember sitting in a nice sunny room. Cynthia provided the food. I think it was mostly snacks. A cold lunch. There was wine. And I was most impressed with how he coped – kept his sanity and sense of proportion aged twenty-four when he could go out and perform in front of between twenty and fifty thousand people, go anywhere in the world and be eulogized, meet presidents and popes, say anything, find it quoted in every language in the world – and *still* sit in his living room and behave like a human being.'

Recalling his 'special relationship' with the Beatles, Junkin recalls the VIP treatment he received from the stars at the London gala première of *A Hard Day's Night*, attended by Princess Margaret and Anthony Armstrong-Jones.

'I walked into this room at the Dorchester Hotel. Every big mogul in the business was there: the whole of Universal Studios (United Artists), Princess Margaret and Anthony Armstrong-Jones. It was full. I walked in and I had not seen the boys for months. I was looking around to see where we could find a drink. George detached himself from the group and came over for the sole purpose of introducing me to his mum and dad, not to the VIPs. He had talked to me about home, his mother and father. And when he saw me, he detached himself from all the money and all the power. They were great fun. They were outrageous. But their manners and their courtesy were instinctive and impeccable. They were instinctive gentlemen.'

Catching up with the boys after the completion of *A Hard Day's Night*, Junkin was asked to attend a party at Annabel's to celebrate John's 'unbirthday' party. His account shows a naff side to the oddball Beatles. 'They told me, "We thought it was John's birthday, but then we found out it wasn't John's birthday. So we're having a party *not* to celebrate John's birthday 'cause we already booked the table. We'd like you to come." So I said, "Smashing." They said, "Will you be bringing the girl you brought to our house?" I said, "I think so." So the following night, without any further communication, this girl and I went to Annabel's. There were three other boys and their ladies and George Martin and his lady. As we arrived, George Martin stood up and said, "Hello, John." He said to this girl, "Hello, you must be Pat." She sat down, and in front of her was the drink she had had when she had been at George[Harrison]'s house. This is the way George always behaved. His manners are impeccable. He said, "John is coming. His girl's name is Pat. She drinks vodka and lime."

A completely different portrait of Lennon is rendered by Eleanor Bron, who played the Indian priestess in *Help*, her first film. Whilst the press were conjuring up all kinds of romance between her and Lennon she was fending off what she considered the Liverpool 'machismo' of the boys.

'Looking back, I think in those days that it was difficult for most men to relate to women as friends. They either related to them as "birds" or something else. It was therefore difficult to get to know them. But,' she cautions, 'that is also to do with my own hang-ups coming from a middle-class background.'

And the groupies?

'Girls would literally throw themselves in front of the car as it moved out of Twickenham Studios. Screaming. The boys moved in a convoy. They couldn't move out.

'I was talking once to John in my dressing room and suddenly there was scrambling at the window. A girl was climbing up the window with tears streaming down her face. "John, John." They couldn't move or walk in the street without being besieged. With the Beatles it was often the "older generation" which would insult them and be rude to them and be totally lacking in any kind of courtesy.'

It was Paul who was the most accessible – the one who was willing to make the greatest social effort and make things a little easier. 'I am talking generally when they met people,' observes Bron. 'They were very nice to me. They were never rude.'

Of all the Beatles she was closest to John (with whom she was rumoured to have had an affair, which she denies emphatically). She got to know him chiefly on the set, and recounts that they would chat in between takes or go to the dressing room on those occasions when Lennon had freed himself of his companions.

There was the odd dinner invitation. 'I was having dinner with him once and it was a great escape. You'd use somebody's car and you'd zoom off to this secret café. It was as if we had escaped from this huge machine. They couldn't go anywhere without being pestered. If they went to a restaurant they would be mobbed. They had no privacy.'

So what happened?

'I became very fond of him. He was a few years younger than I, but not that many. You have to know me to understand the way I reacted to him. He wasn't patronizing. It wasn't that he liked dolly birds. It is how you relate to something which isn't that. It just took a bit longer to get into conversation. But I think that is what he was looking for – something longer. I think that is why he met Yoko Ono. Besides,' she hesitates, 'he *was* married to Cynthia, and I had a boyfriend.'

Whilst she categorically denies being the inspiration for the lonely, deluded spinster in the classic Beatles song 'Eleanor Rigby', Eleanor Bron does recount having talked with John about the prospect of having a daughter and calling her Apple. 'So I was very intrigued when they called their company Apple,' she says.

At the start of her career, with journalists from all over the world hurdling barricades to get an interview, the working relationship in the Bahamas was compromised from the outset.

'We thought it was terrifying, awful,' recalls Eleanor, listing the journalists, the heat and the Mafia as sources of dismay. 'You'd ride along the road and see all this squalor, and then there would be these luxurious places run by the Mob. I stayed at the Balmoral Club. The Beatles had a house.

'And this terrible climate. You got off the plane into this hothouse. I could never stand it, partly because my hair used to do strange things. Now it is fashionable for it to do those things.

'The journalists wanted to know more about you than you know yourself. And if they didn't, they'd invent it.'

Wary on account of fabricated rumours of a romance with Lennon, as well as a fake photo of her wearing a bikini, Bron commiserates with John's phobia about the press.

'They were shrewd about people. They detected fakes. They had a kind of Geiger counter and I think they could tell if someone was not worth much. They could give them a hard time until they felt you were worth something. I don't think they had much brief for journalists, really – sniffing around. They want a story and they will concoct one if there isn't one there.'

Recalling the solicitude of Beatles' manager Brian Epstein, who intervened when Eleanor was at a particularly low point and made it easy for her to get from one place to another, Bron talks about the way the Beatles tended to include third parties by implication. 'I have worked with others from similar backgrounds to the Beatles. The way they make contact with an intelligent and attractive woman is to be combative. The Beatles weren't like that. But when there are four of them and one of you, when you are travelling in a car, you talk to each other. And the other person by implication. You can come from an upper-class background and talk directly to a person and be much ruder. Simply they had a lot to talk about with each other.'

Lennon's sense of self-entitlement is nowhere in greater evidence than in his dealings with the despised 'suit and tie' men who helped to create the music and films for which he is credited. At times, he was an arrogant sod: insultingly condescending toward those of equal talents and abilities.

Nurturing the fantasy, bizarrely realized, that he was somehow anointed and invincible, Lennon proceeded upon the belief that he could get away with murder (no pun intended). In this regard he tried to dispose of the third picture in their three-picture United Artists deal by fobbing off the company with a cartoon feature, believing that it was enough to license use of their caricatures and their voices. United Artists disagreed, and in consequence the Beatles embarked upon yet another film venture, *Let It Be*.

Yellow Submarine producer Albert Brodax explains that the cartoon came about simply because the Beatles 'didn't want to do a third picture. They had the idea that they could go to India and leave the work to me. All they had to do was to sign a piece of paper saying that I could use their caricatures and voices that sounded like their voices. And they could go away. They liked that. That's how we got to do *Yellow Submarine*.'

While it is commonly believed that the project evolved spontaneously, it none the less happened out of one of those merchandising gimmicks for which Epstein has been wrongly blamed. Simply, Brodax had optioned the rights to do a Beatles cartoon series for worldwide syndication by King Features, and consequently liaised with the boys – years before the film was ever envisaged – for songs to intercut with the cartoons.

Like the others, he soon discovered their collective abhorrence of work and inclination to delegate to others. Recalls Brodax: 'I couldn't write my story until they sent me a track. We used songs from *Rubber Soul* and *Revolver*. We even animated a Chuck Berry 'Twist and Shout', which they did.

'This was a network show. Sometimes they had to hurry up and write a song. During that production I made seventeen trips back and forth. I commuted a lot to London. That's why I got the Hill Street flat, because I couldn't take it any more. I didn't have to pack a big bag – I had clothes at the other place.

'Once I couldn't find my little overnight bag, so I took a paper bag and put some underwear, aftershave and so on in it. I went directly to EMI Studios. I was really testy because I hadn't slept the night and I had come across the Atlantic. I started screaming, "You are making all the money and all I am doing is going back and forth over the Atlantic." They started mumbling amongst themselves and Paul said, "You're a rich man, baby. Stop bitching." I said, "I'm not bitching. I'm just tired and I want to get some sleep." So a few weeks later they came up with the song: "Baby, You're a Rich Man" – meaning me. "Keeps all his money in a paper bag". That's how "Baby, You're a Rich Man" came about. They got the idea from the incident.'

Although John is credited with conceiving the idea for the film, it actually evolved from a phone call from Ringo Starr. 'In those days you couldn't dial direct. You had to get the operator to get the number. And my daughter was only about five or six years old. So he called. And she'd say, "Hello." And he'd say, "Hello." And then she'd say, "Goodbye." That happened several times. And from that came the idea for the song, "Hello, Goodbye". We were feeding ideas back and forth.

'It was John's idea to do something about the sea of monsters. He'd ring and say, "Wouldn't it be a good idea to have a sea of monsters? No fish. Just monsters. In water." And he'd hang up.'

The transition from television to film was neither natural nor easy, Epstein putting Brodax through his paces until he produced an acceptable film treatment that was approved (ironically enough) moments before he died. 'You could say we made the *deadline*,' smirks Brodax, abashed by the obvious and bad pun.

Whether it was because Lennon objected to the television series use of voices (Americans doing a Liverpool accent) and drawings (unrepresentative of the boys), or from an obstinacy wholly natural to himself, Brian was obdurate about okaying the start of production, although Brodax had invested considerable sums of money in devising treatments by some very renowned writers including Joseph Heller and Ernie Pintoff. The final treatment was conceived by Brodax in tandem with Erich Segal, then a classics professor at Yale, and Jack Mendelsohn, a Hollywood pro skilled at script construction.

Recounts Albert, 'Brian Epstein wasn't the easiest man to get along with. He was difficult. It was all new to him. All this happened very quickly. He didn't know anything about making movies. He didn't understand scripts. And we had to get his approval before we could go ahead. So I hired a lot of people, because I wanted to get it done quickly. Ernie Pintoff wrote a treatment. Joseph Heller wrote a treatment. He rejected them. He rejected them on a silly basis, which had to do with the colour of the cover. He didn't even read many of them. If he didn't like purple that day, purple was out. If Joe Heller was purple, goodbye Joe Heller. It was getting expensive.'

Arranging to meet Epstein to discuss his reasons for having rejected several treatments, Brodax describes how his anger at the delays got the better of him.

'Epstein was a pain in the ass. He had a flat at the time across from Buckingham Palace. I was really upset with him. This was when he was flipping things in the basket because he didn't like the colour of the treatment. He didn't even read the first page. I don't get violent. But I am a boy from Brooklyn, I had just got off a plane, and I don't take that junk. And he was being silly. So I reached over and grabbed him.

'As I was leaving Brian shouted, "Do you know that I live across the street from the Palace? You're not just dealing with anybody!" He kept alluding to his royalty, and I didn't see any royalty in him.' (Epstein said he was distantly related to the royal family through the marriage of Edwina Cassel Ashley to Lord Louis Mountbatten.)

'What I did was I called the William Morris Agency. What I said was that I needed somebody to collaborate with me – somebody about the Beatles' age who is hip; and somebody local – within twenty-five miles of Westport, Connecticut. They said, "We have a man who has never written a whole script before. He is a translator. He wants to write – Erich Segal." ' He afterwards wrote *Love Story*.

'So Erich came down from Yale. He drove down in his big

old Cadillac. He played the guitar. My twin sons thought he was cool. He played Beatles songs. We started to write a script.

'The script was on Brian's bed when he died that day. Scribbled across the title page was: 'Okay, Brian Epstein'.

The recent release by United Artists of a *Yellow Submarine* cassette grossing $4 million in only four months confirms the film's stature as one of the cinematic cartoon masterpieces.

Virtually dumped with the project after the boys had set off for India, Brodax endeavoured to fulfil the level of expectation. In the end the film exceeded this in both sight and sound.

Liverpool poet Roger McGough's excisions of New Yorkisms – substituting a half-dozen throwaway lines indigenous to Liverpool – combined with Erich Segal's pedantry give the film a one-upmanship which, rather than offending, wholly ingratiates.

Adhering to Lennon's personal preference for Liverpudlian voice-overs, Brodax chose people from the boys' home town. 'Physically they were so different from the Beatles they represented. The guy who did McCartney was about 300 pounds. They actually believed they were the Beatles. They called each other by Beatles names.'

An undoubted distinction is the look of the film, which forms a brilliant marriage to the poetry, conjuring up a kind of surreal sophistication. The look is achieved by a process called 'rotoscope', in which you film live actors and then distort and colour the pictures. 'Lucy in the Sky' was all rotoscope – a real girl riding a real horse. Explains Brodax, 'You take a negative, magnify it and the artist draws it. And frame by frame we colour it and distort it and make an impressionistic thing out of it.'

The cartoonist responsible for the job was Heinz Edelmann, a German illustrator teaching in Cologne. Brodax recalls: 'I had seen some graphics that he had done for a German magazine in London at a dentist's office on Harley Street. I called him in Cologne and told him what the project was. He knew about the Beatles. He was very interested and flew to London. We made a deal and he did the artwork.'

He continues, 'He is a shy man. He didn't want much publicity. He tended to work very hard. He was in his early thirties, and just married. He would lock himself in a room for days and smoke cigars. He drank a lot of gin.

'One night he was working very late and had too much gin. We had two whole floors in Soho. I went to look, and Heinz wasn't in his cubicle. I didn't know where the heck he was. It was late – about two o'clock in the morning. Heinz was on the roof. The bobby saw him and thought there was a man going to jump. So they went up there and took him down and he was not all together. And they said, "Where do you live?" He couldn't remember where he lived. So he said, "Take me to my father's place." (He was aged thirty-one and I was aged thirty-nine.) "Take me to Hill Street." (I lived at 49 Hill Street.) And that is where he spent the night.'

Fatigued by the insurmountable task of rotoscoping hundreds of extras used in the crowd sequences, Edelman suffered a heart attack and then returned to university life in Germany.

Viewing a rough cut of the film following their return from India, the Beatles were keen and asked if they could be in it – hence the tag at the end where they briefly appear.

Responsible for four songs in the film, they had fobbed off on Albert three 'rejects' before departing for India, but were required to do a fourth upon their return.

Recalls Brodax, 'Late at night at the studio I was there with George Martin and George Harrison. We wrote this song for which we didn't have a title. And they were waiting to take the tape to UA in New York. It was an abstract, kind of discordant song and we looked at the music sheet which had these notes on. And it said, "Northern Songs" [Paul and John's publishing company]. And so it became, "It's Only a Northern Song".'

He continues, 'They didn't want to come to this recording. They were getting pernickety. George Martin, who used to sit up in his glass booth, said, "The animals are in their cage now. We can start." George Martin is a classically trained musician and he liked to use classical musicians. There is a lot of classical music on the *Submarine* soundtrack. He used several members of the London Symphony Orchestra. And they came in their tuxedos and what not. And this one night we had several members of the LSO and John Lennon was there being himself. Just to be silly, he came in with a beaten-up coronet bugle from the Salvation Army and wanted to play it. And you could hear Ringo's glockenspiel fall over. By indirection we got a very good piece of music. And George Martin kept saying, "What shall we do, Al?" "Let it run." At the end, we used it. It was fine.

'They liked to work at night and they liked to work in the dark with these pin lights. The only thing that was lit were their music stands and instruments and the cubicle which I was in with George Martin.'

Early tensions surfacing on the television series were exacerbated on the film. 'My first talk with them about *Submarine* was in Paul's house in St John's Wood. I remember he had a dog, Martha; a nice English sheepdog. They were all there. Paul was listening to classical music. He had earplugs on and a cassette. But he was able to listen and talk at the same time.

'John was stand-offish toward me, whilst the others were friendly and outgoing. As a matter of fact I tried to bridge it with him one night at the studio. I said, "Liverpool is very much like Brooklyn, where I come from. So you know, I am nobody special. We went the same route." (You could take a Liverpudlian and put him in Brooklyn and he'd feel at home, and vice versa.) "So stop this crap." It was his attitude. He was dismissive of me. He didn't say anything. He walked away.

'John struck me as introverted and really shy. And his shyness expressed itself in his sharp tongue. That was his way of coping.

'John was less co-operative. If I criticized their work, he wouldn't take that. I'd say, "If this is the story you want to tell, maybe you should slant it that way." He wouldn't tolerate any creative interference. Paul would listen. I intruded upon his lyrics, which I shouldn't have done.'

Adds Albert, 'John wasn't as decent as the others. It was as if he was doing me a favour. I should be grateful and show my gratitude. Paul and I would go for a pint. John kept disappearing.'

Faking visibility, a running joke with Lennon, John 'disappeared' at the start of a press conference to launch the cartoon series on network television.

'John did a funny thing there. The press was there, the Beatles, myself and the vice-president of ABC network and our cartoon voices. We had this table full of drinks. The conference went on. The cameras went on. We realized that John was missing. We saw him come in and the door was locked. They wanted to take a picture of all of us and John was missing. I went to look and saw one boot sticking out from underneath the table. And that was John. He did little tricks like that. Paul and Ringo yanked him out. "Sorry, gents." Then he posed for these pictures.'

One explanation for his difficulty in coping might be that during the film his marriage to Cynthia was disintegrating due to his affection for Yoko Ono. 'The first time I met Yoko,' recounts Brodax, 'they were recording "Revolution" that night. She was lying on the piano – not bothering anybody. That was just the way she positioned herself. She's highly under-rated. Avant-garde. She is a bright and talented woman. I can understand what John saw in her. I don't think it is fair that the press has said *she* broke up the Beatles. I don't think she broke them up at all. I think they were tired of each other and they had to go with their own families – their own ways.

'I remember she was all in white, with this mane of black hair flowing down. When we were introduced, she extended her arm.

'She came to the opening with John in 1968 in Piccadilly. All of the Beatles were there, and someone from the Palace. I think it was Prince Charles. We had a big party afterwards.'

The rift came, according to Brodax, because the boys did not want to work together again – an egocentricity appearing to linger, inflaming old wounds and past rivalries. 'Paul is touring with his family and wants to do that. Ringo is off with his wife. And John is not around any more.'

John's compulsion to carve out some sort of identity independent of the caricature created by the experts in fields of rock and film was fulfilled during the nine years he lived in the United States. And while we may cavil about whether his new self was better or worse than the old, it must be said that his personal and public lives more closely dovetailed beginning with his arrival in New York in 1971.

9

Starting Over (It Was Over!)

When John Lennon departed Britain for the United States in September 1971 he did so, he said, because here was a place where he could be treated as someone more than the guy who won the pools, and Yoko as someone more than the woman who married the guy who won the pools. 'In America, we are both treated as "artists".'

The record shows, however, that John's reasons for leaving Britain were infinitely more complex, and whilst occasionally ruminating about returning, he did in one instance fix up a meeting between Allen Klein and Lord Harlech to discuss the issues obstructing that return. The first was his drug conviction which he wanted quashed. The second was his tax reclassification, aimed to put him in a lower bracket.

Neither to my knowledge came to pass, although Christie's recently auctioned one of Lennon's tax returns. It is also common knowledge that the large and sumptuous homes in which he lived were purchased in the company name, including his aunt's Poole Harbour villa, although it is debatable whether all were used for business purposes.

The least romantic time of his life, John's American Period is consumed by two obsessions – politics and money: the sale of Holstein cows and the purchase of farms used as tax shelters. Buying up flats in New York's WASPish Dakota apartment building displayed a blatantly material obsession. In the past he had at least pretended not to care, although he always lived well.

It was Yoko and the lack of respect accorded her not only by John's friends and business associates, but by the media too, which prompted the move. Whilst she will forever be labelled as 'the woman who broke up the Beatles', Lennon may have suffered as a result of his association with her. He may have exclaimed it from the hilltops that his meeting with this female guru allowed him to express those parts of himself previously covert or only partially revealed. However, from the point of view of marketability the union labelled him as 'box-office poison', and DJs virtually refused to play his records. Lennon's verbal exchange with Andy Peebles on 6 December 1980 on the BBC's *The Lennon Tapes* is a tragic commentary on it all. John asks the interviewer why the BBC no longer plays his records. 'They do,' insists Peebles, offering up as testimony John and Yoko's Christmas classic 'Happy Xmas (War Is Over)', reissued every year for the holiday season.

What Lennon himself described to me in interview as the basis of the Beatles' appeal – 'repressed sex' – did not compete with what came out of the closet. And with the exception of a couple of solos or Yoko collaborations which became standards, most of what he did was too obvious. The public simply did not want to know. Repressed gyrations brought women to orgasm, but downright, outright nudity or copulation in a bag, designed to liberate inhibition, were decidedly *outré*.

Forgetting about the quality of the prose (which was substandard), the DJs refused to play his records on principle. And although Lennon pontificated about the music being somehow purer (because less popular) than his Beatles compositions, the truth is that he grovelled lower than ever to compose songs which were commercial.

Pete Bennett, American press liaison for Apple, conferring with radio and TV DJs, provides background on John's purist ethic. We discussed the flap over the *Imagine* video (to promote the album) and why it was tarted up to appeal to the TV hacks, as well as Bennett's ingenuity in promoting as hits both the American re-mixed version of 'Instant Karma' (sending it to Number Three on the charts) and 'Give Peace a Chance' (which sold 800,000 copies). What he couldn't sell was 'Woman Is the Nigger of the World', even though Lennon was determined that it would become a hit. Too political, the song was banned by DJs, who refused to play it. Nevertheless the album *Some Time in New York City* sold about 600,000 copies, according to Lennon; other estimates, however, put the figure lower.

Whilst the Beatles had always been marketed as a heterosexual group – in contrast with the Stones, whose image was androgynous – they were sympathetic to the homosexual population. Lennon himself was alleged to have had affairs with both men and women, and although he never openly admitted it to me, his condemnation of Britain as a land which feeds on a homosexual subculture persuades me at this late stage that he was speaking from experience.

The fact remains he refused to entertain any of his old cronies and continued in his vehement rejection of Paul McCartney when the junior partner grew in stature and confidence and began dictating the creative course of the Beatles. I am sure that the break-up of the Beatles, or, more specifically, of John and Paul, must have been more traumatic than any of us suspect.

Separating himself from the masculine cult, of which he had been (covert as it may be) an inveterate product, Lennon argued combatively with me against a romantic view of Britain as a mother-loving and feminist country. Attempting to expunge his *angst* in sessions with Arthur Janov in Primal Scream therapy, Lennon also, according to Bill Harry's *The Book of Lennon*, consulted a Los Angeles psychiatrist, Milton Wiess, who attempted to analyse John in 1974 but 'gave up in despair, commenting: "If I was doing this as a job I'd have to send him two bills – one for each personality!"'

Nevertheless in interview Lennon appeared to have resolved his ambivalence, for he protested, 'We all hate our mommies, really. The English have a reputation for being effeminate and sadist. And they don't get that through loving Mommy, I'll tell you that. The largest population of homosexuals come from England. It is no joke that the English are effeminate. It is a fact of life. The British added 'Fair Play' to macho. That is all. That is as phoney as shit! What the hell!'

In my opinion the breach with Paul, who declined to consider playing second fiddle, once he had met up with Linda Eastman, triggered the break-up which separated John not only from Paul but also from others responsible for his success. Whilst collaboration with Ono produced a couple of hits, it was painfully obvious to even the most committed Lennon fan that the man depended upon Yoko for both ideas and composition. Left to his own devices, he was totally incapable of writing anything of the calibre of 'Eleanor Rigby', 'Norwegian Wood', 'Strawberry Fields' and 'Penny Lane'; 'Imagine', by comparison, is a song which cloys as opposed to the hard-edged anti-heroism of the Beatles material.

Although the Beatles were a group renowned for never having less than a Number One, and sometimes four or five hits in succession, Lennon's solo singles arduously reached Number One in Britain only once – the month before he died, on 8 November 1980, with '(Just Like) Starting Over' released from his *Double Fantasy* album, produced after a five-year hiatus. 'Imagine' and 'Woman' went to Number One on 27 December 1980 and 24 January 1981 respectively.

In the States the additional strength of Elton John catapulted to the Number One place Lennon's 'Whatever Gets You Thru the Night', responsible for Lennon's decision to honour his commitment to appear on stage with Elton at Madison Square Garden on 28 November 1974, which turned out to be his farewell concert performance. To all intents and purposes Lennon's career was over, and though the success of '(Just Like) Starting Over' appears to have given him a new lease of life, the follow-up *Milk and Honey* album, released by Polydor Records after John died, failed to reach the same level of visibility. And whilst it would be offensive to suggest that Lennon stage-managed his own death to cope with the failure of being unable to produce works which supported his own transparent self-image or garnered the adulations of the fans, it would be correct to say that the breach created in him a psychological *angst*.

For whatever misguided reasons Lennon hooked up with Ono, the union did generate a psychological safety valve of temporary duration. No mean lyricist or composer, Ono was infinitely better trained as a musician than John and in addition was a masterful poetess, as seen in her anthology *Grapefruit*. Together they were a formidable political unit – the ultimate unisex couple – electioneering for sex equality, race equality, an end to the Vietnam War, prison reform and so on. But the music failed to succeed in the same way that Bob Dylan's protest songs or Arlo Guthrie's political allegories combined conviction with art.

For all the finesse displayed by Yoko in her poetry, the songs she composed with John are comparatively crude. Cleaned up at EMI, 'Open Your Box' was censored in the States on account of its 'suggestive' lyrics; 'Touch Me' appeared instead on the B-side of John's 'Power to the People'. Worse, 'Woman Is the Nigger of the World', scheduled for a British release on 5 December 1972, was withdrawn, although promotional copies were distributed to radio stations. Released in the States, with a B-side of 'Sisters O Sisters', the single entered the charts at Number Fifty-seven and featured in the charts for five weeks. 'Happy Xmas (War Is Over)' was delayed in Britain for a year (being released in America in 1971) due to publishing difficulties over Yoko's composing credits (which had also held up the *Some Time in New York City* album).

While Bob Dylan avoided using four-letter words to articulate anger or protest, Lennon appeared not to be able to communicate in any way other than in an utterance of guttural obscenities. An EMI executive and I cavilled one afternoon about how many four-letter words Lennon actually used in his collection of solo singles. Whether it was five or six is unimportant – obscenities occur as substitutes for poetry in important Lennon songs: 'Give Peace a Chance', 'Working Class Hero,' 'Steel and Glass' and 'Give Me Some Truth'.

If John's motive to surpass the punk cults was commercial, there is no doubt that it was a bet which backfired. And yet, always the poseur, and in spite of what I was told by his Apple PR man, Pete Bennett, Lennon insisted during our meeting that his new persona evolved out of purely idealistic reasons. While he was obviously eating his heart out over the failure of his singles to reach the top of the charts, he was publicly telling me that he didn't care any longer for reaching a maximum audience at 'the expense of his own mind any more'.

Appearing three months earlier in America than in Britain, *Some Time in New York City* entered the US charts on 1 July 1972 at Number 190 and stayed in the Top 100 for twelve weeks. The most controversial of the couple's counter-culture albums, this was also amongst the least successful and prompted our discussion in September 1972 about the path Lennon was musically pursuing and his reasons for deciding to go that way.

The lead song, 'Woman Is the Nigger of the World', was the main talking point – John emphasizing that the idea came from something which Yoko had said in an interview in Britain's *Nova* magazine.

Reflected John, 'I was thinking you don't say things like that – repeating things people were putting down on me. I went through the same business that lots of our Leftish friends would go through – what about this guy and the man doing this and the carpenter? – concerned with what was happening to the men who were suffering and fighting.

'It took me from 1968 until when the record came out last year to begin to comprehend it and Yoko had already written "Sisters". I wrote "Woman Is the Nigger" after hearing "Sisters".'

Banned in Britain, and censored in the States, the lead song has sadly doomed the enterprise from inception; John admitted that it had been difficult to get air play.

'Someone will play it somewhere and then they take it off because of a reaction or whatever it was. Or someone to show that they weren't being (quote) chauvinist or sexist would play it once and say, "Okay, we don't like it." There are those sorts of reasons. You can never get your finger on what was going on.'

Asked if he regretted not being able to change his image, Lennon stoically replied, 'Nobody can get away with anything. That is why Elvis plays it safe and why people play it safe. That puts you out of the ball game. One argument from rock squares as Yoko calls them is for us to concentrate on the music and forget about the words. I can understand that because I've done "Tutti-Frutti" too. But on that score to me the actual sound of it was just rock and I could have been saying anything. It was a record. I wouldn't have put it out just because of what it said and put out a lousy backing or a lousy record. So the fact that it causes all these things is the event itself which I have learned from Yoko. It was called and described as the most talked about record. It was moaned about and talked about so it went through the consciousness one way or the other. It was also on the album which did about half a million which wasn't bad.'

Martin Luther Lennon? The question rankled. Was it real or a pose? Was he purposefully writing down or not?

The pose prevailing, John attributes the appeal to a whole new, although limited, audience. 'We get reviews from places other people don't get them. We get them from all over the States and England. From Bradford, not just from London. And some of the outlying areas, which is to whom we are talking as well. Some people who never bought a rock album for four years bought this one and they were little political types. There is the thing that as one door closes another door always opens.'

Being loyally working-class in his rejection of urbane managers who could have continued to package his career with the expertise of a Brian Epstein, Lennon went along with Ono's cock-eyed, off-the-wall ideas for their musical direction as anti-Establishment balladeers.

'You must understand', she said, 'that the people around us —

the managers and all that – are still dreaming about the Beatles days, and wouldn't understand this.'

The inevitable question surfaced: will the Beatles ever get together again?

'No, no. We are all quite happy. We are not unhappy like the Marx Brothers, separated from each other or something like that – whatever happened to other famous variety acts. *Nobody* is unhappy.'

And the wives?

Protested John, 'That is a lot of rubbish. Linda and Yoko never had an argument. There is a big story about Linda and Yoko. That's the woman thing again. Even though Paul and I were shouting at each other in public almost, people would go back and say, "If it wasn't for Yoko and Linda."'

And yet they refused to let Lennon die, both fans and musicians calling upon him to produce. Both Mick Jagger and Randy Newman criticized his five-year retirement and the low quality of his solo work.

The criticism, while failing to change John demonstrably, nevertheless had an impact. 'One criticism levelled at me recently was, "Please give us some more images, John." I wrote "images" for my own sake. It is like asking some filmmaker please to make films like you did ten years ago. Don't make them the way you do now, 'cause I like the ones you made ten years ago. Well, if you don't like the films I'm making now, well, don't buy it and don't bother me with it 'cause I know what I'm doing and I am not looking for maximum audience for expense of my own mind any more. I've been through the maximum audience bit and while they are there I'll be happy and if it diminishes I'll survive okay. I could probably sit at home and write a lot of nice images that play for a bit. Maybe I could do two albums that would satisfy those critics from Newman to any other. And after that they'd start comparing images with images. "Oh, these images aren't as good as those images." Where can you go? There is no way to please everyone. There is no way out of it. The only kick we get is music, the event and doing it. We hope that it goes through some people's consciousness, even through the intellectualism and their "hypocrisy".'

Following one month after their heroic Madison Square Garden *One to One* concert in August 1972 in aid of retarded children and adults, our interview allowed John to reflect about appearing together on stage.

209

'Yoko and I have been together about five years and about four years publicly. Each time we are hoping that it is different. We get invited to do Madison Square Garden. A guy rings up and says, "John and Yoko, will you do Madison Square Garden?" At the end of it all they were hoping that we were going to bring Brother and Jesus on to sing a few numbers too. So we have to make it clear from the start, "Are you inviting us two?" "Are you asking *us*?" We will do it. But we are not the same as George. We are not quite the same as Elvis or whomever else you might have had in your mind. Try and get out of your head that we are going to do what happened last year. Each time we do something we keep hoping that if we keep appearing as ourselves – John and Yoko – one day, when people arrive there they will expect John and Yoko to do that thing. That is *all* we can hope for.

'One of the criticisms of the show – and this is hysterical – said that "Paul did not come." That was a headline to the show. We are not only fighting chauvinism, Beatleism, Starism. We are also fighting the last event.'

Asked is he had managed to assimilate feminism on a subconscious level, Lennon replied, 'It took me four years. I am still only coming through it. Even though I could sing, "Woman Is the Nigger of the World" and could accept stuff intellectually, there is still an emotional reaction that happens without me even knowing. And that is the real hard thing. It's like starting to have to become ambidextrous. I understand that to make life worthwhile and to make our relationship worthwhile I have to become ambidextrous. And to make it so that both hands are working equally is the thing.

'I learned so much from that last album. Because we weren't making John's album and then Yoko – well she does her avant-garde and John does his rock 'n' roll. We did it *together*, and that was an enormous change for me. It was so new and I was so unsure of what I was doing. I was amazed that I ever got through it. I can't put it in words. I almost pulled the plug on it.'

He paused, 'The only thing in life is to have a relationship with somebody and this [Yoko] is the somebody. Whatever it takes we are going to try and do that. There ain't nothin' else, really. When the record is out and the concert is over – whether they loved it or hated it or described what shoes you were wearing or how you sang, it is irrelevant. We are left there at night or in the evening and wherever anybody goes, that is all that counts. So that is the reality I have been looking for. I never had a relationship with a woman before like the one I have with Yoko.

'It is a relief not to have to be machismo or whatever it is. It is not much fun. There is a borderline between machismo and homosexuality. I feel pretty young to have started waking up and I would hate to have been aged fifty or sixty and found myself on the fifteenth marriage or the thirteenth girlfriend. It is a sad life and I am thankful for all the suffering I go through 'cause there ain't no other reality.'

Asked about the chances for feminism's success, elements of which would be incorporated into mainstream culture, Lennon was optimistic. 'It seems to take about a decade for something to get through. I can only go by what I know and whether or not rock 'n' roll was chauvinist, it was put down, attacked and humiliated. There is still the same thing going on in relation to the Musicians Union as opposed to the Rock Musicians Union. The thing had its own momentum and pushed its way through one way or the other. The next thing is for the women's movement to be pushed through and I hate to say it – 'cause it sounds so horribly conservative, but it will take the same amount of time to get it above sea level.

'We can't conceive of it in the same way that if you conceive of Beatles and Stones you can't conceive of Alice Cooper. But we are what Alice Cooper came from. But if you look at it without knowing what happened before you'd say, "How the hell did it happen? Where did that come from?" What I am saying is that there will be something in the women's movement that will allow the Establishment to earn money from which will allow it to happen. Someone with balls and breasts will probably be singing "Woman Is the Sister of the Sun".'

Confessing that their work was a wholly spontaneous outpouring, Lennon said he never knew what they would do next, a condition confusing to fans and critics alike who tend to want to characterize artists. 'As an artist people can only discuss the thing you have done before. To me that is forgotten and I don't know what we are going to do with the next one. Some of the criticism of people listening to *Some Time in New York City* for Yoko was: "Why didn't she *scream* like she used to?" And for me it was, "Why didn't he do something personal like he did on the first album?" When they slaughtered the first album. There is no way of getting it like they all want it.'

He continued, 'I can't get into that bag of talk discussing what it was or what it could be. We can only discuss what it was at the time and is no more or less important about what happened then. It is all over. That's just me. Not counting her. Not counting every other artist. Not counting the real politics and the real death and the real war. And the traffic jams and the pollution and going to the moon. What's relevant is what we are doing now, not what then, and what tomorrow. What I am hanging on to is now, now, now.

'Talking artistically I wanted to shake off all the classical arrangements – all the trumpets and classical pianists. I enjoy basic blues – basic art. That's the start. What's next? The lyrics which go on top of it. So for nine months I am going to play twelve-bar blues whatever lyrics I want to think about at the time.'

This was an amazing admission for someone who revolutionized twelve-bar blues with musical participles dangling four or five at a go. Dismissive of 'Imagine' as a simple, child's lyric couched in violins with a simple melody, Lennon forswore improvisation for greater simplicity and directness.

'I am tempted to go back into art, because I probably would get less hurt if I concentrated on the music and cut out this political stuff. But it would probably bore me after I had made a few rock symphonies. It is like – to do what you are doing is the only thing you can do. There is no other way of doing it. I am sure that Nature will provide us with subtlety. I've just awakened to it after four years. There was nothing subtle about the awakening. It was like screaming out. It was like when we awoke and discovered that there was no war. Perhaps if the Movement had been more subtle or less subtle in 1968 we would have gotten further – or less further – than we have gotten now. I don't know. But there is no way of discussing what happened in 1968 and saying if we had done that, then in 1972 we would have got rid of Spiro Agnew.'

Manifesting the old Christ complex Lennon objected, 'It is like Jesus. If Jesus had a good PR man he might have been able to do what he did and *not* die on the Cross. Should he have done what he did and ended up on the Cross or should he have been voted in in Israel?'

He continued, 'What we are saying is – "Be naked." It is nicer and it is easier if we weren't and we might prolong whatever is going on longer if we don't reveal ourselves. But whatever is going on, it is time to be completely naked and run that risk.

'I am not going to play the game of that French guy Maurice

Chevalier so that I can survive the Holocaust. I believe that is what is happening now and I am not about to take into consideration the people who are going to fall for this claptrap anyway. I have no time for that. There is no time for art. Things are too desperate.

'It is like subliminal advertising. I believe in shock. I can't intellectualize those things, but presumably Zen is when you go – Pow! There is no discussing it. It just happens.'

Espousing the Communist credo in the midst of such an excess of plenitude is inconsistent, even more so years later when the Lennons compiled acquisitions for sport: their rabbit warren of 11 Dakota Apartment rooms was full of fine furnishings and art treasures.

Objected Lennon, 'The mind is where the real freedom is. We have Christ on the one hand and Communism on the other and they both almost say the same thing. But I heard that [in China] they have a roof over their head. Everybody has one suit and everybody has a meal.

'They do not have to pay, even in England, for medicine. Even if America gets as Socialist as what I term Fascist Britain, then we'd start to move a little. But I can see all the waste on the streets here – clothes lying on the streets of New York. They would have been well-divided where I came from. The only things which matter are clothes, roof and food. And then after that the other bit might be interesting to discuss.

'I don't see any difference between the royalty and aristocracy in America or the old European royalty. Even though it is King Kennedy and Queen Tricia. I don't see any difference. The big families – the Fords. What is the difference? Only the names have been changed.'

Protested John, 'I probably could get more MBEs and more money if I sold out. But I just refuse. There is no way out of that trap. That is why all those fears people put around about an artist running out, they've been putting that on me since I was aged twenty-one. And the artist, like the good dog that he is, goes through the trip and runs out. 'Cause he has blinkers on and he'll go on and on and on repackaging the big hit or whatever it is.'

He paused, 'I go on instinct which is the only thing that man has which hasn't been written by a group of rabbis or mandarins and put in a box and proclaimed for everyone to follow. It is instinct which we are taught to kill from birth. Instinct is the only thing which can make anybody survive if there is a Holocaust. And there are a few of us. It will not be quote good manners, trying to please everybody, education and all the other bullshit which we have been taught and are running around like ballet dancers with spotlights on.'

Denying his past, fearing his future, Lennon's New York persona was marginal at best. No longer the Liverpool Johnny of the London clubs and international tours, he had got himself into a corner as a social outcast. Returning his MBE, being busted for drugs, agitating against Nixon and the Vietnam War all tended to alienate him from whatever passes for New York society. And whether he was invited and rejected invitations to New York social events, he was seldom seen in public as a patron of either arts or charities.

When all is said and done, Lennon was not only a loner but also a misanthrope and a gypsy. What he enjoyed most was hanging out in his bedroom surrounded by his hi-tech gear: sleeping, eating, reading or writing in an almost catatonic – certainly somnambulant – state. *Double Fantasy* producer Jack Douglas, a chum of John's, told me that John told him he hadn't got laid in weeks: Yoko was preoccupied with business details at that time.

Insecure and xenophobic, Lennon's fear of artifice and order must have been imperilled by the precision with which Yoko refined their eleven-room apartment – from all reports, the place sounded as coldly majestic as a palace. One wonders if John ever dared to walk around in muddy shoes or to leave newspapers lying on the sofa?

Similarly alienated from Julian, for reasons which we can only infer, but deriving perhaps from his intimidation by the boy's public school education, Lennon was quoted as having said something to the effect that Julian would never succeed in this cruel old world because he was too gentle (comparing him with Kyoko who appeared harder).

Obtuse with old friends, off-hand with new ones, Lennon is recounted as having accidentally met up on the sidewalks of New York with playwright Adrienne Kennedy – his collaborator on *In His Own Write* – only to greet the lady with despatch. Kennedy, who had wanted to do the Lennon project because of the love her children showed for his books, said that she had no contact with John after he moved to New York. By the same token, John's brief encounters with Sid Bernstein remained simply that.

If not socially ostracized, he was certainly ignored by New York artists and performers on his plateau, and in view of his vast wealth and postion Lennon's pursuit of an underground lifestyle was ludicrous. Garnering friends from the ranks of the underground art and rock worlds, he kept the company of session musicians and artists, neither of whom were competitive or demanding.

Was Liverpool Johnny happy in New York? Subsequently discovering a burst of homesickness welling up in his heart on occasions when Lennon communicated in Britain with family and friends, requesting black puddings and other things English, I have since discerned a decided commitment on Lennon's part to return home to Britain either temporarily or for good.

So what was he like? A pop star with a lot of money attempting to make his way around New York incognito: showing up at Max's Kansas City in jeans and jersey, whilst departing from the splendour of a plush limousine. The inconsistency of it both astounds and appals.

Dakota apartment neighbour, columnist Rex Reed, observes that Lennon was 'shlumpy' and that, while he and Yoko did attend the annual Dakota party, they were not what you would call 'high profile' or conspicuous in society. A toy boy, a has-been, Lennon surfaced at Happenings or pop festivals either as Ono's assistant or as the star making his farewell appearance – thereby excusing lack of rehearsal or programming in performance.

Happiest with an entourage of side men who posed no threat to his status, Lennon recounted to me the social dynamics at a party following his appearance at the *One to One* charity event.

'There were fifteen of us and Elephants and the wives and the girlfriends all talking and chatting. One person suddenly came out with some truth and it was Yoko and there was a silence. And all the males – 'cause they are friends of ours, said, "Why didn't I have the guts to come out with something like that?" But Yoko came out with it. And it was some reality which was underlying the whole situation. And I looked at Rick [the drummer] and he looked at me and I said – "I wish I had said that." I just couldn't get it out.'

Another public appearance occurred on New York's public television Channel 13, where Ono was invited on by experimental film-maker Jonas Mekas to discuss her work. In the course of it she demonstrated several *Grapefruit* exercises, assisted by John – among them cutting bits of string.

Happy being Yoko's straight man, John said, 'I didn't know what I was doing. I was just given the instruction. I was just doing what I was supposed to be doing. I had no idea she was going to scream anything. It shocked me! – I was just following instructions to do what I was supposed to be doing.'

Yoko explained, 'Women are not used to being given a chance, so much so that we have gotten to a point where we can't say anything. That screaming was a typical situation. I was just able to scream because the situation allowed me to. Jonas Mekas gave me the time – gave me the programme. I had John who understands me very well. Jonas who is very kind. All these kind people around me. I was allowed to be myself when I screamed. In a situation like Dick Cavett (I don't want to attack Dick Cavett 'cause Dick is very nice – is there any other talk show that is intelligent?) there is the feeling (and women are human – they are sensitive too) that you shouldn't be sitting there. From the audience. From the reporters. And those little things which you can't describe in words that if I do describe it people say that I am paranoid is detrimental to the female spirit.'

If Lennon was in pursuit of acceptance by New York's intelligentsia, he struck out as often as he scored: one legendary rebuff coming from Andy Warhol whose friendship Lennon solicited for – who knows why? – contacts, financing, companionship? Or because he believed, as he told me in interview, that gays set the trends which heterosexuals follow?

Warhol, conversely, seeing nothing to gain by his friendship, spurned Lennon. According to Warhol's friend Paul Morrissey Andy liked rich people. He saw nothing wrong with being rich: he was eager to increase his own wealth, which was already considerable.

'Andy thought Lennon was a pest – a leech. And worse, he was a professional grouch – an uninteresting, nasty person. A smart-ass,' says Morrissey.

Of Yoko, whose comments about the New York art scene being run by the gay Mafia are well noted, Morrissey is no more sanguine. 'My first recollection of her is in 1966 or 1967. I went to some stupid benefit with Andy Warhol – the Jazz Club on Fourth Street in Greenwich Village. There was a group and we had to go. It was crowded. It was about 2a.m. And Yoko who considered herself some sort of art person was contributing her art to the evening. It was crowded. And her art consisted of a canvas five feet high by four feet wide. And there was a hole in the middle of the canvas and there was this little arm sticking out and you were supposed to shake hands with the work of art. And everybody wanted to see what moron was doing the 'shake hands' art? Going to the toilet is art. Shaking hands is art. Who gives a shit? It was little Yoko Ono and she had this very young baby on her breast. At 2a.m. in the morning at this jazz nightclub with rock 'n' roll blaring. People like this take themselves too seriously.'

When Yoko and John married, Warhol was supposed to have expressed condolences for John, for whom he felt Yoko was unsuitable.

Morrissey recalls, 'Then she married John Lennon and would come around with him when she had nothing better to do. She never let him out of her sight, because she was afraid that someone would grab him and run off with him. She was with him twenty-four-hours-a-day. She went to the toilet with him and stood outside the door at a nightclub. She was obsessed with him. All you could say was that he was the kind of person who needed that kind of thing.'

And the attraction to Andy?

'For some reason Andy had this art with a capital "A" reputation and John had been in graphics in some grammar school and did these little drawings. So instead of telling a kid I'm bringing you to the zoo, it's I'm bringing you to the art world today. And it took up an hour or so of the day. They'd call up Andy and he'd ride around in their limousine like a rock 'n' roller. They'd go to the East Village. I used to live on Sixth Street and they used to go to a macrobiotic restaurant on Sixth Street. One day they came across to my house. I was watching TV. Andy said, "Oh, we were across at the macrobiotic with Yoko and John and I told them what a great house you have here. And they have to see your house." I owned it but it was a rickety run-down tenement. Nothing to show off. But poor Andy was so desperate. He was there by himself with these two people and had no one else to talk for him.

'They were not fun. They were deadly serious. Andy made it all a joke. People like Yoko who took it all deadly seriously were silly.'

Whilst it was obvious that the Lennons didn't need the support, financial or critical, of the New York underground to pursue their art, there is in Morrissey's account of Yoko's behaviour a need to prove her artistic worth. Typically, the harder she tried to impress, the less successful she was. Too much pressure always put people off.

'Yoko tried to talk about some sort of art that she was doing or going to do. I remember being in a limousine with them. She did all the talking. He was making these nasty remarks which weren't so funny.'

Contemptuous of rock 'n' roll, wrapping it all up under the umbrella of bubblegum music, Morrissey says that he never had a particularly high opinion of Lennon – even as a Beatle.

'Nobody in the rock 'n' roll world ever had much of a mind, personality, charm or humour. Mick Jagger is an exception. He is like Andy. He likes meeting people. He likes meeting rich people. Jagger has money. So did Andy. But they all want more. Don't ask me why.

'Andy was harmless. He was well-behaved and he was likeable. He went after the rich and they accepted him. He was lame and shy and awkward and didn't know what to say. People felt sorry for him and wanted to take care of him. He was always a very likeable character.

'In interviews Lennon came off with smart-ass remarks. But not in real life. It fell flat. Yoko was into taking everything seriously and working hard, keeping up her profile as an artist. Wasn't *his* great fantasy that she was some great artist whom men wouldn't accept because she was a woman? He was bananas.'

And yet in spite of her vigilance, the romance faded precisely one year after our own interview, when Lennon had pledged fidelity and embraced monogamy. In October 1973 John and Yoko separated after four and a half years of marriage, Lennon pursuing a 'lost weekend' of fourteen months with their Chinese-American PA, May Pang: the camp follower whom Sid Bernstein identifies as a fan of the Rascals had finally got herself a legitimate place in the rock scene.

Whilst the public is under the impression, formulated by Pang and the TV media, that May was John's real true love, the truth is actually less romantic. Jack Douglas told me during our interview that Lennon was on the make for lots of girls, and, following his reunion with Ono in March 1975, that he had made overtures to film actress and model Maud Adams.

Recounts Douglas, 'A request had gone out for a particular lady – Maud Adams. He was nuts about her. It was weird. He used to say, "Do you think she'll like me?" '

Was the marriage having problems? Douglas concurs: 'John was complaining about not getting laid enough. Because he never saw her. She was in her office all the time. Doing business. The cows. She was always downstairs, working all hours.'

Abstinent? Lennon's definition could mean not getting laid six times a day.

Maybe so, for as Douglas recounts: 'Lennon was *wildly* in love with Ono. He said, "You don't know anything about women until you have been with a Japanese woman." But she was so manipulating and conniving. And when she felt she was losing her chance she would go mad. She would imagine it most of the time.'

Douglas, who accompanied Lennon on that Los Angeles 'lost weekend', refers to Pang as his secretary, 'although he was sleepng with her. She was there doing a job. He needed women to do things for him. He called Yoko "mother". It used to make me sick.

'May didn't think it would last. I don't think he was seeing her at the end. But he really dug her. Absolutely. They were great together. It was a weird situation. I don't think John gave it any thought. I don't think he was able to give much of anything very much thought at that period. He was very drunk. He was awful when he was drunk. He bashed out the back of my car.'

Photographer David Nutter, who shot Lennon's wedding photos, met up again with him in New York when he was seeing May.

'John was wonderful with May Pang. We used to sit up all night in the apartment on the East Side – her apartment. We used to sit up laughing all night long at these funny English things. I think May was very good for John at that time. I think what happened was that Yoko snapped her fingers. It was almost like Svengali. She had remote control. He went straight back. Of course May was devastated. She used to call me up and she would be in tears. She expected him to stay with her. But obviously Yoko had the upper hand here. When he went back to Yoko, none of us saw John for a long time.'

Both sustaining and erotic is the picture of their relationship portrayed by Pang in the book she co-authored with Henry Edwards, entitled *Loving John*.

Observes Nutter, 'In Los Angeles there was a bad scene. Here [in New York] it was wonderful.' He pauses. 'I think May has been a bit naughty. I saw her on TV saying about how John was physically aggressive with her. I thought it was tacky. Why bother? Why say it? Naughty, naughty girl, I thought.

'One of the last things as far as John was concerned is a frantic phone call from May Pang one night saying that John had been shot. I said, "Don't be ridiculous. Don't be silly." "Yes," she said, "it was on the radio." She was in a terrible state and I thought: it can't be true. And of course it was. She called me back a couple of hours later and said it was.'

Pang's literary account of the Lennons' marriage is that it was a travesty: Lennon comes out as selfish and deceitful, playing women off against each other whilst compromising his wife's sensibility and reputation. Apparently other women besides Pang were made to feel superior to Ono by being told by John that 'Yoko deserves what she gets' or 'My wife wants me to . . . [get] laid. If she knew I *cared* anything for you, she'd be hurt.'

Creating the impression that Yoko was the kind of woman to whose moods John was susceptible, his return appears to emanate as much from obligation as passion. If one is to believe any of his confidences to Pang, the consequent image of the marriage is of a conflict interlocking the two. True to form and self-definition, Lennon once again is the complete bastard.

Much had changed since the secret Gibraltar marriage which captured the hearts of the world. One of the few people in the world to have been present is David Nutter, whose account of the wedding prefaces an ugly side to Lennon.

'After the wedding we all piled into a private jet. It was wonderful. All we did was laugh and they were blissfully happy. We just laughed at the funny old English things. I think Yoko felt a bit left out. She didn't quite understand about old English comedy shows. It was almost like one had known him forever. John is very working-class English. And when somebody is sort of an outsider or from a different culture and they start talking about wartime radio programmes – and then Yoko started coming up with all these wonderful schemes for her art Happenings.'

And the reunion?

John's return to Ono amazed May, who years after the affair and the account of the affair and the media hype of the account of the affair, talks about it all in view of her own marriage to a recording company executive and her pregnancy. In conversation an envy of Yoko creeps into her voice from time to time. 'John told me', she recounts with indignation, 'that "Yoko has *allowed* me to come home."'

And yet, in spite of all speculation, there was something lingering: May possesses John's prayer book as well as his first edition of Elizabeth Barrett Browning's poems.

Present at the Madison Square Garden reunion of Yoko and John, Nutter recounts, 'I didn't see anybody until afterwards. They had a party at a place called Hippopotamus. John was alone. That was my first introduction to everybody – to Elton and the whole world. I didn't know the politics of what was going on. It was magical.'

Godfather to the Lennons' son Sean, Elton John took Nutter along on one of his visits to see him. 'I went over with Elton one day to see the baby,' recalls Nutter. 'He said, "Let's go over and see the little godson." John had the baby in a shoebox, because it was so unexpected. They didn't have anything to put the baby in.

'The Dakota is a weird place – very gloomy. We had to come up the back way, because Yoko didn't want anyone to see John. You had to go into the basement which is like a city down there. I used to get lost in all the rooms. There were mannequins in each room: throwing up in the darkroom and S-M mannequins with handcuffs. She wanted me to photograph all these mannequins. "Listen, I want you to photograph all these mannequins in different positions doing different things, and I want to put them in a catalogue. If there is one standing by the fridge I will sell the fridge with the mannequin."

'Of course John awoke when we arrived. And he was fine. I thought: why the paranoia about anyone talking to John? It is so silly.

'It was the afternoon. Elton had a day off from the show. Yoko had a woman there to serve tea. It was pleasant. John was the proud father.'

Hailed to the royal flat to photograph an album cover of Ono songs due for release six months after John's death in June 1981, Nutter recalls the controversy over *Season of Glass* on account of the bloodstained pair of glasses used on the cover, which critics condemned for being in bad taste.

'Yoko asked me to come up to the flat after John died at 6a.m. Why so early, I don't know. There were bodyguards all over the place outside her flat. She said, would I do an album cover for her? She brought out this pair of bloodstained glasses which I sort of cringed at. I thought: "Oh, my God." Half of me wanted to do it. Half of me said, "I don't really think it is in the best taste." I said, "Why don't we use this room and we can put the glasses by the window? I can use a 28mm wide angle lens, this, that and the other. We can use available light." And she said, "Yes. Yes." It was pleasant. And then she started crying, because she said she was so lonely. She said, "I'll call you in a couple of days and we'll do it." And I never heard another word. She did it herself in her own way. I just felt a little bit used.'

'Used' is the operative word describing Nutter's first encounter with Lennon when the superstar purloined the copyright to the wedding photos without settling up, putting Nutter out of pocket on expenses too.

Recounts Nutter, 'A phone call came in from Peter Brown. He said, "Do not ask any questions. I cannot mention it on the phone. Just get the next plane to Gibraltar. I'll meet you there. You'll see what happens." I realized because it was Peter, because it was Apple, that it must have something to do with the Beatles. The wedding I had no idea about. No idea at all. They didn't want anyone to know, on account of the fuss with McCartney's wedding. John and Yoko wanted a very quiet secret ceremony.

'John had wanted to get married immediately and Peter had found that Gibraltar was the only place where you can fly in and out and get married.

'I stayed overnight. Peter had booked me into an hotel and he told me what it was. I couldn't believe it. Let me just treat this as if it is a movie. Because if I really think about it I am going to go mad. I was living on nothing at the time. I had a little old camera with a few rolls of film. I thought: "This is ridiculous."'

He continues, 'The next day John and Yoko flew in and they were wonderful. They really were. It was the first time I had met John.

'The wedding was very quiet. Nobody knew. It was like in a little registry office and we took the pictures. They needed two witnesses for the wedding, so I ran up and signed the thing. Peter and I were the two witnesses to the marriage (Brown is immortalized in 'The Ballad of John and Yoko').

'We got to Paris and I thought – "This is ridiculous. I am in a private jet. I do not know how I am going to get back from London airport. I haven't even got the money for a taxi." They didn't know and I didn't want to tell them I was poverty-stricken. One of the guys on the plane said, "Do you want a lift back to England?" I said, "Okay." So I am sitting on this luxurious jet thinking: Isn't life ridiculous? Here I am sitting on this plane, without a pound in my pocket.'

Frequently at Apple when a photographer was needed, since David's brother Tommy had a tailor's shop on Savile Row, Nutter was asked to drive up to Golspie in Scotland to rescue the couple after the car crash.

He recounts, 'They had bandages all over. We had Yoko's daughter with us who drove us absolutely crazy. Every time she would say something John would look at me and I would look at him and we'd raise our eyebrows. She was just a persistent child.'

He continues, 'Another time I remember John's white Rolls Royce picking me up when I lived in Kilburn. We went to their house in Kenwood. Yoko was making these horrible macrobiotic cucumber things. I thought: "God, how can I eat this?" No wonder they look so ill. I thought, "Have a nice cheeseburger dear."'

The success of John's comeback album, *Double Fantasy*, as living proof of the victory of an androgynous marriage, belies the facts as recounted by producer Jack Douglas, who describes the couple's marriage as a truce between two super egos.

Feminist vs. chauvinist? Produced after John had had five years of indoctrination as a househusband, devoted to rearing the couple's only child, son Sean, *Double Fantasy* contains the best of the twenty-two cuts recorded, the others appearing on the posthumous *Milk and Honey* album.

Commencing production on 4 August 1980, the album was released on 29 November only days before John was shot. It was distributed by Geffen Records, then a fledgling company, and the original idea had been to hook up with a major which would match McCartney's advance of 18 million dollars and 23 per cent. David Geffen offered Yoko a million dollars for *Double Fantasy*, but did so in such a way that she accepted his offer. Ironically *Milk and Honey*, released by Polydor, bore the same label of the Dutch company which released the single on which John played back-up to Tony Sheridan.

Recounts Douglas, 'We didn't know what label it was going to be on. Yoko was doing that. I was shocked when I saw David Geffen walk in the door. I must say. Geffen came to the Hit Factory before we came to the Record Plant. I expected to see a major. Now David was starting his label. But David was so gung-ho. He could hustle my grandmother. The others – Yoko wouldn't talk to them. Geffen was smart. He didn't intimidate her by putting a piece of paper in front of her. He said, "Don't worry, Yoko. We'll make a great deal. Here is a million dollars."'

Douglas's opportunity to produce came after years of working as a sound engineer on other Lennon albums, starting with *Imagine* when additional tracks were laid over what John had recorded at Tittenhurst in his home-based 'Ascot Sound Studios'. In addition, he worked on many of Ono's albums.

In New York for *Mind Games* and in Los Angeles for *Rock 'N' Roll*, Douglas was a keen observer of the dynamics between two rock legends, Lennon and Phil Spector – who produced many Lennon albums including *Imagine* and *Rock 'N' Roll*.

Douglas gives his own opinion: 'I heard a lot of stories about Phil before like he's insecure; that the 'Phil Spector Sound' can't be taken at face value, and that many of his songs were inspired by other people. The Phil Spector sound of turning the speakers back on in the studio to reverberate was the result of a collaboration. I said, "No way, man. The guy is brilliant." After working with him I tend to question the extent of his achievement.'

The falling out in Los Angeles over the *Rock 'N' Roll* album was prefaced on *Imagine* when John, in interview with me, disparaged Spector's contributions as being sugary.

'At the time he thought it was great,' says Douglas. 'I heard the tracks before Spector added his "wall of sound". They sounded complete already. We did a lot of work at the end.

'Phil was in charge and Lennon let him mix it. John didn't oppose it. When the strings came in, it was such an impressive sound John couldn't help going for it. He did respect Phil.'

Privy to the origins of the *Double Fantasy* concept which began, according to Douglas, as John's solo album, it was only when Yoko involved herself in the project that it became the love duet which Lennon boasted was a testament to their unity. As a matter of fact, John boasted to Douglas that the next album was going to be all rock 'n' roll, all John and all male.

'When we started to do the *Double Fantasy* album it was that *John* was coming in to make an album,' recounts Douglas. 'Not John and Yoko. Then Yoko asked me to come out to their country house. She played me a bunch of songs and I recorded them. She said to me, "Listen, when you and John talk, don't tell him about these songs." I said, "Okay. You two work that out. I am not going to get in the middle of it." So it was that the double album was to have been two single albums.'

Comparing Douglas to John's Liverpool friends whom I interviewed, I perceive that he is as solid and middle-class as Sunday lunch. Having a stabilizing influence upon Lennon, it was Jack who, when John arrived in New York, acted as a buffer – separating good from bad amongst the hippies, yippies, underground artists and politicos seeking John's friendship or support.

'The day I met John after not seeing him for a few years I ran into him in a health food store coming from giving Sean swimming lessons at the Y [somewhere on the East side].

'He was intimidated by the city at first. I was born and raised here. I know everybody – where to go and where not to. So when we were doing *Imagine* we talked and he said, "I want you to go out with me. There are people and I don't know if they want to take advantage of me or what they want. Tell me who these people are who we are meeting as we go along." We'd go to see Abbie Hoffman, and Julian Beck – all these people would have these parties and John would be invited. He'd ask, "Are they after me for something? Do they want me to front some cause?"

'I remember one time when he was with Abbie Hoffman and he was talking about revolution. John went crazy. He grabbed the guy and shouted, "Do you all want to die?" He scared the hell out of them. He said to me, "They don't know anything – these people." It got him so upset. It was great. He was not in tune with that. They want you to front for some bullshit. It was selfish and insincere here. He saw through it.'

Admittedly abstinent when recording, Lennon's schedule was obsessed with work. And in the rare intervals between sessions, he confined his socializing to Jack Douglas, with whom he developed an almost incestuous attachment.

'We would go out after a session for something to eat at 4a.m. And we lived one block from each other. He would get up at 9a.m. We would have breakfast. He would go back to bed. I would go do the Yoko session.

'He would get home. Maybe he'd go to bed. Maybe he'd stay up for a while. But at 9a.m. he'd expect to see me for breakfast at the Opera Café. Then he would go back to the house and I'd go on to work wth Yoko. I would see him again at 7p.m. I had no sleep. But it was so much fun I did not care.'

The same routine prevailed on the night that Lennon was shot – 8 December 1980 – except for slight deviations.

'We were both working on "Walking on Thin Ice", Yoko's

song. We were both producing her session. That was a single and John and I had done all the work on that song. We were very excited about it. We thought it was the best thing she had ever done. The hope was that she would be so well-received by the critics for that record, she would be able to go off and stand on her own.

'After the session we didn't go out for a drink. I had another session with a girl from RCA so I stayed on at the Record Plant and John went home with Yoko to the Dakota.'

When I enquire of Douglas whether John had a premonition about the presence of the fan, Mark Chapman, lingering around the Dakota Apartment building, he replies in the affirmative. 'I think John knew his life was over. He knew something was definitely wrong that afternoon. While we were working, we talked about it. He said he'd be more famous than Elvis when he died. He was talking about death all day. He said, "Don't tell Yoko." He was explicit.'

Whether out of shock or perversity, Ono phoned Douglas the day after John died and asked him to meet her in the studio to record something.

Recalls Douglas, 'I would have done anything for her. But the day after his death I had gone to pieces. She rang and said, "Meet me in the studio." I thought, "My God, what are we going to do?" It was a B-side of something.

'Because the night he died we had finished it. We were supposed to meet at a master lab. But I didn't go home with him. It was the only time I didn't go home with him.

'First I thought, maybe what we are doing is like a funeral service. A friend wanted to fly me out of the country, because I was like bruising it, to his ranch up in Canada. He said, "I have the plane at the airport. I want you to get out of here, Jack. I want you to get away from that woman. She is crazy." Yoko rattled on like a drill sergeant. "This is what I want you to do. Get out the David Spinozza tapes which we did with the classical guitar solo. Take John's words and put them over."'

Whatever Yoko's motives in this instance, it is true that whilst John was chasing after other women, Ono was professionally involved with Sam Havadtoy, a Hungarian interior decorator who doubled as her production manager. 'I used to see Havadtoy at her sessions. He used to bring her some goodies. Food and stuff.'

Was John concerned?

'He didn't know. There are a lot of secrets which I was privy to which would have made her paranoid. But not in a million years would I betray Yoko to John or betray John to Yoko.

'Yoko had a private room behind the control room. Sam used to come in, they would go in the back room and I would wait for them to come out. I would say at that time, their friendship was strictly professional.'

Some Time in New York City, their finest collective effort, celebrates in song not only the issues but the people who were important – Angela Davis, who was on trial for conspiring in the prison escape of her husband, George Jackson; and John Sinclair, imprisoned for ten years for the possession of a small amount of marijuana.

Although a miss with the fans – Lennon's own friends trivializing his commitment to the politics of protest by minimizing his camaraderie with Chicago Seven defendants Jerry Rubin and Abbie Hoffman – the album was probably the most direct and honest thing Lennon had ever done. Recorded whilst waging his own battles with Immigration, it is almost a musical diary of the events of a time when John experienced greater pain than he had for years.

A copy of Lennon's FBI file, obtained under the United States Freedom of Information Act, documents the full extent of Lennon's paranoia as the spurious grounds for his deportation become manifest. Whatever the underlying reasons for his application for permanent residency in the United States, Lennon's stated intentions for prolonged domicile had to do with their search for Yoko Ono's daughter by Anthony Cox: Kyoko, who had been illegally spirited away by the father in violation of a Houston court ruling.

Whilst the Federal government believed, as endorsed in the FBI memos, that Lennon's entry was prompted by an intention to disrupt the Republican National Convention in an election year (1972), and in consequence ensure the defeat of Richard Nixon, the reasons given by the Immigration Service for his deportation concerned both Lennon's British drug conviction and the expiration of his US visa. Only after the scandal of his 'selective deportation' was exposed did New York Immigration Director Sol Marks admit that he had 'received orders from Washington not to give this man a break'.

Appearing on *The Dick Cavett Television Show* on 11 May 1972, Lennon made claims about being followed by government agents and about the tapping of his telephone. He felt that he was being deported due to outspoken remarks regarding US policy in South-east Asia. His lawyer, Leon Wildes, applied on his behalf to the Justice Department for information.

An FBI memo dated 18 September 1973 records: 'Would you please supply us with electronic surveillance information pertaining to the individual named on the attached list . . . should your files reveal that the individual or the premises in which he had a proprietary interest were subjected to electronic surveillance, we would appreciate your furnishing . . . with the following. . . .' The reply was negative, the FBI replying: 'Such a review failed to indicate that Lennon or premises in which he had a proprietary interest have been subjected to any lawful electronic surveillance.'

The ultimate victory in 7 October 1975 – merely two days before his son Sean's birth – granting Lennon possession of his Green Card, was an admission that, whilst free of political surveillance, he *was* the object of selective deportation. The judge noted that 'the court cannot condone selective deportation based upon secret political grounds'.

An FBI memo of 1972 confirms this, advising the Bureau 'to initiate discreet efforts to locate subject and remain aware of his activities and movements [and] to handle inquiries only through established sources and discreet pretext inquiries, in view of subject's avowed intention to engage in disruptive activities surrounding the Republican National Convention'. Lennon ultimately dropped his plans to go to Miami for the RNC.

Another memo cites fear of possible disruption of the Republican National Convention, advising surveillance by 'mature, experienced agents'.

What was the profile which the FBI sought to create, characterizing Lennon as a security threat? The issue raises the question of whether the Bureau, without first issuing a writ, should be allowed to monitor the activities of both citizens and residents of the United States. The Bureau's file on Lennon creates a picture of a moral reprobate, a drugged cretin. But a serious revolutionary? No way!

Although he had publicly forsworn dependency upon drugs, Lennon was evaluated by the FBI as a sustained 'user', one memo advising, 'Lennon appears to be radically oriented, however he does not give the impression he is a true revolutionist since he is constantly under influence of narcotics.'

Although Lennon claimed he had kicked the habit, Morrissey

perceived an addiction, ascribing the lethargy in his personality to the use of drugs.

'Whatever New York is, God knows, it never bought this shit about rock 'n' roll, hippies and drugs. What they have always taken a cocktail party interest in is something they call the modern art world.

'My point is that he was unbelievably uninteresting. It was horrendous how pathetic he was. Staying in bed. Putting dog shit on the floor. Taking the drugs and taking heroin. I read biographies. But when you are reading the case history of a drug character – they're just vegetables. And anything they do, even if they function, is stupid. Very few of these people ever really get off drugs. Especially if they have the money. They get their blood changed and go back.'

When interviewed about drugs, Lennon assured me he was 'clean': a condition supported by Jack Douglas, who recalls John going 'cold turkey' with Yoko while driving cross-country in a chauffeured limo – in order to kick the heroin habit. 'He had this theory if you mixed with heroin – three days on and three weeks off – it was okay. If not, within eleven months you would be hooked. He knew how to take drugs.'

A controlled junkie, Lennon had diet-conscious eating habits that minimized any addictive effects. Recalls Jack, 'He was such a health freak. The Fat Beatle. I thought he was too thin at the end. I used to call him skinny head, because of when he tied his hair back. His head was so narrow. Toward the end my wife was bringing him up cheeseburgers and pizza and he would have to hide them so that Yoko wouldn't see.'

One of John's last cover photos, emphasizing his slim, taut body, focuses on tight-fitting, hip-hugging jeans virtually glued to the crotch. Forever the repressed lover, embarrassed by the erotic photos in which Yoko made him take off his clothes, Lennon proclaimed that he was proud of being forty and still virile. 'He was thin and muscular – did push-ups every day,' recounts Douglas. 'He was happy being in the greatest shape of his life. And *drug-free*. Colonic.'

As it transpires, the erotic photos contributed to a damaging FBI profile. Lennon's *Two Virgins* nudes formed the basis of a complaint from a person described as 'an employee' in 'a Minnesota company' against Lennon as a man who undermines 'the standards of US youth'. Although there was no violation of any obscenity laws, the complaint is given credence in an FBI memo citing: 'The cover of the album was a photograph of Lennon and Ono (his latest flame) completely nude; and believe me they didn't hide a thing . . . most discolored and vulgar display of garbage. . . .'

Drugs no, politics yes. While it would be unfair to assume that Lennon entered the United States for the purpose of disrupting the Republican National Convention, or for mobilizing to bring an end to the Vietnam War, it is nevertheless true that his activities whilst a temporary resident fighting deportation were aligned with left-wing causes and individuals.

Surveillance terrifies. Whatever the legal outcome of his case against the Bureau, the reality of living in fear had an effect, and Lennon changed his plans to attend the Republican National Convention in consequence. An FBI memo dated 30 August 1972 confirms: 'The subject did *not* travel to Miami for RNC as he had previously planned. . . . For the past several months there has been no information received to indicate that the subject is active in the New Left.'

And yet there is no doubt that Lennon wanted to see Nixon defeated and the Vietnam War ended; his commitment to anti-war protest groups and Democratic fringe groups supporting George McGovern's candicacy, such as EYSIC (Election Year Strategy Information Centre) and YES (Youth Election Strategy), con-sumed much of his time and money.

Of course, as we know, Nixon *was* a second-term President but was forced to resign in 1974 after serving only two years on account of the Watergate scandal. Lennon was amongst the first to notice Nixon's ominous downslide, Jack Douglas recalls: 'John was the first person to tell me about Watergate. He read some small article in the *Times* and told me, "This is the beginning of the end for Nixon." He despised Nixon and he despised Reagan as well.'

Whilst the charge of using Lennon has been levelled against Hoffman and Rubin, the basis is unfounded: John was as keen to maintain the alliance as they. Champion of the Yippies, it was Lennon who argued for Rubin's appearance on CBS-TV's *The Mike Douglas Show*, a popular American chat programme, during the week of 14-18 February 1972 when John and Yoko were co-hosts. Mike Douglas introduced Jerry Rubin, stating that his feelings were quite negative concerning Rubin but that John Lennon wanted him on the show; also that he had heard Rubin was against drugs and that that was the reason he was in favour of having him on the show.

Lennon stated that Rubin was not at all like his image and that he and his wife were not like their image. He said that he found something in Rubin that was artistic.

Mike Douglas asked, 'What is Jerry Rubin thinking about these days?'

Rubin answered, 'We're going to support Nixon for President. . . . I'm just kidding! What he has really done is automate the war in Vietnam so that its machines killing people create a situation where forty-three people can be murdered at Attica, create a situation where four kids can be killed at Kent State and people are afraid. . . . I'm working very hard with people all over the country to defeat Nixon.'

When asked about the 'Movement', Rubin stated that 'The way the Movement has changed is the pressure is so heavy that if anybody does anything, gets arrested, jailed, killed, people are very pessimistic.'

When asked about voting, he said that 'We ought to go to both conventions in Miami and San Diego, non-violently make our presence felt – and stand on the issues.'

There are those who credit Lennon single-handedly with bringing about an end to the Vietnam War; he certainly did an enormous amount to effect its termination. What he was, in essence, was a political activist, except that the focus of his attention had become, rather than a pop group, select political issues.

It is not trivial to consider that, fifty-five hours after the Ann Arbor, Michigan rally for John Sinclair, he was freed on bail. A left-wing writer, Sinclair had been jailed for ten years in 1969 for possession of two marijuana cigarettes. Lennon's song, entitled simply 'John Sinclair', turned a victim into a martyr. It was sung that night before sixteen thousand people who had congregated at the University of Michigan rally at the Events Building at 7.15p.m., and Lennon reversed the man's fate when he sang: 'They gave him ten for two' and 'What more can Colombo, Nixon, Rockefeller and Agnew do'.

Civil rights lawyer William Kunstler dramatized the situation: 'John is in jail for two essential reasons: first of all he is a political person who calls into question the validity of the superstate which seeks to control all of us and destroys those it cannot readily dominate. Secondly, his harsh sentence dramatizes the absurdity of our marijuana laws which are irrational, unjust and indefensible.'

But it was Lennon's presence which augured a positive change in Sinclair's condition, Jerry Rubin cheering:

'This is the first event of the Rock Liberation Front and it is really incredible that John Lennon and Yoko Ono are going to be here tonight . . . 'cause it's really a committed act by people who are very involved in music, who are identifying to the culture you and I are part of . . . and for them to come on this stage and for John to sing his song 'It ain't fair, John Sinclair' and for John and Yoko to sing a song about the IRA and Attica State it's really incredible. It shows that right now we can really unite music and revolutionary politics and really build the movement all across the country. . . .'

Was Lennon a tool of the Left – pursuing a guilt trip, the relief from which was to bite the hand that fed? Or was he honestly committed to political change through music? The woeful course determining the end of his life suggests a kind of divine fulfilment, retribution for having been an example of moral corruption and commercial decay. At least, that was the rationale of his assassin, defining the motive for the vendetta as giving Lennon his retribution. In a penetrating account of Lennon's death in his book entitled *The Murder of John Lennon*, Fenton Bresler postulates that the assassin, Mark David Chapman, was brainwashed by the CIA to carry out the murder by rationalizing that he was acting as a henchman for the betrayed masses of Lennon fans.

Writes Bresler, 'Mark David Chapman, a twenty-five-year-old fan or ex-fan . . . had got it into his head that . . . Lennon was a "phoney", a billionaire rock star who preached peace and denial while enjoying the fruits of his vast wealth like any other super-rich capitalist. . . .'

Hanging around the Dakota with other fans so that he was a recognizable face, Chapman first saw John and Yoko at five o'clock on the night of 8 December, on their way to the Record Plant for the last working session on the *Double Fantasy* tapes.

Having got John's autograph, he waited around for Yoko's, remaining with the others for about five hours. At 10.50p.m. the limousine arrived back at Central Park West and 72nd Street, and John and Yoko departed into the Dakota.

Chronicles Bresler,

Yoko got out first, with John clutching the tapes from their session in his hand and trailing a few steps behind. As he passed under the ornate archway leading to the building's interior courtyard, a voice called out from behind: 'Mr. Lennon'.

He half turned to see Mark crouched in a combat stance less than twenty feet away. Five times his .38 fired at point-blank range, pumping four bullets into Lennon's back and left shoulder. One went astray as Lennon, almost killed outright by the first explosion of steel particles shattering into his body, staggered up the five steps to the entrance office to fall flat on his face, gurgling and bringing up blood.'

If, as Bresler argues, the wounds to Lennon were in the back and shoulder, why one wonders was he incapable of being saved?

The account at the hospital is mystifying. 'Although doctors pronounced Lennon dead on arrival at the Roosevelt Hospital . . . a team of seven surgeons laboured desperately to try and save him. But his wounds were too severe.'

Mourning for Lennon invoked a pomposity surpassing that for presidents and popes. Enjoying life as an idol, death as a saint, Lennon had become, in Paul McCartney's words, 'Martin Luther Lennon'. His smart-ass remarks, social exhibitionism and political hooliganism suddenly took on the mantle of respectability. The area of parkland across from the Dakota was consecrated as a bit of Holy Land in Central Park. Christened Strawberry Fields, the 22-acre tract of parkland, dedicated to John, was purchased by Yoko with a million-dollar gift, with an additional $400,000 maintenance allowance. The meadows and lawns have been landscaped to commemorate Lennon: a plaque lists those countries which have contributed gifts of new trees, shrubs and perennials, whilst a marble mosaic dedicated to *Imagine* and donated by Italy graces the cobblestone-edged path near the 72nd Street entrance.

That our own sense of loss over John Lennon surpasses what we felt when John Kennedy died or for any of the great New York philanthropists whose energies were spent in the enhancement of and dedication to New York City is a condition as awesome as it is disturbing. The lunacy of it all is well expressed by columnist Rex Reed, a Dakota neighbour, who bridles at the excess of adulation lavished upon Lennon. Reed, who received a *TV Guide* subscription as a gift after signing Lennon's Immigration petition, was largely unmoved by his death – 'If it was Cole Porter, I would have understood the extent of the mourning,' he says.

Annoyed by the increased security on the premises in view of Yoko's continuing to live there, Reed objects: 'After the death it was a nightmare. People moved to hotels. We were under siege by the police. Christmas parcels were checked by the bomb squad. Fans prostrated themselves in front of the building. Radios played nothing but Lennon songs. We were no better than prisoners in our own homes,' he complains.

There are those who believe that Lennon actually died on that fatal December day. But I prefer to put faith in the fantasy of faking his own death, so that he can live out the rest of his days in peace and solitude, unbothered by fans.

Who knows? The fat, bald-headed man with a moustache walking down some Geneva street could be John Lennon.

POSTSCRIPT

The aftermath to the ordeal is as bizarre as the event itself. After John died, Yoko began living with her production manager, Sam Havadtoy. Executor of the Lennon estate, she attends regular Apple business meetings and has come to be accepted by the very Beatles who once opposed her. She herself has dropped the bohemian façade and enjoys being a *grand dame*. Her unabashed wealth, captured on film in her introduction to Andrew Solt's *Imagine* feature, is in plain view: the apartment looking every bit the palace or the museum, replete with period furnishings and fine art works. She has also become a sort of historian of the Lennon cult, mounting shows of his art and tributes to his music around the world – which is perverse since it was she who turned his head from things Beatles into more esoteric areas.

John's son Julian, a former public school boy, is a pop singer and has had his personal battles and career upheavals. There has been some acrimony about getting his money from the estate, but this appears to have been resolved. His singing career falters, although he seems to have an aptitude for films. Calmer and less aggressive than John, he could become the Clint Eastwood of the nineties.

Married a couple of times, Cynthia Lennon appears not to have got over John. Enshrining his memory in various business enterprises, she is currently involved in mounting with promoter Sid Bernstein a Lennon memorial concert, whilst having abandoned her role as a partner in the London café Lennons. She appears to have struck up a rapport with May Pang; one wonders if Yoko will be next.

George, Paul and Ringo grow more orthodox as they get older. Plans are under way for a reunion concert. None of them has ever done anything which equals the awesome originality of the Beatles. Paul has, however, had enormous success with a succession of bands, and along with Linda has done a great deal to highlight the indignity of slaughtering animals for food and clothing.

John's music, solo or with the Beatles, survives as a reminder of the Flower Power era: a dream of Strawberry Fields and Penny Lanes – of prodigious English countryside. The verger at St Peter's, Woolton, where John was a choirboy for a brief time, says that he hopes Lennon will be remembered as someone who has taken the values of the English town or village into the world. I believe that to be the most significant thing about John's life, transcending his death. For, as I have previously said, it is my opinion that John Lennon was the best unpaid advert that the Church of England ever had.

BIBLIOGRAPHY

BEST, Pete, and Patrick Doncaster, *Beatle!* Plexus, London, 1985
BRESLER, Fenton, *The Murder of John Lennon*, Sidgwick and Jackson, London, 1989
COLEMAN, Ray, *Brian Epstein: The Man Who Made the Beatles*, Viking, London, 1989
COLEMAN, Ray, *John Lennon*, Futura, London, 1985
EDWARDS, Henry and May Pang, *Loving John*, Corgi, London, 1983
FAWCETT, Anthony, *One Day at a Time*, New English Library, London, 1977
FEDERAL BUREAU OF INVESTIGATION, *Freedom of Information: John Lennon.* Justice Department, Washington, DC, 1981
FLIPPO, Chet, *McCartney*, Sidgwick and Jackson, London, 1988
GOLDMAN, Albert, *The Lives of John Lennon*, Bantam Press, London, 1988
HARRY, Bill, *The Book of Lennon*, Aurum Press, London, 1984
HOPKINS, Jerry, *Yoko Ono*, Sidgwick and Jackson, London, 1987
LENNON, Cynthia, *A Twist of Lennon*, W. H. Allen, London, 1978
LENNON, John, *In His Own Write and A Spaniard in the Works*, New American Library, New York, 1964
LENNON, John, *Skywriting by Word of Mouth*, Harper and Row, New York, 1987.
LEWISOHN, Mark, *The Complete Beatles Recording Sessions*, Hamlyn, London, 1988
McCABE, Pete, and Robert D. Schonfeld, *Apple to the Core*, Martin Brian and O'Keeffee, London, 1977
ONO, Yoko, *Grapefruit*, Peter Owen, London, 1970
PEEBLES, Andy, *The Lennon Tapes*, BBC, London, 1981
SCADUTO, Anthony, *Mick Jagger*, W. H. Allen, London, 1974
SCHAFFNER, Nicholas, and Pete Shotton, *John Lennon: In My Life*, Coronet Books, London, 1984
SOUTHALL, Brian, *Abbey Road*, Patrick Stephens, Wellingborough, 1982

PHOTOGRAPHIC CREDITS

1. Tom Hanley
2. Thelma McGough (supplier)
3. David Redfern Photography
4. Popperfoto
5. Uniphoto Press Inc
6. The Hulton–Deutsch Collection
7. The Hulton–Deutsch Collection
8. David Redfern Photography
9. The Hulton–Deutsch Collection
10. The Hulton–Deutsch Collection
11. Chris Arthur
12. Popperfoto
13. Syndication International
14. Walter Shenson Collection
15. Rex Features
16. The Hulton–Deutsch Collection
17. The Kobal Collection
18. The Hulton–Deutsch Collection
19. Popperfoto
20. Rex Features
21. Camera Press
22. Syndication International
23. The Hulton–Deutsch Collection
24. Syndication International
25. Syndication International
26. The Hulton–Deutsch Collection
27. Syndication International
28. Rex Features
29. Camera Press
30. Syndication International
31. Associated Press
32. London Features International
33. Rex Features
34. Popperfoto
35. The Hulton–Deutsch Collection
36. Rex Features
37. Syndication International

INDEX